Sustainability Prospects for Autonomous Vehicles

The Autonomous Vehicle (AV) has been strongly heralded as the most exciting innovation in automobility for decades. Autonomous Vehicles are no longer an innovation of the future (seen only in science fiction) but are now being road-tested for use. And yet while the technical and economic success and possibilities of the AV have been widely debated, there has been a notable lack of discussion around the social, behavioral, and environmental implications. This book is the first to address these issues and to deeply consider the environmental and social sustainability outlook for the AV and how it will impact on communities. Environmental and social sustainability are goals unlike those of technical development (a new tool) and economic development (a new investment). The goal of sustainability is development of societies that live well and equitably within their ecological limits. Is it reasonable and desirable that only technical and economic success comprise the swelling AV parade, or should we be looking at the wider impacts on personal well-being, wider society, and the environment?

The uptake for AVs looks to be lengthy, disjointed, and episodic, in large measure because it faces a range of known and unknown risks. This book assesses the environmental and social sustainability potential for AVs based on their prospective energy use and their impacts on climate change, urban landscapes, public health, mobility inequalities, and individual and social well-being. It examines public attitudes about AV use and its risk of fostering a rebound effect that compromises potential sustainability gains. The book concludes with a discussion of critical issues involved in sustainable AV diffusion.

George Martin is currently Emeritus Professor in the Sociology Department at Montclair State University. He is also Visiting Research Associate at the University of California, Santa Cruz, and Visiting Professor at the Centre for Environment and Sustainability, University of Surrey. He has served as Senior Editor of *Capitalism Nature Socialism* since 2010 and is author of *The Ecology of the Automobile*.

Sustainability Prospects for Autonomous Vehicles

Environmental, Social, and Urban

George Martin

Routledge
Taylor & Francis Group

LONDON AND NEW YORK

First published 2019 by Routledge

2 Park Square, Milton Park, Abingdon, Oxon, OX14 4RN
605 Third Avenue, New York, NY 10017

Routledge is an imprint of the Taylor & Francis Group, an informa business

First issued in paperback 2020

British Library Cataloguing-in-Publication Data
A catalogue record for this book is available from the British Library

Library of Congress Cataloging-in-Publication Data
Names: Martin, George T., author.
Title: Sustainability prospects for autonomous vehicles : environmental,
   social, and urban / George Martin.
Description: New York, NY : Routledge, [2019] | Includes bibliographical
   references and index.
Identifiers: LCCN 2019003555 | ISBN 9780815363316 (hardback) |
   ISBN 9781351109956 (ebook)
Subjects: LCSH: Autonomous vehicles.
Classification: LCC TL152.8 .M373 2019 | DDC 303.48/32—dc23
LC record available at https://lccn.loc.gov/2019003555

ISBN: 978-0-8153-6331-6 (hbk)
ISBN: 978-0-367-78627-4 (pbk)

Typeset in Bembo
by Apex CoVantage, LLC

To the memory of Peter Freund (1940–2014), collaborator, colleague, friend, and fellow walker.

Contents

Preface

The autonomous vehicle (AV) was a challenging subject about which to write a book. It required dense use of the contingent voice (could, would, etc.) as it is an emergent technology – a moving target! Anticipating its sustainability prospects required thorough and timely judgments of new data and analysis on a daily basis. Meeting this challenge was made possible by the talented and efficient bibliographic assistance of Stan Jacobsen, a veteran editor with Nolo Press in Berkeley (and a good neighbor). His digital mining of hundreds of freshly published documents allowed me time to concentrate on writing. The work also was supported in kind through my on-going institutional affiliations: Emeritus Professor, Sociology Department, Montclair State University, Montclair, New Jersey; Visiting Professor, Centre for Environment and Sustainability, University of Surrey, Guildford; and Research Associate, Sociology Department, University of California, Santa Cruz.

The AV is a technology and a business with a laundry list of under-studied environmental and social implications bearing upon an array of weighty realms – climate change, public health, and urban transportation. I crafted its sustainability profile from the multidisciplinary perspective of an urban environmental sociologist. The prime venue for AV development and deployment is the US, and one hotspot is the San Francisco Bay Area (and its Silicon Valley), my home. I also have lived and worked in the UK, and the experience added appreciably to my grasp of the subject. In addition to the US and the UK, I judged seven countries as being most active in AV endeavors – China, France, Germany, Italy, Japan, the Republic of Korea, and Sweden. These nations comprise a group I designated as the AV9 and followed through the book. Several others were referenced in a variety of contexts – Australia, Canada, and the Netherlands – while another dozen or so were occasional sources of material.

It is my hope that readers find something here that pricks their interest and satisfies their concern and curiosity about uncertain changes in daily life that may follow on the heels of an autonomous vehicle deployment, changes of considerable consequence for the sustainability of environments, societies, and cities.

Abbreviations

AEV	Autonomous Electric Vehicle
AICV	Autonomous Internal Combustion Vehicle
APEV	Autonomous Public Electric Vehicle
APTV	Autonomous Public Transit Vehicle
ARSV	Autonomous Ride Share Vehicle
ASEV	Autonomous Shared Electric Vehicle
AV	Autonomous Vehicle
AV9	China, France, Germany, Italy, Japan, ROK, Sweden, UK, US
BEV	Battery Electric Vehicle
BFI	British Film Institute
CBD	Central Business District
CEV	City Electric Vehicle
CO_2	Carbon Dioxide
COPD	Chronic Obstructive Pulmonary Disease
EPA	Environmental Protection Agency (US)
EU	European Union
EV	Electric Vehicle
ft	feet
GDP	Gross Domestic Product
GHG	Greenhouse Gases
GPS	Global Positioning System
ha	hectare
HEV	Hybrid Electric Vehicle
ICE	Internal Combustion Engine
ICV	Internal Combustion Vehicle
kgs	kilograms
km	kilometer
lbs	pounds
LBW	Low Birth Weight
LCA	Life Cycle Assessment
mi	mile
mj	megajoule
mph	miles per hour

NGO	Non-Governmental Organization
PHEV	Plug-in Hybrid Electric Vehicle
PM	Particulate Matter
PTOD	Public Transit On-Demand
ROK	Republic of Korea
ROW	Right of Way
SDSD	Social Development for Sustainable Development (UN)
SUV	Sport Utility Vehicle
TNC	Transportation Network Company
TOD	Transit Oriented Development
UK	United Kingdom
UN	United Nations
US	United States
VKT	Vehicle Kilometers Traveled
VMT	Vehicle Miles Traveled
WHO	World Health Organization (UN)
WTWA	Well-to-Wheel Assessment

1 Setting the scene

PROLOGUE: **THE AUTONOMOUS VEHICLE TAKES THE STAGE**

The back story of the autonomous vehicle depicted in a drama with three acts:

> *Act I reveals the backstory. Its opening scene introduces an aging antagonist: The internal combustion vehicle and its boorish and confident entourage led by hyper automobility and including super highways, super congestion, and super-sized vehicles. The second scene shifts to the present day grievances of an emergent protagonist, sustainability, representing a chorus of plaintive campaigning voices about climate change, public health, public transit, mobility equity, and green cities. Scene one of Act II introduces the autonomous vehicle (Av), a talented and hopeful newcomer with potential to resolve the conflict but who must choose between the present benefits offered by hyper automobility or the prospective opportunities afforded by sustainability. In the second scene conflict mounts. The antagonist demands a stay-the-course role for Av that maintains private automobile benefits and avoids uncertainties of change. The protagonist offers a new path with a shared mobility. Act III is in process. Its denouement will favor either the default option for Av – stepping into the internal combustion vehicle format and its personal mobility role – or choosing to premiere an electric format in a new role as a public vehicle.*

1.1 Introduction: Transforming automobility's character and role

Fantastic self-driving automobiles periodically have been imagined for public consumption. A notable example was Isaac Asimov's *automatobile* in a 1953 short story in *Fantastic Magazine* (Asimov 1969). Today, the autonomous vehicle is moving from a role in a science fiction story to one in a reality show. The uncertainties surrounding this transition are illustrated by the range of its numerous designations, including driverless, self-driving, robotic, and automated. Here, autonomous is the chosen term. Automobiles have featured some bits of automation for a surprisingly long time. The first hydraulic automatic transmission appeared in the 1940 model year of the *Cadillac* and *Oldsmobile* cars of *General*

Motors (Seams 2017). Cruise control was introduced with the 1958 *Chrysler Imperial* (Varney 2018). In 2003 *Toyota* offered automatic parallel parking as an option in its *Prius* (Andreev 2018).

In its essence the AV is a motorized vehicle that can guide itself without hands-on human direction. Given the mass consumption of cars it is understandable that its eminent arrival commands a great deal of attention in news media. An analysis of *Google* searches found that interest in autonomous vehicles nearly quadrupled between 2015 and 2017 (Claypool 2017). Stimulating this curiosity is popular expectation of major changes in the everyday travel experience, changes that seem to have some promise – at least on their surface (Martin 2018).

The media attention is given a boost by the copious investments of money and time being made in autonomous vehicle development by multinational automotive and digital corporations. One result is frenetic competition to get a foot in the door of the emerging industry so as to have a piece of its future. The introduction of test AVs on public roadways has compelled a growing reach of regulatory oversight by government agencies. Moreover, civic institutions as well as businesses and governments are moving forward with anticipatory adjustments; for example, many universities in the US now factor "the autonomous vehicle thing" into their campus planning (Prevost 2017, B6).

Since *Google* announced in 2010 that it was beginning development of self-driving cars, a wealth of media attention has created a halo-like effect of positive expectations. Realistic and critical appraisals of possible consequences have been marginalized by the sheer scale of the favorable coverage. However, more balanced commentaries are making their way into the public arena. For example, one journalist used a religious metaphor in dividing AV potential impacts into hellish or heavenly (Chase 2014). Another journalist has used a secular version of the metaphor – utopian or dystopian outcomes (Leslie 2018).

The AV attracts such widespread attention because motorized mobility is a critical and ubiquitous feature of contemporary life. About 1.3 billion vehicles are used widely and regularly throughout the world to carry people and goods for a multitude of purposes. They are highly concentrated in more developed nations (OICA 2017a; UN 2017), and that is where motor vehicle production and use have been used as key indicators of economic development since the first decades of the 20th century. Today, more developed nations have 49 percent of the world's vehicles with only 13 percent of its population. However, rapidly developing China has overtaken the US to lead in vehicle production and is nearly overtaking it in vehicle stocks.

Generally defined the motor vehicles examined here are mechanized, have a minimum of four wheels, and operate on roadways. This excludes two- and three-wheeled vehicles, farm tractors, etc., but includes vans, buses, and trucks. The most numerous category is the passenger automobile (or car), which represents about three-fourths of the world's vehicles. All vehicle types are prospects for mobile autonomy, but the personal automobile is the most socially and environmentally consequential, and it is the focus of attention here.

In public discourse the benefits of AVs appear to be sound while the costs are speculative. Literature and online posts, both academic and popular, focus on the technical and business progress of their build-out and on their promise, not their peril. Reviews of writings about autonomous vehicles are in agreement with regard to this bias. Papa and Ferreira (2018) pointed out that a focus on technology makes the autonomous vehicle literature weak on broader impacts. Cavoli et al. (2017) researched the comprehensive *Scopus* technical database relative to autonomous vehicles and found that 61 percent of references were to engineering and computer sciences, while less than 10 percent cited social and environmental sciences.

Clearly then, the present AV discourse is deficient in addressing its broader impacts. A major reason for this is that a new technology has to be fully deployed before the whole range of its consequences is revealed. However, the course of autonomous vehicle deployment can be anticipated and to some extent predicted. Looking forward is a basis for preventing or ameliorating negative impacts rather than reacting to them down the road. Mobility technologies have major repercussions for environments, societies, and cities, as we have learned in over 100 years of living with the automobile.

Systematic attention to environmental, social, and urban prospects will cross boundaries of the natural and behavioral sciences, in which measures of impacts differ from the technological (a new tool), the regulatory (a new law), and the economic (a new investment) ones. A broadening of academic and public attention to include mobility in all of its facets is critically integral to the sustainability program for humanity: To live well and equitably within Earth's ecological limits. Currently, motorized mobility is a prominent impediment to this program, making it important to anticipate the AV's social and environmental ramifications. The assessment of impact here focuses on the opportunities for the autonomous vehicle to improve the wanting sustainability profile of today's stock of motor vehicles.

As we have learned from the eventual courses taken by many technological innovations, an initial route may prove difficult to abandon or even to alter. A convenient and popular course may turn out to be damaging to environments, societies, and cities. Such path-determining choices create unanticipated liabilities for subsequent generations. Passing on inter-generational environmental burdens was the social encumbrance that brought the concept of *sustainable development* to the world in the *Brundtland Report* (WCED 1987).

In the case of automobile technology more developed nations have become dependent on it as a consumer product, casting long shadows over prospects for bequeathing socially and environmentally sustainable mobility to their progeny (Dauvergue 2008). If AVs are fitted to use internal combustion engines (ICE) and fossil fuel it will serve to darken and lengthen these shadows. However, their deployment offers an opportunity to segue to a propulsion system that enhances sustainable automobility – perhaps considerably. The perspective here is that the autonomous vehicle offers the possibility of transforming both the *character* (internal combustion) and the *role* (personal use) of the automobile.

A case is made here that an AV deployment's best sustainability path forward is to play a role in rewriting the legacy of the personal internal combustion vehicle (ICV) rather than accepting it as is. In becoming a vehicle that is used to promote change it could be part of yet another historic stepwise transformation in automobility. According to the US National Traffic Safety Administration's policy statement concerning automated vehicles (NHTSA 2016, 1): "Motor vehicles and drivers' relationships with them are likely to change significantly in the next ten to twenty years, perhaps more than they have changed in the last one hundred years." For such a change to take a sustainable turn autonomous vehicle deployment will have to deal with burdensome historical legacies. The critical analysis fashioned in this book can serve as a signposting for the directions that are available in order to turn legacy burdens into sustainability opportunities.

1.2 Legacy of environmental troubles

A legacy is something that is handed down to us by our predecessors, and here it comprises automobility's contemporary *status quo*. It can be continued as is, reformed, or rejected. With regard to the historical development of the automobile, one of its best known figures, Henry Ford, commented on the nature of progress: "The remains of the old must be decently laid away, the path of the new prepared" (Ford 1922). Today, the progress required for environmental sustainability requires the laying away of the internal combustion vehicle. The autonomous vehicle will be deployed in mobility systems dominated by super-sized, greenhouse gas (GHG) emitting, passenger ICVs. The potentials for autonomous vehicles to challenge this dominance are analyzed in Chapter Two.

The internal combustion engine

Carl Benz began the first commercial production of motor vehicles with internal combustion propulsion in 1886 in Mannheim. It competed with two other power sources, steam and electricity. In the US, which became the principal locale of technological development, ICVs were only about one-fifth of sales in 1900 (Orsato and Wells 2007, 996). The competition over propulsion systems ended a few years later, in 1905, when the *Ford Motor Company* launched the first mass-produced vehicle with an internal combustion engine, the *Model T*. It rolled off assembly lines in Detroit, as well as in Manchester and cities in continental Europe (Melosi 2004).

The major reason for choosing ICE propulsion was economic – specifically a newfound availability of cheap gasoline and lubricants that was ignited by the gigantic Spindletop oil strike in southeast Texas in 1901. Assembly line mass production and cheap oil lowered the cost of making and using cars and they became widely available for the first time. In 1912 the *Model T* cost $US 650 ($US 16,000 in purchasing power in 2018 dollars), while competitor electric vehicles sold for about 3 times as much (Matulka 2014). It was produced until 1927, by which time its cost was down to about $US 300 ($US 4,000 in 2017 dollars).

Today's ICE propulsion is a major obstacle to the environmental sustainability of automobility. Its GHG emissions are a substantial contributor to global climate change. We are entangled in the web of consequences of a path-deciding option chosen more than a hundred years ago (Freund and Martin 2009). An autonomous vehicle deployment has potential either to alter or to follow this path's direction.

Super-sized vehicles

The development of superhighways (see below) prompted a substantial rise in the number of super-sized sport utility vehicles (SUVs). They are larger descendants of the station wagon in the US, the *Kombi* in Germany, and the estate car in the UK. In 1990 they represented only 5 percent of US motor vehicle sales; in 2004, 21 percent; in 2016, 30 percent (EPA 2017; WSJ 2017). The growth has been led by their largest models, which grew from 11 percent to 49 percent of SUV sales between 1990 and 2004 (*Statista* 2017). These vehicles are considerably larger and heavier than other passenger cars. They range between 4,000 and 6,000 lbs in weight, nearly double that of mid-size vehicles and more than double that of small cars (NMEDA 2011). As a result of the shift to larger vehicles, the overall industry vehicle footprint (defined as the area bounded by its tires) increased by 0.6 ft^2 between 2008 and 2016 (EPA 2017).

Superhighways spurred the upsurge in sport utility vehicles by increasing traffic, which in turn posed newly perceived safety threats to drivers. As a result many Americans developed an appetite for the sense of security that larger, higher vehicles offered (Oge 2015, 105). Not just Americans, however. Popular European SUVs include the British *Land Rover* and the German *Audi Q7*. Commonly voiced reasons that consumers offer for buying them include the improved road vision provided by their height and the greater crashworthiness afforded by their mass (Davis and Truett 2000). (The additional interior space for goods and passengers is another reason given for buying them.) Sport utility vehicle popularity prods drivers of smaller cars with less roadway vision and vehicle crashworthiness to purchase them.

The upsizing of cars has had a major negative impact on environmental sustainability. Fattening automobiles is a principal reason that average fuel economy has stopped improving in the US – moving more weight against more wind resistance requires more energy and releases more emissions (Hakim 2004). Their greater mass also consumes more natural resources in the vehicle production stage and emits more greenhouse gas emissions throughout its life cycle. From an environmental perspective the SUV can be viewed as a Seriously Unsustainable Vehicle. If autonomous vehicles replicate them they will fall well short of possible environmental sustainability gains.

1.3 Legacy of social troubles

The ascendance of the automobile in post-war Western Europe and North America has left a social legacy highlighted by public health deficits and mobility inequities.

Public health deficits

With regard to public health the legacies are high levels of toxic emissions, and injurious and lethal roadway crashes. These problems carry threats of premature death for millions of human beings yearly around the globe, constituting an on-going harm to social sustainability. Road crashes are largely a result of human error, at least in countries of the global North (see Chapter Three), and the machine intelligence of the autonomous vehicle promises to reduce the bulk of these errors, although it also will produce its own brand of errors (presumably at a much lower rate than human drivers).

Higher rates of premature respiratory and cardiovascular mortality are linked to breathing in vehicle tailpipe exhaust and non-exhaust emissions of particulates from brake and tire wear. An unknown number of deaths can be attributed to deficiencies in regulatory air quality standards. They are often too low, based on the average person in a population rather than on any number of atypical persons who are more vulnerable. Thus, a national study in the US reported that risks from short-term exposures to particulate matter and warm-season ozone occurred at levels *below* current air quality standards. Research has demonstrated that older adults, children, and people with chronic diseases are particularly vulnerable to toxic air (Di et al. 2017). An additional problem is that enforcement of healthy air standards as with many regulatory standards can be lax, in part because it is an often underfunded public duty.

Air pollution is an on-going general health threat for urban dwellers (see below). Additionally, they face somewhat more place-specific and intermittent problems. One is the ambient noise created by conventional vehicles. The other is driver stress stemming from repetitive negotiation of heavy traffic congestion.

Mobility equity (see next) is about a fair provision of local transport. This is accomplished by the accessible and affordable protocols of public transit. Lack of access and affordability carries with it an added health risk; thus, it constitutes a public health problem. Mobility exclusion has both social and health consequences (Carr and Ott 2010). Motorized mobility provides for "personal independence, reduction in social isolation, and access to essential services" (Anderson et al. 2014, 17). For example, according to a UK National Travel Survey about one-fifth of households without an automobile faced some difficulties getting to markets and to doctors (DFT 2005).

Mobility inequities

With regard to inequality a legacy of hyper automobility has been to disenfranchise large sub-groups of populations from access to monetarily affordable and physically accessible mobility. There are large groups of people who are currently circumscribed, prohibited, or discouraged from driving vehicles, and this considerably limits their participation in all-too-common auto-centered transport systems (Freund and Martin 2001, 2002). These groups include people living in poverty and those with disabilities and infirmities. Lack of affordable and accessible mobility is one of the most generalized social injustices in more developed societies because travel plays a critical role in the demands of everyday life such as getting to work, and in the quality of life such as reduced social isolation.

Thus, mobility equity is a social problem and a social sustainability issue. It exemplifies the larger problem of socioeconomic inequality. While inequality refers to a hierarchically distributed quantity such as income, inequity refers to the absence of a quality of justice or fairness. Mobility reflects both: Inequality sorts those who can buy a personal vehicle from those who cannot, while inequity describes the situation of those who do not have access to public transit services. Over time and under the right conditions inequality and inequity can synergize to promote a level of division and conflict in societies which threatens their stability and hence their sustainability.

Lack of mobility access is in large measure a product of prevailing social inequities, and it has a negative effect on social sustainability. There are secondary or indirect inequities as well as the primary ones. One such equity concerns parking space, a large land use in urban areas. Parking represents a largely unrecognized factor in transport-related inequity, as noted in the following:

> Because the driving population tends to skew older, whiter, and richer on average, the hidden costs of parking also raise distributional and social equity concerns: free parking is in many ways a subsidy for older, richer, whiter drivers paid disproportionately by the younger, poorer, and non-white non-drivers.
>
> (Phillips 2017, 324)

Such indirect inequities are commonly not subjected to public policy reform measures and remain, in effect, a hidden and unfair tax.

1.4   Legacy of urban troubles

The negative legacies of the conventional automobile for cities are concentrated in their supporting infrastructures and in their hyper use. A major sustainably negative outcome has been the depreciation of public transit systems. An autonomous vehicle deployment will likely begin in cities and holds some promise for rectifying the clutch of unsustainable ills bequeathed by the hypermobility of internal combustion vehicles.

Superhighways and super congestion

Several decades on from the *Model T* the mid-century period following World War II saw a widespread construction of limited-access, multi-lane superhighways in the more developed world – *super* here meaning enormity. Like adoption of the internal combustion engine and fossil fuel, they illustrate the unintended negative consequences that can shadow sociotechnical change. Despite their political selling point as long-distance roadway systems connecting national population centers the superhighways' greatest users have turned out to be local commuters. Thus, the vehicle miles traveled (VMT) on US urban superhighways is now more than twice that traveled on non-urban ones (FHWA 2015). Superhighways function primarily to support the heavy vehicle traffic within urban areas rather than the more modest traffic between them.

The automobile and its infrastructures played a vital role in the recoveries of World War II combatant nations. The construction of superhighways and the manufacture of motor vehicles were primers for re-orienting war economies and providing jobs to millions of military veterans. Auto use reached new highs that are now justifiably designated as *excessive* based on the scale and intensity of their negative impacts. These include new levels of land-eating low-density urban sprawl with its adverse consequences for public transportation (Freund and Martin 2007; Martin 1999).

An excessive, or hyper, increase in automobility took place throughout the more developed world but most noticeably in the US, nurtured by the construction of a massive roadway infrastructure. Its Interstate Highway System ("I" roads) was launched by the Eisenhower Administration in 1956 and completed in 1992, inspired by Germany's *Reichsautobahnen* national road system. Eisenhower had commanded the allied forces in Western Europe in World II and was impressed by the autobahns' logistic contributions to the war effort of their German adversaries. He is reported to have stated that "after seeing the autobahns of modern Germany and knowing the asset those highways were to the Germans, I decided, as President, to put an emphasis on this kind of road building" (FHWA 2017b, 3).

Superhighways have continued to expand from a base of four traffic lanes to as many as 20 in some large metropolitan areas in the US. The common justification offered for their expansion is that it is a rational economic reaction to user demand. However, research has demonstrated that new lanes attract yet more vehicles. The now-fundamental *maxim of road congestion* is that building more superhighways or adding lanes to existing ones increases VMT proportionally. The result is that increased travel demand absorbs the congestion-relief benefits of additional lanes (Duranton and Turner 2011). The misbegotten rationale of demand still is used to justify adding lanes, so that "the dismal cycle of road-building and sprawl has continued" (Wasik 2017, 20).

However, the public mood in the more developed world has shifted away from having superhighways bisect cities (Kurutz 2017). In the US, opposition to building them was heralded by years of public resistance to constructing Westway in New York City's Manhattan Borough. Put forward in 1971 the project was finally abandoned in 1985 (Buzbee 2014; Gratz 2010). The work of Manhattan resident Jane Jacobs was instrumental in building public opposition (Jacobs 1961). Planned roads were abandoned in a number of cities, including the Spadina Expressway in Toronto in 1971 and the North Western Expressway in Sydney in 1976 (*The Guardian* 2018).

The defiant reaction to urban superhighways spread. In its next phase their *re*-building was resisted as well. A signal target was San Francisco's waterfront Embarcadero Freeway. It was opened in 1959 and acquired the reputation of being "the blight by the bay" (Van Niekerken 2017). Subsequently, it was torn down rather than rebuilt after being damaged by an earthquake in 1989. Resistance to urban superhighways led to a third, current phase – tearing them down. It is exemplified by a digital listing entitled "Freeways Without Futures" (CNU 2017), in which particular urban freeways across the US are highlighted to encourage their demolition. This shift in public attitudes toward superhighways in cities led the nation's shift into its present post-superhighway era (Mohl 2012).

A similar transition has occurred in cities in other parts of the more developed world, including Paris (Grabar 2016), Seoul, and Madrid (Walker 2016), even though far fewer superhighways were built outside North America. The development of opposition in London had parallels to that in New York City (Beanland 2011). It is important to note that while city superhighways have reached a saturation point in the global North they remain highly congested. In fact, congestion has continued to creep slowly upward, especially during the morning and evening commuting hours. Furthermore, superhighways continue to be built apace in cities of developing countries – China presently being the leading example.

Hyper automobility and public transit erosion

Superhighways constitute vast multi-lane infrastructures (of 47,000 miles length in the US) that became material platforms for hyper automobility and auto-centered transport systems – serving as the bones of, first, suburban, and then exurban sprawl. Hyper automobility, measured by auto use (in per capita VMT), progressed apace in the US between 1956 and 1996, corresponding to the period when its superhighway system matured and public transit atrophied. In that period per capita vehicle miles experienced steady rapid growth – an average annual increase of 3.7 percent. Subsequently it has leveled off to an average annual increase of 0.3 percent (BOC 2017; FHWA 2017a).

In addition to the US other more developed nations built massive superhighway systems that encouraged hyper automobility from the 1950s into the early 1990s. The UK superhighways, designated as Motorways ("M" roads), were inaugurated in 1958 and the last one was opened in 1994 (DFT 2016). They served as infrastructures for an eight-fold increase in vehicle miles between 1951 and 2014 while population rose by a much smaller 25 percent. In 2016 the Motorway system comprised only 1 percent of the UK's roadways but carried 21 percent of its vehicle miles.

It appears to be the case that average automobile travel has leveled off (or peaked) since 1996 – at about 10,000 miles per year (Newman and Kenworthy 2011). However, this leveling off may not continue (Focas and Christidis 2017; Goodwin and Van Dender 2013; Martin 2015; Metz 2013; Millard-Ball and Schipper 2010; Stokes 2013). The vehicle miles traveled rose substantially in

2015 and 2016 in the US, largely due to recovery from the 2008 economic crisis (FHWA 2017a). Thus, the current leveling may represent an interruption in VMT growth that will be resumed (Goodwin 2012), perhaps as the current car-declining Millennial generation ages (Delbosc and Currie 2013; Kuhnimhof, Zumkeller, and Chlond 2013; Kuhnimhof et al. 2012), or from the uncertain effects of an AV deployment. Moreover, an apparent vehicle miles peak may not become a global phenomenon; it presently features in developed countries but not in developing ones.

Looking back, it is apparent that the development of hyper automobility in auto-centered transport systems in the US served to replace many of its public transit services. Between 1969 and 1995 there the proportion of commuters who traveled to and from work on public transit declined by about 40 percent (FHWA 2011, 46). Moreover, hyper automobility continues to support auto-centered transport systems, mitigating a full recovery of public bus, tram, and rail services. This displacement remains in force even as car use stagnates at saturation levels.

The US leads a parade of seven highly motorized nations in per capita vehicle kilometers traveled (VKT) with 19,800 (FHWA 2010). It is followed by a group consisting of Canada, China, the UK, Germany, and France, all within a range of 12,400 to 14,100. Japan, like the US, stands alone – with the *lowest* VKT per capita, at 5,200. However, some more developed nations that traveled an automobilization path similar to that of the US also have managed to maintain healthy public transit systems. According to surveys in 2012 they were used frequently by 35 percent of respondents in the UK and by 32 percent in Germany – but only by 15 percent in the US (IC 2014).

The relatively low population density in urban sprawl continues to dictate a preference for automobile transport. While hyper automobility has helped to make the US "clearly the most auto-dependent society on earth," other nations have caught up (Handy 2002). In 2015 it had 821 motor vehicles per 1,000 persons, 4.5 times the global figure. Two nations – Australia and Canada – were not far behind (OICA 2017b). Canada, the US, and Australia are the giant nations of the highly developed world and they accommodate much lower urban population densities than do the nations of Western Europe (*Demographia* 2018). Their largest cities – Toronto, New York City, and Sydney respectively – average 2,200 inhabitants per square kilometer. The three largest urban areas in Western Europe – in order, Paris, London, and Madrid – average 3 times as much.

Data for transportation modal shares in cities consistently show those in the US to be the most automobilized. Its historically newest metropolitan areas lead the world in auto commuting – 89 percent of trips in Dallas and 84 percent in Los Angeles. Some cities in other developed nations also have high rates of automobility – 80 percent in Melbourne, for example. The lowest rates for cities in more developed nations are in East Asia – only 12 percent of Tokyo's commuter trips are by automobile. In between these highest and lowest rates are cities with moderate levels of use. They include the oldest cities of the US as well as

European ones: New York City's auto share of trips is 31 percent; London's, 33 percent (*Journeys* 2011).

1.5 The debut

By 2017 autonomous vehicle tests had multiplied to include public roads in urban areas of six countries on three continents (Valen 2017). Hundreds operate on streets of the Silicon Valley metropolitan area that is home to a great deal of AV digital development. Present California law requires all tests to have backup drivers, but regulators have promised to move quickly to the next step (Said 2017). However, fewer than half of US states have enacted necessary regulatory legislation (NCSL 2017). The cloudy outlook for the pace and character of autonomous vehicle deployment illustrates the truth of a humorous epigram: "It's tough to make predictions, especially about the future" (FQQ 2017, 1). The autonomous vehicle debut is improvised, happening without a shared script.

Locales of rehearsal

Because AV technology is still in the experimental testing stage there is variation in expert forecasts as to when it will become available to consumers and when consumers will embrace it. One expert forecast predicts initial consumer adoption by 2025, with general acceptance arriving by 2050 (Bertoncello and Wee 2016). A market research study predicts the leading locales for uptake by 2035 will be China with 5.7 million on the road, the US with 4.5 million, Europe with 4.2 million, and Japan plus South Korea (the Republic of Korea [ROK]) with 1.2 million (IHS 2016; Voelcker 2014). Still, at that point in time, 2035, a projected 21 million autonomous vehicles will represent only about 1 percent of the world's motor vehicles. The center of gravity for the numerous forecasts of the timing and scale of their deployment has been summarized as follows: "AVs will become an emergent phenomenon by 2020, an accepted technology by the 2030s, and come to dominate personal transportation by 2050" (Greenblatt and Shaheen 2015, 79).

The countries leading autonomous vehicle development and deployment are characterized by three structural features:

1 *Motorization:* High levels of vehicle production and use, the latter measured in vehicle registrations per 1,000 people
2 *Infrastructure:* Extensive, high quality roadways accompanied by first-rate traffic management, measured by the proxy of national per capita income
3 *Digitalization:* Formidable cyber hardware and software production, measured by the presence of influential, AV-involved information technology enterprises and research universities

All three features play important parts in rolling out autonomous vehicles for testing. Advanced motorization provides a manufacturing and consumption base for vehicles. A well-developed infrastructure provides safe built environments for experimental operations. A robust digital capacity provides for the creation and application of essential mapping, surroundings-sensing, and artificial intelligence programming.

Based on an analysis of data for these features the US sets the pace in pursuing AV development and deployment, as it is potent in all three. The state of California is the "hotbed for robot-car development, with 50 companies testing 387 autonomous vehicles" (Said 2018, A1). The companies doing the testing have been led by automotive and digital giants – *General Motors, Apple, Tesla*, and *Alphabet* are operating 55 percent of the test vehicles. It is followed by a small group of eight nations in East Asia and Western Europe that are relatively strong in the three measures: China, France, Germany, Italy, Japan, the ROK, Sweden, and the UK; here these nations will be referred to as the AV9 (DFT 2015; *Forbes* 2017; Gibbs 2016; Greenblatt and Shaneen 2015; Herrmann, Brenner, and Stadler 2018; Kohl et al. 2018; Mercer 2017; Muoio 2017; Navigant 2018; OECD 2015; OICA 2017b, 2017c; Sawyer 2018; Schreurs and Setuwer 2016; *Statista* 2018; Taeihagh and Lim 2018; Trommer et al. 2016; West 2016; *Worldatlas* 2017; *World Bank* 2016). English is the global language of science and technology, and these nine nations lead the world in the production of English-language literature, academic and non-academic, related to autonomous vehicles (Cavoli et al. 2017).

Like many technological innovations autonomous vehicles are being sparingly developed in nations of the global South. Still, as one public opinion study in Pakistan found, they will "impact the opinions and lives of the people living there" (Sanaullah et al. 2017, 561). The poor roadway infrastructures of rapidly growing and traffic-choked cities in the developing world such as Nairobi (Rausch 2016) will face considerably more challenges to an AV uptake than lack of consumer purchasing power. For example, in Lebanon the road system has been described as having the structure of a jellyfish and as featuring a disregard for traffic rules (Waddell 2017).

Thus, autonomous vehicle deployment makes most sense in more developed countries because of their widespread availability of good road and communication infrastructures. Of course, as is often the case with the present structure of global inequality, it is the less developed nations that have more need for the AV's potential benefits, especially its promise to considerably reduce roadway fatalities. There is a reasonable possibility that some megacities in less developed countries will be able to provide a level of required complex technical services to support limited autonomous vehicle operations (Herrmann, Brenner, and Stadler 2018, 377–8). Bangalore, India's equivalent of a Silicon Valley city, is an example.

Despite lacking a significant presence in the global South the AV staging areas are somewhat more decentralized regionally than those for the historic emergence of the automobile. Early 20th century auto production and use were exclusively located in Western Europe and North America. Thus, in 1920 Canada, France, and the US produced nearly all of the world's motor vehicles – 94 percent by the US. With regard to automobile use, in 1921 the same two

North American countries, plus three in Western Europe, France, Germany, and the UK, together had 95 percent of world motor stock – 83 percent was in the US. It was not until the 1970s that a non-Western European, non-North American nation – Japan – became a major global producer, consumer, and exporter of motor vehicles (Martin 2015). It has been joined since by two neighbors, China, and the ROK.

Today there is far less automobile concentration, providing for broader participation in AV development. The Western European-North American share of world vehicle stock is down to 42 percent; the US share, to 21 percent (OICA 2017a). There is now a great deal of variable dispersion in use levels around the world, largely reflecting the inequality that exists between more and less developed countries. For example, the continent of Africa had only 4 percent of global vehicle stock in 2015 while it had 17 percent of population. Its motorization rate was only about one-fourth the global figure. The great majority of African nations fall into the less developed category. The very few that do not are developing, led by South Africa, its most automobilized country (*World Bank* 2016).

Plateaus of incremental change

The cloudy autonomous vehicle uptake looks to be lengthy, disjointed, and disputed – in some measure because it poses a variety of environmental and social risks. Its deployment is laid out in incremental changes that are measured not in years but in decades. When they are made available to the public AVs probably will be first used in fleets rather than as individually owned vehicles. The likely first adopters are commercial ride-providing (carshare) digital platforms, buses, taxis, light to heavy trucks, and vans (McGrath 2018, 67–9; West 2016, 7). One carshare enterprise, *Lyft*, started using self-driving vehicles in Boston in late 2017 – with on-board backup human drivers as required by law (SFC 2017).

Intercity freight haulers rather than passenger cars look to be the first autonomous vehicles to operate on the road – in systematized groupings or platoons (Dougherty 2017a). The incentives for trucking firms to digitalize their vehicle fleet operations are strong: A potential of lower labor and fuel costs combined with lower accident rates. The industry's large scale makes it a premium target for an early AV deployment (Dougherty 2017b). Local commercial van services likely will follow the lead of the larger, better capitalized haulage companies.

Any autonomous vehicle deployment will be required to meet governmental regulatory safety standards. The vehicles and their operators probably will be licensed at each interval in ascending stages, following the levels of automation developed by the International Society of Automotive Engineers (Anderson et al. 2014; NHTSA 2016; Reese 2016; SAE 2016). The levels are as follows:

0   No Automation.
1   *Function-Specific Automation* (or Driver Assistance): Some automated functions can be activated by the driver.

2 *Combined Function Automation* (or Partial Automation): The driver is dis-engaged from specific automated functions but monitors them and can intervene.
3 *Limited Self-Driving Automation* (or Conditional Automation): The driver is limited to specific safety functions but can monitor others and intervene if necessary.
4 *Full Self-Driving Automation* (or High Automation): The vehicle is fully automated but limited to an operational domain that excludes specific environments; e.g., dirt roads, extreme weather conditions. This level is predicted by mid-century.
5 *Full Automation*: The vehicle is fully autonomous and operates in all con-ditions and environments – the truly driverless car, which is predicted by the end of the century.

There are some practical ways to understand these stages and the questions they raise for users. For example, at what point will one be able (permitted) to go to sleep while managing an AV? The answer is Level Four. The final stage, the Fifth or driverless one, is a lifetime away and bears a mythic quality. One forecast refers to it as the coming of *autopia* (Azmat, Schuhmayer, and Kummer 2016). Such a slow uptake to saturation is historically characteristic of motor vehicle technological innovations; for example, air bags took 25 years and automatic transmissions took 50 years (Litman 2016, 11).

A 2014 report on an AV-dedicated conference of 500 experts revealed that one-half did not expect Level Four until 2030, one-fifth not until 2040, and one-tenth never (Gomes 2014). Progressing through the levels of deployment will be progressively more difficult. Preparing accurate up-to-date mapping of streets is proving to be quite nettlesome. One analyst writes that "the slightest variation on the road – a construction zone that pops up overnight, or a bit of debris – could stop a driverless car in its tracks." Such "freak" events ultimately may make autonomous vehicles unworkable at the proposed Four and Five levels (Bergen 2018, D2).

There are a number of compelling reasons for a slow autonomous vehicle deployment above and beyond those relating to technical, regulatory, and busi-ness concerns. Such a major vehicle change will have to gain public approval and trust – it will need to become socially accepted. Furthermore, a full digitalization will be far more complex for users to take in than have been singular changes in vehicles such as automatic transmissions. Driving a car is a learned and licensed skill that eventually becomes an ingrained habit – managing an AV will require a comparable but unknown amount of training and hands-on experience.

Rules of engagement

An autonomous vehicle roll-out will be complex and contested as its deploying enterprises compete vigorously for market share. This competition requires vigi-lant government oversight: "Policy will need to be agile in managing disruptive innovation in transport" (OECD 2017, 2). Integration of vehicular traffic is likely to be even more socially fraught than was the historical transition from horse-and-carriage to automobile. In that shift some localities required a person to walk ahead of a horseless carriage waving a red flag as a warning of danger to all within sight (Said and Evangelista 2017).

Today's automobiles travel much faster, are much more numerous, and are considerably more complex to operate than ever before. The safe roadway blending of autonomous vehicles with conventional ones will require active and comprehensive public regulation of traffic. This likely will lead to vehicle segregation on multi-lane roads. Perhaps there will be licensed lanes for autonomous vehicles – comparable to the High Occupancy Vehicle lanes presently on many US superhighways. Another possibility is that cities will create circumscribed urban areas in which AVs can be used, perhaps using the congestion pricing zone models of London, Singapore, and Stockholm (Anderson et al. 2018).

The most contentious aspect in development of regulatory regimes for deployment likely will be a three-party tug-of-war involving autonomous vehicle start-up enterprises, established transportation businesses, and government regulators. They will feature disparate, sometimes overlapping interests. Private sector entrepreneurial and corporate profit-seeking will test the public sector's mission to protect the safety of vehicles and roadways, as well as that of cyclists and walkers – and at the same time to generate compensatory state income for the task.

It is possible that autonomous vehicle deployment will follow the disruptive business model adapted by digital carsharing start-ups. *Uber* has set a pattern that consists of forging ahead with operations without waiting for regulatory approval, pioneering disruptive intervention on public roads. Digital carshare enterprises challenge established businesses such as taxi cab and car rental companies, as well as local government regulators who have oversight authority for motor vehicles and roadways (Said 2018). With these moves the enterprises have shown they hold the white pieces in their chess match with regulators.

1.6 Uncertainties

The history of the automobile represents a quintessential example of the unwinding of unintended consequences. In its initial deployment more than a century ago its promoters promised to provide safe and congestion-free road transport (Norton 2018). However, both promises have become two of the most notorious banes of contemporary auto use. Because of the acceleration of technological innovation spurred by digitalization, forecasting the impacts of technical and social change is at the same time more necessary but also more difficult. Unknown consequences await discovery. They remain behind a curtain and "will not become obvious until they are put into widespread use at a scale impossible to turn back" (Dean 2008, F1). The known impacts are already onstage but their roles are small and have not yet been scripted – that is, they have not been defined and calibrated.

Uncertainties feature in all major technological innovations. There are expectations as to risks but they defy specifications. These will emerge from the course of a technology's use. In the analysis here, "Uncertainty signifies that one knows the kind of things that might happen but not the probability of their occurrence" (Douglas and Wildavsky 1982, 22). One result is that defining uncertainty relies on the subjunctive tense – this or that impact would, should, or could (or not) hypothetically occur. While risk is defined by calculation, uncertainty depends on judgment (Adams 1995, 26). Thus, assessment of autonomous vehicle impacts here will be informed by data but decided by acumen. Not all technical innovations are equal with regard to the caliber of their uncertainties. Motor vehicles historically have been "implemented more slowly than other technological changes due to their high costs, slow fleet turnover and strict safety requirements" (Litman 2016, 17).

The deployment of AVs likely will be subject to five major uncertainties: Disruption, public resistance, digital failures, ethical dilemmas, and rebound effects. All five potentially will have relevance to the sustainability of autonomous vehicle mobility. They rather dramatically illustrate the known unknowns flowing from sociotechnical change. While they can be identified, their specific applications and outcomes remain quite variable.

Disruption

The AV is popularly depicted as an innovation, or breakthrough, with a decidedly positive aura. However, it has at this moment a disruptive or breaking asunder potential as well (Bissell 2018). Not all technological innovations can be disruptive across such a wide range of life activities as the automobile. In great measure that is because it is a large machine operated at speed by an individual in public space. At this point it appears that the autonomous vehicle has potential to be at least as disruptive as the original automobile was over a hundred years ago.

Disruption theory has developed in economics and describes the process in which a small company, often today a digital start-up, directly challenges incumbent enterprises (Christensen, Raynor, and McDonald 2015). The impact of car-sharing digital platforms such as *Uber* on the taxicab industry is a popularly used example. There is a rather long list of known targets of disruptions of unknown magnitudes on the business side of AV deployment. These include challenges to the auto industry itself, as well as to vehicle insurance companies, the trucking industry, and rental car companies (McGrath 2018).

Aside from its implications for the operation of auto-related businesses, autonomous vehicle deployment will be socially disruptive to road traffic and safety, as well as to licensing and regulation. The potential social disruptions are led by the threat of job losses in a number of businesses (see Chapter Three). The most general disruptions will likely take place in the management of road traffic and the regulation of AV licensing. Autonomous and conventional vehicles will have to share the same congested roadways. In addition, autonomous vehicles and their users, like conventional vehicles and their drivers, will face qualifying licensing tests as well as periodic examinations of the safe operating conditions of both vehicles and their managers.

Public resistance

Resistance to AV use will take a passive and an active form. Both are rooted in the habituation of conventional automobile use over the last one hundred years. It became part of family life – as in taking family drives on weekend afternoons and going to drive-in movies in the evenings. Such cultural customs have developed in all highly motorized nations, but they seem to be pronounced in the US. As one commentator noted: "As the car transformed the American lifestyle, so did it colonize the American imagination" (Wasik 2017, 18). Canadians and Australians as well have developed a particularly strong affinity to motoring, perhaps resulting from living in expansive territories combined with high levels of development. Australia and Canada rank just behind the US in vehicles per capita (OICA 2017a).

For many, driving an automobile can be a source of joy and pleasure as well as boredom or stress. In the end, even after a full autonomous vehicle deployment it is likely that an unknown proportion of motorists still will not use one; many of them will choose not to give up driving because they like it (Quain 2016). If AV deployment does reach saturation levels conventional vehicles may end up becoming the urban horses of their time, to be used for sport and recreation and in designated venues.

There is some strong public reaction to the possibility of driving being taken away by the arrival of AVs. One anecdote may foreshadow the intensity of public reaction. Of six autonomous vehicle crash reports in California in the first two months of 2018, "two involved a human approaching the car and attacking it" (Mitchell 2018, C3). Some in the automobile business express a passionate criticism of AVs: "Don't brainwash the new generation with autonomous driving – it's so beautiful, driving" (Mathews 2017, E3). Others make a patriotic defense, illustrated by the cover of a *New York Magazine* edition in October, 2016. It was highlighted by bright red letters reading, "Is the Self-Driving Car Un-American?" Perhaps such discord will become the basis of yet another cultural war, at least in the US, prosecuted by campaigning "right-to-drive" motorists who espouse such slogans as "make America drive again" (Atkin 2018).

Digital debacles

A challenge to human adaptation of autonomous vehicle use will be getting accustomed to being a passenger and leaving the driving to a machine. It represents a further and more risky extension of the on-going digitalization of daily life. The global internet of things apparently is on its way to include a global internet of vehicles (Datta 2008). One internet pioneer referred to this by saying that "software is eating the world" (Andreessen 2017, 2). AVs will share the characteristic technical demands of digital devices, such as fluency in the use of windowing touch screens, but they will be considerably more complex to operate. Thus, another digital doyen has described the autonomous vehicle as becoming "one of the largest mobile devices out there" (West 2016, 1).

We are used to being passengers in motor vehicles controlled by other people – for example, taxi and bus drivers. However, they are practiced and licensed, and are driving in our presence. Turning control over to a remote machine will create uncertain levels of anxiety and bewilderment. Generally, it has been the case that public concern is especially high to major changes in mobility technologies. Objectively they can be, or subjectively can seem to be, abrupt new threats to personal safety. Public reactions to the past advents of steam trains, conventional automobiles, and airplanes serve as examples. Ceding car driving to computers will represent a new threat to one's sense of safety as a commentator has noted:

> Driverless cars tap deep into the human psyche. We want to be in control, or at least to give control to trained professionals. . . . We don't want computers to be in charge.
>
> (Leonhardt 2017, A21)

Based on our experience so far with digital systems it is reasonable to anticipate there will be autonomous vehicle failures. The common mantra in computer programming, "garbage in, garbage out," may become "garbage in, danger out," indicating a qualitative increase in the gravity of digital operations. After all, AVs will be moving and interacting at speed with other moving vehicles, as well as with cyclists and walkers. Failures could be random errors or could be produced by hackers and cyber terrorists. In an online survey of 5,000 people in 109 countries, the respondents' greatest concern about autonomous vehicles was software hacking (Kyriakidis, Happee, and de Winter 2015).

There is some early experimental evidence about the random error frequency in autonomous vehicle deployment. In 2017 five companies tested them on public roads in California. The vehicles were managed by engineers who could intervene and take control; interventions were defined as "disengagements." One took place an average of every 1,674 miles driven (Baker 2018). In the same year autonomous vehicles reported 27 road accidents (CA 2018), or one in an average of 18,472 miles. In comparison the average US driver has an accident about every 165,000 miles (FHWA 2016). While the nine-fold difference may be concerning it is not a basis for prediction as AVs were in their early experimental days in 2017, and none of their road crashes in California that year resulted in death or bodily injury.

The potential human costs flowing from digital failures are real, and they will serve to subtract from benefits of a prospective AV reduction of road crashes. An additional consideration is that contemporary social heightening of the global terrorism threat may spill over into autonomous vehicle deployment, making it yet another travel modality refereed by state security agencies. This likely will raise an unknown level of concern from the public about yet another threat to personal privacy.

Ethical dilemmas

Autonomous vehicle discourse is exploring relationships between ethical rules and binary algorithms, and much remains to be debated and decided. It has been taken up as a public health issue in a number of fields (Fleetwood 2017). For example, one analyst has suggested that constructing artificial intelligence to negotiate traffic should become a major focus of cognitive science research (Chater and Griffiths 2017). Ultimately, there will be no perfect answer but at least decisions should be thoroughly thought through and transparently arrived at with meaningful public input.

Ethics will mix with law and business practices in an autonomous vehicle deployment. Who will own the damages stemming from a system failure or malfunction: The operator or owner of the vehicle, the manufacturer of the vehicle, or its software (Raghuram 2018)? Allowing the manufacturer to market autonomous vehicles with different software platforms may result in outcomes that are not equitable and therefore not socially sustainable. Automobile businesses may use AV digital programming packages as a marketing ploy; such ploys are currently used with cruise control, GPS, and rear camera technologies. As one analysis pointed out, if unregulated, autonomous vehicle salespersons could offer self-preserving software to wealthier prospective buyers (Bergmann et al. 2018, 7). On the tech side, while digital platforms such as *Facebook* and *Google* have succeeded in keeping secret their algorithms for searching, sorting, and selling personal data, it likely will not be permitted by regulators with autonomous vehicle data (Nida-Rumelin 2018, 253). AV-sourced data will be directly and immediately relevant to the personal safety of all connected vehicle occupants.

Rebound effects

In addition to digital failures and ethical dilemmas there are social and environmental ramifications stemming from the rebound effects that will follow AV deployment. Such technological innovations historically have led to behavioral and systematic changes as a result of an expansion of their applications. The rebound is similar to the common human reaction to unexpected or unwanted events, such as the break-up of personal relationships. In environmental science rebound refers to a characteristic feature of human consumption that was originally promulgated by the British economist William Jevons (1906) in his 19th century treatise on the use of coal for fuel in the new railway industry. Essentially, a rebound effect occurs when efficiency gains reduce the price of a resource, product, or service, which in turn serves to increase its consumption. The consumption from a rebound effect has two facets: Magnitude and direction.

A rebound effect may have more than an initial economic result. Thus, like a stone cast into a calm lake it may produce ripples in the same direction beyond the initial impact. For example, autonomous vehicles may result in a direct rebound of fewer crashes, which is turn produces a ripple of less vehicle materials consumption because vehicles will live longer and more repair-free lives. Furthermore, a rebound's onward effects may not be direct or be restricted to economics but like a bullet hitting an obstacle will ricochet and take another direction. For example, an autonomous vehicle rebound effect (from programmed driving) may be less traffic congestion, which in turn may produce a ricochet of increased urban sprawl (as the same commuting time will cover longer distances). The most commonly expected rebound effect of autonomous vehicle deployment is an increase in vehicle miles traveled due in part to the appeals of its conveniences – for example, not having to park. The uncertain increase in VMT will present a wide range of potential impacts on energy consumption (OEE 2013). An estimate of the rebound effect to enhanced fuel efficiency (in conventional vehicles) is an increase of 25 to 65 percent in fuel use (Chitnis et al. 2014).

Rebound effects are crucial unknown variables that will influence any prospect for autonomous vehicles' sustainability prospects. Secondary ripples and ricochets are even more uncertain. The rebound is a dynamic reaction to change, not a linear and one-dimensional one. The term is used popularly to refer to reaction to the end of a personal relationship – that is, to start another one "on the rebound." The English word is traced to the Old French *rebondir*, meaning to re-bounce. It connotes an uncertain quality and quantity of reaction – as a post break-up, new relationship may lead to unexpected ripples and ricochets.

There is no debate about the validity of the rebound effect. The on-going disagreement, based in ecological economics, lies in its magnitude and direction. Some researchers argue that it may entirely wash away any AV efficiency gains, referred to as a rebound backfire. Others argue that there is little support for the backfire hypothesis (Gillingham, Rapson, and Wagner 2015), and still others argue that a nil VMT rebound is possible through a redirection of efficiency savings into green investments (Druckman et al. 2012), illustrating the flexible character of rebound effects.

Whatever their direction and magnitude the rebound effects of autonomous vehicles will not be certain until they are widely deployed, and this will take time. Ripples and ricochets in particular likely will not be evident until Level Four, Full Self-Driving Automation. In the meantime, forecasts and scenarios are useful tools that produce probabilities or hints based in data and observations already at hand.

1.7   Toward sustainability for environments, societies, and cities

Technological innovations commonly develop without consideration of the full range of their sustainability impacts. It takes the widespread adoption of innovation – its embeddedness as a routine consumer product – to create a scale sufficiently robust to produce notable impacts. However, while mass diffusion of the AV is decades away its potential to enhance sustainability still can be anticipated and usefully projected.

The automobile serves as a prime example of how the maturation of material technologies involves on-going *dynamic* and *reciprocal* connections to their contexts. In the human imagination a new tool can be a marvel and an unmitigated boon while in practice it is likely to become mundane and to produce unintended consequences or side effects. The development of the automobile, now well over a century in duration, is a good example. We are dealing today with both the positive and negative legacies of its mass adoption. While the car has provided for an unprecedented level of convenient and flexible personal mobility its hyper development has led to unacceptably high levels of traffic congestion, fatalities, injuries, toxic pollutants, and GHG emissions (Freund and Martin 2009).

This troublesome legacy of conventional vehicles sets the stage for deployment of the AV. Its character and role will be shaped by the infrastructures and practices with which it interacts. Significantly, this will be a two-way interaction. The autonomous vehicle will influence its surroundings as it is being shaped by them. A consequence of this fact is that deployment can be steered by public policy in the direction of neutralizing the negative legacies of conventional automobility.

There are three impact areas of autonomous vehicle deployment that warrant detailed sustainability scrutiny: Environments, societies, and cities. They overlap considerably; for example, internal combustion vehicle emissions are an issue for societies (public health) and cities (air pollution) as well as for environments (climate change). Still, the categorization is a helpful tool for analysis as it breaks a complex subject into more manageable bits that facilitate easier and fuller comprehension.

With regard to environments ICVs make major contributions to climate change with their greenhouse gas emissions. Autonomous vehicles may have a capacity to maximize eco-motorization for individual vehicles, and to multiply their energy efficiencies within connected vehicle groupings. Developing eco-motorization programming across a wide variety of potential vehicles could also reduce the traffic congestion that intensifies vehicle emissions. Autonomous vehicle deployment has potential to make an even greater contribution to environmental sustainability through additional gains that could be achieved by its electrification. Fully electric AVs will reduce the GHG emissions from their operation. Taking advantage of electric power would add yet other gains – downsized powertrains and reduced mechanical complexities. This would provide for enhanced sustainability through the full life cycle of vehicles, not just in their operations. Moreover, electrification could be an effective compensation for the anticipated autonomous vehicle rebound effect of increased vehicle miles. These environmental sustainability prospects are analyzed in detail in Chapter Two.

In relation to societies, autonomous vehicles have promise to provide two major public health benefits – lowering of road crash injuries and deaths and toxic tailpipe emissions. Even moderate reductions in crash and emission levels could make for a major drop in the large number of humans who are subjected to motor vehicle related mortality and morbidity. AVs also will have potential to provide mobility access and affordability to persons generally excluded because of the physical demands and costs of driving a personal vehicle. New autonomous vehicle users could include large numbers from several groups, notably persons with disabilities and those with physical infirmities of aging. Assessment of the potential autonomous vehicle impacts on social sustainability are taken up in Chapter Three.

Cities merit categorical attention with regard to an autonomous vehicle sustainability prospectus for several reasons. They are home to a growing majority of humans and motor vehicles. They are also the principal arenas where autonomous vehicles are being tested and where they likely will be publicly deployed as well. These facts mean that AVs will have their most immediate impacts in cities. At present urban landscapes in the more developed nations are permeated with auto-centered transport systems, based in space-eating infrastructures of roadways, vehicle service facilities, and parking places (WEF 2015). In some US cities parking lots and structures cover more than one-third of total land area (Ben-Joseph 2012). The promise of fewer automobiles on the road and less need for parking space could lead to opportunities for a new wave of urban greening. There is a potential to turn concrete and asphalt roads and parking facilities into parks and community gardens, as well as into a bounty of walking and cycling paths (Martin 2018).

Autonomous vehicle deployment could make a major contribution to the revitalization of public transit systems in many cities. AVs of various passenger capacities could extend public transit's reach into lower-density suburban and exurban areas. They could provide support for developing sustainable, low cost, and accessible multi-modal systems by adding options to fill current service gaps. Urban sustainability as it relates to autonomous vehicle impacts is analyzed in Chapter Four.

This monograph's final Chapter Five fashions an evaluative scorecard for assessing the sustainability impacts of an autonomous vehicle deployment, and goes on to parse five looming wildcards that likely will have major but uncertain effects on deployment. At this point, now that parameters for an AV roll-out's setting have been suggested, its character and role on different sustainability stages can be examined in some detail – beginning with environments.

References

Adams, John. 1995. *Risk*. London: UCL Press.
Anderson, Christina, Winnie Hu, Weiyi Lim, and Anna Schaverien. 2018. "Should New York Look Abroad to Get Out of Its Traffic Jam?" *The New York Times*, February 27, p. A15.
Anderson, J., N. Kalra, K. Stanley, P. Sorensen, C. Samaras, and O. Oluwatola. 2014. *Autonomous Vehicle Technology: A Guide for Policymakers*. Santa Monica, CA: RAND Corporation.
Andreessen, M. 2017. "Why Software Is Eating the World." Available at: https://bcourses. berkeley.edu/files/64332569/download?download_frd=1 [Accessed November 18, 2017].

Andreev, Nik. 2018. "A Brief History of Car Parking Technology." *Confused*, June 13. Available at: www.confused.com/on-the-road/gadgets-tech/parking-technology-brief-history [Accessed October 4, 2018].

Asimov, Isaac. 1969. *Nightfall and Other Stories*. New York: Doubleday.

Atkin, Emily. 2018. "The Modern Automobile Must Die." *Mother Jones*, August 21. Available at: www.motherjones.com/environment/2018/-the-modern-automobile-must-die [Accessed October 3, 2018].

Azmat, M., C. Schuhmayer, and S. Kummer. 2016. "Innovation in Mobility: Austrian Expert's Perspective on the Future of Urban Mobility with Self-Driving Cars." *Innovation Arabia 9: Quality and Business Management Conference (Business Innovation – Imperative for Knowledge Economy)* 9: 142–60. ISSN 2414-6110.

Baker, David R. 2018. "Robot Cars Need Less and Less Human Help." *San Francisco Chronicle*, February 1, pp. C1, C6.

Beanland, Christopher. 2011. "London: Roads to Nowhere." *Independent*, February 8. Available at: www.independent.co.uk/arts-entertainment/architecture/london-roads-to-nowhere-2207351.html [Accessed August 10, 2018].

Ben-Joseph, E. 2012. "Taking Parking Lots Seriously as Public Spaces." *The New York Times*, January 8, p. 15.

Bergen, Mark. 2018. "Google Tries to Win Map War Again." *San Francisco Chronicle*, February 26, pp. D1, D2.

Bergmann, Lasse T., Larissa Schlicht, Carmen Meixner, Peter Konig, Gordon Pipa, Suzanne Boshammer, and Achim Stephan. 2018. "Autonomous Vehicles Require Socio-Political Acceptance: An Empirical and Philosophical Perspective on the Problem of Moral Decision Making." *Frontiers in Behavioral Neuroscience* 12: 1–12. doi: 10.3389/fnbeh.2018.00031.

Bertoncello, M. and D. Wee. 2016. "Ten Ways Autonomous Driving Could Redefine the Automotive World." *Our Insights*. Available at: www.mckinsey.com/industries/automotive-and-assembly/our-insights/ [Accessed September 6, 2016].

Bissell, David. 2018. "Automation Interrupted: How Autonomous Vehicle Accidents Transform the Material Politics of Automation." *Political Geography* 65: 57–66. https://doi.org/10.1016/j.polgeo.2018.05.003.

BOC. 2017. *Population Clock*. Washington, DC: US Bureau of the Census.

Buzbee, William W. 2014. *Fighting Westway: Environmental Law, Citizen Activism, and the Regulatory War that Transformed New York City*. Ithaca NY: Cornell University Press.

CA. 2018. *Report of Traffic Accident Involving an Autonomous Vehicle*. Sacramento: Department of Motor Vehicles, State of California. Available at: www.dmv.ca.gov/accidents [Accessed February 6, 2018].

Carr, D. and B. Ott. 2010. "The Older Adult Driver with Cognitive Impairment." *Journal of the American Medical Association* 303: 1632–41.

Cavoli, Clemence, Brian Phillips, Tom Cohen, and Peter Jones. 2017. *Social and Behavioural Questions Associated with Automated Vehicles a Literature Review*. London: UCL Transport Institute, January. Available at: www.ucl.ac.uk/transport-institute/pdfs/social-and-behavioural-literature-review.pdf [Accessed February 24, 2018].

Chase, Robin. 2014. "Will a World of Driverless Cars be Heaven of Hell?" *Citylab*, April 3. Available at: www.citylab.com/transportation/2014/04/will-world-driverless-cars-be-heaven-or-hell/8784 [Accessed August 14, 2018].

Chater, Nick and Nathan Griffiths. 2017. "Negotiating the Traffic: Can Cognitive Science Help Make Autonomous Vehicles a Reality?" *Trends in Cognitive Sciences*, December. doi: 10.1016/j.tics.2017.11.008. Available at: www.researchgate.net/publication/321814210 [Accessed January 22, 2018].

Chitnis, M., S. Sorrell, A. Druckman, S. Firth, and T. Jackson. 2014. "Who Rebounds Most? Estimating Direct and Indirect Rebound Effects for Different UK Socioeconomic Groups." *Ecological Economics* 106: 12–32.

Christensen, Clayton, Michael Raynor, and Rory McDonald. 2015. "What Is Disruptive Innovation?" *Harvard Business Review*, December, pp. 4–11.

Claypool, Henry. 2017. *Self-Driving Cars: The Impact on People with Disabilities*. Boston: Ruderman Family Foundation. Available at: www.rundermanfoundation.org/wp-content/uploads/2017/08/Self-Driving-Cars_FINAL.pdf [Accessed March 21, 2018].

CNU. 2017. *Freeways without Futures*. Washington, DC: Congress for the New Urbanism. Available at: www.cnu.org/highways-boulevards/freeways-without-futures/ [Accessed August 10, 2018].

Datta, S. 2008. *Auto ID Paradigm Shifts from Internet of Things to Unique Identification of Individual Decisions in System of Systems*. Cambridge, MA: Engineering Systems Division, Working Paper ESD-WP-2008–09, MIT. Available at: https://dspace.mit.edu/bitstream/handle/1721.1/102863/esd-wp-2008-09.pdf?sequence=1 [Accessed June 22, 2018].

Dauvergue, P. 2008. *The Shadow of Consumption: Consequences for the Global Environment*. Cambridge, MA: MIT Press.

Davis, S.C. and L.F. Truett. 2000. "An Analysis of the Impact of Sport Utility Vehicles in the United States." Available at: https://citeseerx.ist.psu.edu/viewdoc/download?doi=10.1.1.500.4646&rep=rep1 [Accessed December 5, 2017].

Dean, C. 2008. "Handle with Care." *The New York Times*, August 12, p. F1. Available at: www.nytimes.com/2008/08/12/science/12ethics.html [Accessed August 29, 2009].

Delbosc, Alexa and Graham Currie. 2013. "Causes of Youth Licensing Decline: A Synthesis of Evidence." *Transport Reviews* 33: 271–90.

Demographia. 2018. *World Urban Areas 14th Annual Edition*. Belleville IL. Available at: www.demographia.com/db-worldua.pdf [Accessed August 17, 2018].

DFT. 2016. *Road Use Statistics for Great Britain*. London: UK Department for Transport. Available at: www.licencebureau.co.uk/wp-content/uploads/road-use-statistics.pdf [Accessed December 1, 2017].

DFT. 2015. *The Pathway to Driverless Cars Summary Report and Action Plan*. London: UK Department for Transport, February. Available at: www.gov.uk/government/uploads/system/uploads/attachment_data/file/401562/pathway-driverless-cars-summary.pdf [Accessed February 24, 2018].

DFT. 2005. *Focus on Personal Travel*. London: UK Department for Transport.

Di, Q., L. Dai, Y. Wang, A. Zanobetti, C. Choirat, J. Schwartz, and F. Dominici. 2017. "Association of Short-Term Exposure to Air Pollution with Mortality in Older Adults." *Journal of American Medical Association* 318: 2446–56. doi: 10.1001/jama.2017.17923.

Dougherty, C. 2017a. "When the CB Radios All Go Quiet." *The New York Times*, November 13, pp. B1, B3.

Dougherty, C. 2017b. "Autonomous Trucks Closer Than They Appear." *San Francisco Chronicle*, November 14, pp. D1, D3.

Douglas, Mary and Aaron Wildavsky. 1982. *Risk and Culture: An Essay on the Selection of Technological and Environmental Dangers*. Berkeley: University of California Press.

Druckman, A., M. Chitnis, S. Sorrell, and T. Jackson. 2012. "Missing Carbon Reductions? Exploring Rebound and Backfire Effects in UK Households." *Energy Policy* 39: 572–81.

Duranton, G. and M. Turner. 2011. "The Fundamental Law of Road Congestion: Evidence from US Cities." *American Economic Review* 101: 2616–52. doi: 10.1257/aer.101.6.2616 [Accessed December 3, 2017].

EPA. 2017. *Highlights of CO2 and Fuel Economy Trends.* Washington, DC: US Department of Environmental Protection. Available at: www.epa.gov/fuel-economy [Accessed February 5, 2018].

FHWA. 2017a. *Historical Monthly VMT Report.* Washington, DC: Federal Highway Administration, US Department of Transportation. Available at: www.fhwa.dot.gov/policyinformation/travel_monitoring/historicmt.cfm [Accessed November 28, 2017].

FHWA. 2017b. *Highway History: The Reichsautobahnen.* Washington, DC: Federal Highway Administration, US Department of Transportation. Available at: https://fhwa.dot.gov./infractructure/reichs.cfm [Accessed December 1, 2017].

FHWA. 2016. *Facts & Statistics.* Washington, DC: Office of Highway Policy Information, Federal Highway Administration, US Department of Transportation. Available at: www.fhwa.dot.gov/accidents [Accessed February 6, 2018].

FHWA. 2015. *Annual Vehicle Distance Traveled in Miles by Highway Type and Vehicle Type.* Washington, DC: Federal Highway Administration, US Department of Transportation. Available at: www.fhwa.dot.gov/policyinformation/statistics/2013/vm.1.cfm [Accessed November 29, 2017].

FHWA. 2011. *Summary of Travel Trends: 2009 National Household Travel Survey.* Washington, DC: Federal Highway Administration, US Department of Transportation. Available at: https://nhts.ornl.gov/2009/pub/stt,pdf [Accessed December 6, 2017].

FHWA. 2010. *Vehicle Travel by Selected Country;Vehicle Kilometers of Travel-Automobile.* Washington, DC: Federal Highway Administration, US Department of Transportation. Available at: www.fhwa.dot.gov/policyinformation/statistics/2008/pdf/in5.pdf [Accessed January 13, 2018].

Fleetwood, Janet. 2017. "Public Health, Ethics, and Autonomous Vehicles." *American Journal of Public Health* 107: 532–7. doi: 10.2105/AJPH.2016.303628.

Focas, Caralampo and Panayotis Christidis. 2017. "Peak Car in Europe?" *Transportation Research Procedia* 25: 531–50. doi: 10.1016/j.trpro.2017.05.437.

Forbes. 2017. "The World's Biggest Public Companies." *Forbes Magazine.* Available at: www.forbes.com/global2000/list/#industry:Software%20%26%20Programming [Accessed November 16, 2017].

Ford, Henry. 1922. *Ford News,* May 15, p. 2. Available at: www.thehenryford.org/collections-and-research/digital-resources/popular-topics/henry-ford-quotes [Accessed September 23, 2018].

FQQ. 2017. *Famous Quotes & Quotations.* Available at: www.famous-quotes-and-quotations.com/yogi-berra-quotes.html [Accessed November 22, 2017].

Freund, Peter and George Martin. 2009. "The Social and Material Culture of Hyperautomobility." *Bulletin of Science, Technology & Society* 29: 476–82.

Freund, Peter and George Martin. 2007. "Hyperautomobility, the Social Organization of Space and Health." *Mobilities* 2: 37–49.

Freund, Peter and George Martin. 2002. "Risky Vehicles, Risky Agents: Mobility and the Politics of Space, Movement, and Consciousness." Pp. 105–20 in J.P. Rothe, ed., *Driving Lessons: Exploring Systems That Make Traffic Safer.* Edmonton: University of Alberta Press.

Freund, Peter and George Martin. 2001. "Moving Bodies: Injury, Dis-Ease and the Social Organisation of Space." *Critical Public Health* 11: 203–14.

Gibbs, S. 2016. "Self-Driving Cars: Who's Building Them and How Do They Work?" *The Guardian,* May 26. Available at: https://theguardian.com/technology/2016/may/26/self-driving-cars-whos-bulding-them-and-how-do-they-work/ [Accessed July 30, 2017].

Gillingham, K., D. Rapson, and G. Wagner. 2015. "The Rebound Effect and Energy Efficiency Policy." *Review of Environmental Economics and Policy* 10: 68–88. Available at: https://doi.org/10.1093/reep/rev017 [Accessed December 10, 2017].

Gomes, L. 2014. "Urban Jungle a Tough Challenge for Google's Autonomous Cars." *MIT Technology Review*, July 24. Available at: www.technologyreview.com/news/529466/urban-jungle-a-tough-challenge-for-googles-autonomous-cars [Accessed October 2, 2018].

Goodwin, P. 2012. *Peak Travel, Peak Car and the Future of Mobility: Evidence, Unresolved Issue, Policy Implications, and a Research Agenda*. Paris: International Transport Forum, Discussion Paper No. 2012–13.

Goodwin, P. and K. Van Dender. 2013. "'Peak Car': Themes and Issues." *Transport Reviews* 33, Special Issue on "Peak Car." Available at: https://doi.org/10.1080/01441647.2013.80 4133 [Accessed June 21, 2018].

Grabar, Henry. 2016. "Paris Is Turning Its Central Highway into a Park." *Slate*, September 13. Available at: www.slate.com/blogs/moneybox/2016/09/13/paris-html [Accessed August 14, 2018].

Gratz, Roberta B. 2010. *The Battle for Gotham: New York in the Shadow of Robert Moses and Jane Jacobs*. New York: Nation Books.

Greenblatt, Jeffrey B. and Susan Shaheen. 2015. "Automated Vehicle, On-Demand Mobility, and Environmental Impacts." *Current Sustainable Renewable Energy Reports* 2: 74–91. doi: 10.1007/s40518-015-0038-5.

The Guardian. 2018. "Unbuilt Cities: The Outrageous Highway Schemes Left as Roads to Nowhere." January 5. Available at: www.theguardian.com/cities/2018/jan/05/unbuilt-highways-urban-development-roads-nowhere [Accessed August 25, 2018].

Hakim, D. 2004. "Average U.S. Car Is Tipping Scales at 4,000 Pounds." *The New York Times*, May 3. Available at: www.nytimes.com/2004/05/05/./average-us-car-is-tipping-scales-at-4000-pounds.html [Accessed December 6, 2017].

Handy, Susan. 2002. "Accessibility vs. Mobility-Enhancing Strategies for Addressing Automobile Dependence in the U.S." European Conference of Ministers of Transport, May. Available at: www.des.ucdavis.edu/faculty/handy/ECMT_report.pdf [Accessed February 23, 2018].

Herrmann, Andreas, Walter Brenner, and Rupert Stadler. 2018. *Autonomous Driving: How the Driverless Revolution Will Change the World*. Bingley, UK: Emerald.

IC. 2014. "Transportation Statistics by Country." *International Comparisons*. Available at: http://internationalcomparisons.org/environment/transportation.html [Accessed December 10, 2017].

IHS. 2016. "Autonomous Vehicle Sales Set to Reach 21 Million Globally by 2035." *Information Handling Services*. Available at: www.ihs.com/automotive-industry-forecasting.html?ID=115737/ [Accessed December 20, 2016].

Jacobs, Jane. 1961. *The Death and Life of Great American Cities*. New York: Vintage.

Jevons, W.S. 1906 [1865]. *The Coal Question*. London: Macmillan.

Journeys. 2011. "Passenger Transport Mode Shares in World Cities." November 11. Available at: www.studylib.net/doc/7972629/passenger-transport-mode-shares-in-world-cities [Accessed February 25, 2018].

Kohl, Christopher, Marlene Knigge, Galina Baader, Markus Bohm, and Helmut Krcmar. 2018. "Anticipating Acceptance of Emerging Technologies Using Twitter: The Case of Self-Driving Cars." *Journal of Business Economics* 88: 617–42. https://doi.org/10.1007/s11573-018-0897-5.

Kuhnimhof, T., J. Armoogum, R. Buehler, J. Dargay, J. Denstadlii, and T. Yamamoto. 2012. "Men Shape a Downward Trend in Car Use among Young Adults: Evidence from Six Industrialized Countries." *Transport Reviews* 32: 761–79.

Kuhnimhof, T., D. Zumkeller, and B. Chlond. 2013. "Who Made Peak Car, and How? A Breakdown of Trends over Four Decades in Four Countries." *Transport Reviews* 33: 325–42.

Kurutz, Steven. 2017. "Exit the Expressway." *The New York Times*, October 21, p. ST1.

Kyriakidis, M., R. Happee, and J. de Winter. 2015. "Public Opinion on Automated Driving: Results of an International Questionnaire among 5000 Respondents." *Transportation Research Part F: Traffic Psychology and Behaviour* 32: 127–40.

Leonhardt, D. 2017. "Driverless Anxiety, and Then Relief." *The New York Times*, October 17, p. A21.

Leslie, Jacques. 2018. "Will Self-Driving Cars Usher in a Transportation Utopia or Dystopia?" *YaleEnvironment360*, January 8. Available at: http://e360.yale.edu/features/will-self-driving-cars-usher-in-a-transportation-utopia-or-dystopia? [Accessed August 22, 2018].

Litman, T. 2016. *Autonomous Vehicle Implementation Predictions*. Victoria, BC: Victoria Transport Policy Institute, September 1. Available at: http://vtpi.org/AVIP.pdf [Accessed March 16, 2017].

Martin, George. 2018. "An Ecosocial Frame for Autonomous Vehicles." *Capitalism Nature Socialism*. Available at: https://doi.org/10.1080/10455752.2018.1510531 [Accessed August 22, 2018].

Martin, George. 2015. "Global Automobility and Social Ecological Sustainability." Pp. 23–37 in A. Walks, P. Hess, and M. Siemiatycki, eds., *The Political Economy and Ecology of Automobility: Driving Cities, Driving Inequality, Driving Politics*. Abingdon: Routledge.

Martin, George. 1999. *Hyperautomobility and Its Sociomaterial Impacts*. Guildford: Centre for Environment and Sustainability, University of Surrey, CES Working Paper No. 02/99.

Mathews, J. 2017. "Ferrari's Grand Touring Car Drives Home Lessons." *San Francisco Chronicle*, February 5, p. E3.

Matulka, Rebecca. 2014. *The History of the Electric Car*. Washington, DC: US Department of Energy. Available at: https://energy.gov/articles/history-electric-car [Accessed January 4, 2018].

McGrath, Michael E. 2018. *Autonomous Vehicles: Opportunities, Strategies, and Disruptions*. San Bernardino, CA: Independently Published. ISBN-13: 978-1980313854.

Melosi, M.V. 2004. *The Automobile and the Environment in American History*. Dearborn, MI: Science and Technology Studies Program, University of Michigan-Dearborn. Available at: www.autolife.umd.umich.edu [Accessed December 6, 2017].

Mercer, C. 2017. "12 Companies Working on Driverless Cars: What Companies Are Making Driverless Cars?" *techWorld*. Available at: www.techworld.com/picture-gallery/data/-companies-working-on-driverless-cars-3641537/ [Accessed November 18, 2017].

Metz, David. 2013. "Peak Car and Beyond: The Fourth Era of Travel." *Transport Reviews* 33: 255–70.

Millard-Ball, Adam and Lee Schipper. 2010. "Are We Reaching Peak Travel? Trends in Passenger Transport in Eight Industrialized Countries." *Transport Reviews* 31: 357–78.

Mitchell, Russ. 2018. "2 Crashes of Autonomous Cars Were Attacks in S.F." *San Francisco Chronicle*, March 7, p. C3.

Mohl, R.A. 2012. "The Expressway Tear Down Movement in American Cities: Rethinking Postwar Highway Policy in the Post-Interstate Era." *Journal of Planning History* 11: 89–103.

Muoio, Danielle. 2017. "RANKED: The 18 Companies Most Likely to Get Self-Driving Cars on the Road First." *Business Insider*. Available at: www.businessinsider.com/the-companies-most-likely-to-get-driverless-cars-on-the-road-first-2017-4/#18-baidu-1 [Accessed November 21, 2017].

Navigant. 2018. *Navigant Research Leaderboard: Automated Driving Vehicles*. Ann Arbor, MI: Navigant Research. Available at: www.navigantresearch.com/reports/navigant-research-leaderboard-automated-driving-vehicles [Accessed September 20, 2018].

NCSL. 2017. *Self-Driving Vehicles Enacted Legislation*. Washington, DC: National Conference of State Legislatures. Available at: www.ncsl.org/research/transportation/the-transporter-ncsl-s-transportation-newsletter636473721.aspx [Accessed November 30, 2017].

Newman, Peter and Jeffrey Kenworthy. 2011. "'Peak Car Use': Understanding the Demise of Automobile Dependence." *World Transport Policy and Practice* 17, January. Available at: www.researchgate.net/publication/267944725 [Accessed February 26, 2018].

NHTSA. 2016. *Preliminary Statement of Policy Concerning Automated Vehicles*. Washington, DC: National Highway Traffic Safety Administration, US Department of Transportation. Available at: www.nhtsa.gov/nhtsa.doc.gov/files/documents/automated_vehicles_policy.pdf [Accessed December 29, 2017].

Nida-Rumelin, Julin. 2018. "Statement by Julian Nida-Rumelin." P. 253 in A. Herrmann, W. Brenner, and R. Stadler, eds., *Autonomous Driving: How the Driverless Revolution Will Change the World*. Bingley, UK: Emerald.

NMEDA. 2011. "How Much Does Your SUV or Van Weigh?" *Automotive Mobility Solutions*. Available at: www.nmeda.com [Accessed December 6, 2017].

Norton, Peter. 2018. "Special Report: Autonomous Vehicles." *The Economist*, March 1. Available at: https://media.economist.com/news/science-andtehnology/21696925 [Accessed April 9, 2018].

OECD. 2017. *ITF Transport Outlook*. Paris: Organisation for Economic Co-Operation and Development. Available at: https://doi 10.1787/9789282108000-en/ [Accessed October 30, 2017].

OECD. 2015. "Road Traffic, Vehicles and Networks." Pp. 61–5 in *Environment at a Glance 2015*. Paris: Organisation for Economic Co-Operation and Development. Available at: http://dx.doi.org/10.1787/9789624235199-17-en [Accessed September 25, 2018].

OEE. 2013. *Autonomous Vehicles Have a Wide Range of Possible Energy Impacts*. Washington, DC: Office of Energy Efficiency, US Department of Energy.

Oge, Marge T. 2015. *Driving the Future: Combating Climate Change with Cleaner, Smarter Cars*. New York: Arcade.

OICA. 2017a. *World Vehicles in Use: All Vehicles, 2015*. Paris: Organisation internationale des Constructeurs d' Automobiles. Available at: www.oica.net/wp-content/uploads/Total-in-use-All-Vehicles.pdf [Accessed November 15, 2017].

OICA. 2017b. *Passenger Vehicles in Use, 2015*. Paris: Organisation internationale des Constructeurs d' Automobiles. Available at: http://oica.net/wp-content/uploads/PC-Vehicles-in-use.pdf [Accessed November 15, 2017].

OICA. 2017c. *2016 Production Statistics*. Paris: Organisation internationale des Constructeurs d' Automobiles. Available at: www.oica.net/category/production-statistics/2016-statistics/ [Accessed November 16, 2017].

Orsato, R.J. and P. Wells. 2007. "U-Turn: The Rise and Demise of the Automobile Industry." *Journal of Cleaner Production* 15: 994–1006.

Papa, Enrica and Antonio Ferreira. 2018. "Sustainable Accessibility and the Implementation of Automated Vehicles: Identifying Critical Decisions." *Urban Science* 2: 1–14. doi: 10.3390/urbansci2010005.

Phillips, Eric. 2017. "The Future of Autonomous Vehicles in American Cities." *Journal of Law and Public Policy* 21: 287–336. New York: New York University School of Law.

Prevost, L. 2017. "College Campuses Prepare for a Future with Fewer Cars." *The New York Times*, September 6, p. B6.

Quain, J.E. 2016. "Not Everyone's Ready to Give Up the Wheel." *The New York Times*, June 17, p. B4.

Raghuram, Anchit. 2018. *Robust Localization of Research Concept (RCV) in Large Scale Environment*. Masters Thesis, School of Computer Science and Communication, KTH Royal Institute of Technology, Stockholm.

Rausch, Tom. 2016. "Autonomous Vehicles Can Save Emerging Markets from Gridlock But It May Be a Bumpy Ride Getting There." *Medium*, September 28. Available at: https://medium.com/startup-grind/autonomous-vehicles-can-saveemerging-markets-from-gridlock/ [Accessed February 20, 2018].

Reese, H. 2016. "Updated: Autonomous Driving Levels 0 to 5: Understanding the Differences." *TechRepublic*, January 20. Available at: www.techrepublic.com/article/autonomous-driving-levels-0-to-5-understanding-the-differences/ [Accessed November 19, 2017].

SAE. 2016. "U.S. Department of Transportation's New Policy on Automated Vehicles Adopts SAE International's Levels of Automation for Defining Driving Automation in On-Road Motor Vehicles." *Society of Automotive Engineers*. Available at: www.sae.org/news/3544 [Accessed November 28, 2017].

Said, Carolyn. 2018. "Driverless Cars Await State's OK." *San Francisco Chronicle*, February 25, pp. A1, A4.

Said, Carolyn. 2017. "Fleets of Robot Taxis Set to Roll in '19, GM Says." *San Francisco Chronicle*, December 1, pp. C1, C3.

Said, Carolyn and Benny Evangelista. 2017. "S.F.'s Tough Rules for Robots." *San Francisco Chronicle*, December 7, p. C1.

Sanaullah, Irum, A. Hussain, A. Chaudry, K. Case, and M. French. 2017. "Autonomous Vehicles in Developing Countries: A Case Study on User's View Point in Pakistan." Pp. 51–69 in N. Stanton, ed., *Advances in Human Aspects of Transportation*. Berlin: Springer. doi: 10.1007/978-3-319-41682-3_47.

Sawyer, Tom. 2018. "Smart Cities in Many Guises." *Engineering News-Record*, September 3/10, pp. 36–41. New York.

Schreurs, Miranda A. and Sibyl D. Setuwer. 2016. "Autonomous Driving: Political, Legal, Social, and Sustainability Dimensions." Pp. 149–71 in M. Maurer, J. Gerdes, B. Lenz, and H. Winner, eds., *Autonomous Driving: Technical, Legal and Social Aspects*. Berlin: Springer.

Seams, Clayton. 2017. "Shifting Times: The Rise of the Automatic Transmission." *Postmedia*, January 6. Available at: https://driving.ca/chevrolet/corvette/auto-news/hail-hydra-matic-the-rise-of-the-automatic-transmission [Accessed August 22, 2018].

SFC. 2017. "Self-Driving Lyfts in Boston." *San Francisco Chronicle*, December 7, p. C3.

Statista. 2018. "Ranking of the Countries with the Highest Road Quality in 2017." *Statista, the Statistics Portal*. Available at: www.statista.co/statistics/268157/ranking-of-the-20-countries [Accessed September 11, 2018].

Statista. 2017. "Light Vehicle Retail Sales in the United States from 1976 to 2016 (in 1,000 Units)." *Statista, the Statistics Portal*. Available at: www.statista.com/statistics/199983/us-vehicle-sales-since-1951/ [Accessed December 5, 2017].

Stokes, Gordon. 2013. "The Prospects for Future Levels of Car Access and Use." *Transport Reviews* 33: 360–75.

Taeihagh, Araz and Hazel Si Min Lim. 2018. "Governing Autonomous Vehicles: Emerging Responses for Safety, Liability, Privacy, Cybersecurity, and Industry Risks." *Transport Reviews*. Available at: https://doi.org/10.1080/01441647.2018.1494640 [Accessed August 1, 2018].

Trommer, Stefan, V. Kolarova, E. Fraedrich, L. Kroger, B. Kickhofer, T. Kuhnimhof, B. Lenz, and P. Phleps. 2016. *Autonomous Driving: The Impact of Vehicle Automation on Mobility Behaviour*. Munich: Institute for Mobility Research, BMW Group. Available at: www.ifmo.de/files/publications_content/2016/ifmo_2016_Autonomous_Driving_2015_en.pdf [Accessed October 24, 2018].

UN. 2017. *List of Countries by 2015 Population*. New York: United Nations Department of Economic and Social Affairs. Available at: http://statisticstimes.com/population/countries-by-population.php [Accessed November 15, 2017].

Valen, A. 2017. *The ATaxi Revolution: Autonomous Vehicle Implementation and Rise-Sharing Optimization in the United States and China.* Princeton, NJ: B.S. Thesis, Department of Operations Research and Financial Engineering, Princeton University. Available at: http://orfe. princeton.edc/~alaink/ThesesSeniorTheses%2717/Antigone-VAlen-Te%20ATaxi%20 Revolution.pdf [Accessed November 28, 2017].

Van Niekerken, Bill. 2017. "An Ode to the Embarcadero Freeway, the Blight by the Bay." *San Francisco Chronicle*, August 1. Available at: www.sfchronicle.com/thetake/article/an-ode-to-the-Embarcadero-Freeway-the-blight-by-11543621.dhp? [Accessed August 15, 2018].

Varney, Vincent. 2018. "The Evolution of Cruise Control." *Here 360*, April 19. Available at: https://360.here.com/the-evolution-of-cruise-control [Accessed October 4, 2018].

Voelcker, John. 2014. "1.2 Billion Vehicles on World's Roads Now, 2 Billion By 2015: Report." *GreenCarReports*. Available at: www.greencarreports.com/news/1093560_1-2-billion-vehicles-on-worlds-roads-now-2-billion-by-2035-report [Accessed November 23, 2017].

Waddell, Kaveh. 2017. "Prepping Self-Driving Cars for the World's Most Chaotic Cities." *Wired*, October 29. Available at: www.wired.com/story/self-driving-cars-chaotic-cities-traffic/ [Accessed February 21, 2018].

Walker, Alissa. 2016. "Six Freeway Removals That Changed Their Cities Forever." *Gizmodo*, May 25. Available at: https://gizmodo.com/6-freeway-removals-that-changedtheir-cities-forever-1548314937 [Accessed August 14, 2018].

Wasik, B. 2017. "Life after Driving, Introduction." *The New York Times*, November 12, p. 18.

WCED. 1987. *Our Common Future.* New York: UN World Commission on Environment and Development. Available at: www.are.admin.ch/are/en/home/sustainable-development/ international-cooperation/2030agenda/un-_-milestones-in-sustainable-development/ 1987-brundtland-report.html [Accessed December 2, 2017].

WEF. 2015. *Self-Driving Vehicles in an Urban Context.* Geneva: World Economic Forum.

West, D. 2016. *Moving Forward: Self-Driving Vehicles in China, Europe, Japan, Korea, and the United States.* Washington, DC: Brookings Institution. Available at: www.brookings.edu/ research/moving-forward-self-driving-vehicles-in-china-europe-japan-korea-and-the-united-states/ [Accessed November 18, 2017].

Worldatlas. 2017. "Which Are the World's Largest Technology Companies?" Available at: www.worldatlas.com/articles/which-are-the-world-s-largest-technology-companies.html [Accessed November 15, 2017].

World Bank. 2016. "Gross National Income Per Capita, Atlas Method and PPP." Available at: http://databank.worldbank.org/data/download/GNIPC.pdf [Accessed November 29, 2017].

WSJ. 2017. "What's Moving: U.S. Auto Sales." *Wall Street Journal*, December 1. Available at: www.wsj.com/mdc/public/page/2_3022_autosales.html [Accessed December 6, 2017].

2 Environmental sustainability

2.1 Introduction

The prospective environmental sustainability of an autonomous vehicle (AV) can be evaluated in the way that it is for conventional vehicles. This requires a detailed examination of motor vehicle cradle-to-grave lifespan. These lifetimes are measured in successive stages with a Life Cycle Assessment (LCA): Resourcing and processing of raw materials, manufacture and assembly of components, and then on to a vehicle's operational use and end of life (EPA 2017c). Each includes assessments of its constituent elements such as in-stage transportation requirements.

The automobile is an industrial product with an uncommonly complex sustainability profile in that it has "an extensive environmental footprint in all phases of its life cycle" (Orsato and Wells 2007, 1001). Overall, emissions from the use or operational stage dominate its impact and they are measured by a Well-to-Wheel Assessment (WTWA). It identifies the sources of the energy (well-to-tank segment) required for vehicle motive power and the tailpipe emissions (tank-to-wheel segment) it releases. This analysis focuses on tailpipe greenhouse gas (GHG) emissions, particularly CO_2, as they are the single most critical target for improving the environmental sustainability portfolio of automobiles. Reducing the GHG emissions of internal combustion vehicles (ICVs) would make a substantial contribution to the amelioration of climate change. (Additionally, it would benefit public health by lowering air pollution levels of toxics and particulates, addressed in Chapter Three.)

Diesel fuel is not separated out for attention in this analysis. Globally, about 20 percent of new cars sold are diesel powered. While it has better fuel economy than gasoline it emits more toxic pollution (Lloyd and Cackette 2001). There is a wide variation in its use around the world; for example, only 3 percent of new automobile sales in the US in 2014 were diesel powered; in Europe, 50 percent were (DOT 2016). Diesel's future is not promising due to a combination of tighter emissions controls by governments and the growing popularity of electric vehicles (De Aenile 2015). The scandal concerning the German auto industry's efforts to circumvent regulatory standards will hasten diesel's decline (Sumantran, Fine, and Gonsalvez 2017, 103–4; Wehrmann 2018). Throughout Europe where it is has been most popular its future is quite cloudy (Ewing 2017).

The chapter begins by detailing the environmental legacy of fossil fuel powered internal combustion vehicles (ICVs). This is followed by an examination of how individual vehicles, digitally operated, and vehicle groupings, digitally connected, might reduce energy use and emissions by maximizing eco-motorization and minimizing traffic congestion. The perspective taken here is that the autonomous vehicle provides an opportunity to make extensive reforms in automobile sustainability – a re-scripting of its character.

The next section of the chapter presents a case for the integration of autonomous vehicle deployment with the on-going take-up of electric vehicles, so that the first operational AVs can be autonomous electric vehicles (AEVs). The combination of digital eco-motorization and electric propulsion would make a significant dent in emissions. This is followed by examination of another of the AEV's potential environmental benefits – the simplification and downsizing of the automobile-as-machine. The chapter then moves to an analysis of rebound effects expected from an autonomous vehicle deployment, highlighted by an expected increase in vehicle travel.

2.2   Legacy problems of the internal combustion engine

Conventional motor vehicles are a major contributor to global climate change and are not environmentally sustainable. The internal combustion engine is extremely inefficient in converting resources into useful energy (Orsato and Wells 2007, 1003). Petroleum used in motor vehicles loses about two-thirds of its energy, most of it as heat dissipated in the combustion process (NRC 2013). This is a prime reason why transportation has such a voracious appetite for fuel. Globally, in 2015 road vehicles used 75 percent of petroleum's final consumption. In sum, the ICV's operation produces a sequenced triad of detrimental environmental impacts: *Inefficient* use of an *unsustainable* fossil fuel that releases GHG *emissions*. From an environmental sustainability perspective, it is fair to say that at the end of the day petroleum is a bad fuel, used badly, with bad side effects.

Internal combustion engines produce 16 percent of human-made CO_2 emissions (EIA 2016). Among the nine leading national locales for autonomous vehicle development and deployment (the AV9), the US leads (and also leads the world) in per capita road vehicle emissions with about 6 times the global average. China is the low outlier of this group of nations, having per capita emissions that are 35 percent below the global average (BP 2017; EIA 2017; IEA 2017a, 2017b). With regard to absolute levels of carbon emissions from fuel use, China, the US, Japan, Germany, and the ROK, in that order, are five of the world's top seven nations (*EnerData* 2018a). It is fitting then that these countries are among the AV pioneers as it offers potential to reduce carbon emissions where most needed.

The passenger car dwarfs other motorized transport modes in energy use and carbon emissions. (For reference purposes the combustion in the typical US passenger car releases nearly 9,000 grams of CO_2 for each gallon of gasoline that is burned [EPA 2017a, 2017b].) Automobile use accounts for about one-half of global transport energy – equal to the combined shares of trucks, planes, ships, and trains (EIA 2016; IEA 2017a, 2017b). Households are the principal domiciles for cars and in the US they are responsible for about one-fifth of domestic carbon emissions (Jones and Kammen 2011).

In economic terms driving an automobile produces a high level of per mile environmental costs associated with its emissions that are not part of the vehicle sticker price. In the US motoring in congested traffic generates 43 percent of an automobile's external costs; CO_2 emissions are responsible for another 18 percent and toxic emissions for another 15 percent (Anderson et al. 2014, 11–12). These external environmental costs are sizeable, adding up to being equivalent to the cost of fuel. The ICV also has high out-of-pocket expenses. It is highly energy intensive compared to other mobility modes, as the data in Table 2.1 illustrate:

Table 2.1 End-use energy intensities of mobility modes in per passenger mj/km

Modality	Intensity	Fuel
Non-motorized:		
Walk	0.2	Food
Bike	0.1	Food
Motorized, private:		
Automobile	2.1	Fossil
Motorbike	1.6	Fossil
Motorized, public:		
Bus	0.5	Fossil
Tram	0.6	Electric
Metro	0.3	Electric

Source: IIASA. 2012. "Energy End-Use: Transport." *Global Energy Assessment.* Cambridge: Cambridge University Press. International Institute for Applied Systems Analysis, Laxenburg, p. 623.

The high intensity use of fossil fuel makes for substantially more greenhouse gas emissions. On a per passenger-kilometer basis at average load factor the petrol automobile with only a driver emits 1.9 times those of the bus, 2.4 times those of a tram, and 3.6 times those of a metro train (Vaze 2009).

Reducing GHG emissions in transportation has become a prime goal of multifaceted international efforts. A focused targeting on the passenger car, sparked by public interest in the AV, offers promise for measureable sustainability gains in the face of what lays ahead. Transportation's share of global crude petroleum use rose from 45 percent in 1973 to 64 percent in 2013 (IEA 2015), and it is expected to continue to increase. Moreover, it is projected to increase nearly 50 percent by 2030 and 80 percent by 2050, led by automobiles and airplanes (IEA 2009). According to one scenario the number of cars is predicted to grow from just over 1 billion to 4 billion in 2050, prompted by economic growth in developing countries (IEA 2016). Part of the interest in autonomous vehicles is generated by the possibility that their use will retard the expected growth in petrol consumption.

Thus, the AV offers a window of opportunity to ameliorate the enormous negative environmental impacts of the projected four-fold increase in vehicles. This opening could be exploited through digitally based operational efficiency improvements and traffic congestion reduction, both of which would flow from maximizing the currently low level of eco-motorization. Vehicle operations are the prime sustainability target as they account for about three-fourths of the GHG emissions in vehicle life cycles (Maclean and Lave 2003, 5448). Furthermore, the deployment of electrified autonomous electric vehicles offers an even more compelling prospect – eliminating the ICV's operational environmental degradation. Presently, its deficits are being tackled piecemeal by incremental and diminishing engine and fuel efficiency improvements. Autonomous electric vehicles could overcome the legacy of internal combustion's GHG-rich propulsion system. This new AEV could then in time become road transportation's first operationally sustainable motor vehicle.

2.3   Sustainability opportunity: Digitalization

Digitalized and connected autonomous vehicles present an opportunity to act as a transformative agent of change in the character of automobiles. Digital applications have been introduced in piecemeal fashion in cars for decades. Examples include the voice-assisted global positioning system (GPS) in the early 1990s by *Mazda* and *Toyota* (Arlt 2016) and the backup camera that reached global consumers with the 2002 *Nissan Infiniti* (Nwosu 2017). The autonomous vehicle represents a two-pronged holistic change in automobility's environmental character: Considerably more fuel efficient driving and considerably less traffic congestion.

Eco-motorization

The AV digital management, even applied in the ICV character, can benefit environmental sustainability by lowering fuel use and GHG emissions through vehicle eco-motorization. It would serve to minimize road traffic congestion, producing further reductions in fossil fuel consumption and its emissions. Eco-driving has been promoted for decades as an educational method for improving fuel use efficiency. It has direct appeal to drivers as it saves them money.

Eco-driving already utilizes some automated machine assistance, such as cruise control for longer journeys on superhighways. If practiced resolutely it can induce up to 20 percent savings in fuel consumption (Andrieu and Saint Pierre 2012). However, it has not been popularly accepted, at least not in the US. One reason is a lack of public health campaigns as in, for example, successful drunk-driving reduction programs: "One action item overlooked in the United States has been changing driver behavior or style such that eco-driving becomes the norm rather than the exception" (Barkenbus 2012, 762).

Eco-motorization is viewed here as the AV/digital successor to eco-driving that promises even larger gains in fuel use efficiency. In eco-motorization vehicles consume less fuel by optimizing the timing of gear shifts, avoiding idling, reducing rapid acceleration and deceleration, and consistently maintaining the most efficient speed. Digital management would smooth vehicle movement, replacing the inconsistency that features in human driving. The individual gains could be multiplied by a connected grouping of autonomous vehicles because, unlike eco-driving, eco-motorization would be both individual and collective. Vehicles could be linked to others operating on the same digital platform. Such systematic digital management could minimize stop-and-go traffic congestion; for example, by reducing vehicle-to-vehicle headways. Thus, eco-motorization represents a new, collective gain that has not been possible in individualized eco-driving.

One study indicates that autonomous vehicle eco-motorization will result in 20 percent additional savings in a vehicle's fuel use over that of eco-driving (Brown, Gonder, and Repac 2014; Wu, Zhao, and Ou 2011). More specifically, in another study, researchers modeled a road intersection control system using vehicle-to-vehicle and vehicle-to-infrastructure connectivity to reduce deceleration and acceleration (Zhixia et al. 2015). The control system was an enhanced reservation-based algorithm titled *Autonomous Control of Urban TrAffic*. The modelers found that compared to conventional four-way stop activity it reduced energy consumption by about 15 percent. Other research confirms that the use of vehicular digital systems at intersections and superhighway on-ramps reduces energy consumption and emissions (Rios-Torres and Malikopoulos 2017). For a literature review of other research on the potential of AV eco-motorization's fuel efficiency gains, see Milakis, Van Arem, and Van Wee (2017). (The systems could also reduce roadway crashes, a subject taken up in Chapter Three.)

Truck fleets likely will be among the first adopters of autonomous vehicle eco-motorization. They have a major incentive as fuel accounts for about two-fifths of their operating expenses. In the US heavy trucks are only 4 percent of road vehicles but account for 25 percent of fuel consumption (Wang 2015). Multiple trucks that move in convoys may be digitally connected throughout in-line platoons. Such a procedure would add to sustainability gains provided by individual AV trucks. The platoon reduces the wind resistance on all but the lead vehicle, and it enables shorter vehicle headways (Herrmann, Brenner, and Stadler 2018). An autonomous vehicle fleet eco-motorization is generally viewed as fit for purpose within the trucking industry: "By combining partial automation with vehicle-to-vehicle and vehicle-to-cloud communication, these fleets can see massive fuels savings and safety improvements in the near term" (Switkes and Boyd 2016, 195). As an example of potential gains a demonstration research study involving three fully automated trucks using a test track and a superhighway produced a fuel savings of 14 percent and a CO_2 reduction of 2 percent (Tsugawa, Kato, and Aoki 2011).

De-congestion

Today's excessive traffic congestion is a product of the hyper automobility generated in auto-centered transport systems (Freund and Martin 2009; Martin 1999). It is due to traffic bottlenecks caused by vehicle densities exceeding (even) superhighway capacities. The result is a slowing down of traffic flow to stop-and-go pace, at times reaching full-stop gridlock. With engines continuing to run, emissions are multiplied (Parry, Walls, and Harrington 2006, 11) and fuel is squandered.

The superhighways that were built to speed traffic flow have become instead the principal locales for routine super congestion. During the development of hyper automobility between 1982 and 1997 traffic congestion in the US almost doubled, raising the average annual delay per commuter from 18 to 34 hours. While the growth rate has since slowed it continues to rise steadily. In 2014 the average delay was 42 hours – the equivalent of 1.75 days lost to traffic delays in that year (TTI 2015, 2). The loss has been projected to rise to 47 hours per car commuter in 2020. Loss is the appropriate word because stop-and-go traffic prevents drivers from safely engaging in a simultaneous activity. Thus, conducting telephone conversations while at the wheel has been prohibited in many regulatory jurisdictions. Another measure of the growth in congestion is a slowdown in the speed of urban traffic, as indicated by a study of London, Los Angeles, Paris, and Stuttgart (*INRIX* 2014). In London it was 21 miles per hours (mph) in 2013 and was projected to fall to 16 mph in 2030; in Los Angeles, from 21 to 15 mph.

Urban traffic congestion has been increased by the popularity of new ride-hailing (carshare) digital platforms. Research using US national demographic and travel data found that Transportation Network Companies (TNCs), a category dominated by *Uber*, added nearly 6 billion vehicle miles to the streets of nine large metropolitan areas, led by New York City and San Francisco (Schaller 2018). A report from the San Francisco County Transportation Authority assessed local traffic changes between 2010 and 2016 (SFCTA 2018). Congestion was marked by a significant increase, and one-half of it was due to carshare trips (Said 2018).

Roadway congestion effects comprise the major external environmental cost of driving an automobile. It leads to more engine operating time, intensifying fuel use and carbon emissions. In 2011 traffic congestion accounted for about 2 percent of CO_2 emissions in the US and the figure has been on the rise. The congestion-dissipated fuel in 2011 was almost 6 times the level it was in 1982 and was forecast to increase by almost 90 percent from 2011 to 2020 (Schrank, Eisele, and Lomax 2012, 1).

The additional CO_2 emissions produced in traffic congestion have been estimated for all US metropolitan areas. The percent emitted during congestion relative to that of free-flow traffic is 3.9 percent for larger cities and 2.1 percent for smaller ones (Schrank, Eisele, and Lomax 2012). Because they would be able to process complex information faster than humans, autonomous vehicles operating in connected systems can minimize the safe distance needed between moving vehicles, thereby increasing road capacity as well as ameliorating congestion. One common human driving practice that adds to traffic congestion is rubbernecking – slowing down to take a look at road crashes. Autonomous vehicle software will not be distracted by day-dreaming or crash-viewing drivers.

Eco-motorization can provide what humans cannot – consistent vehicle speeds, thus reducing the tailpipe emissions caused by accordion-like congestion:

> It is commonly known that as traffic congestion increases, CO_2 emissions (and in parallel, fuel consumption) also increase. In general, CO_2 emissions and fuel consumption are very sensitive to the type of driving that occurs. As highlighted as part of many "eco-driving" strategies, traveling at a steady-state velocity will give much lower emissions and fuel consumption compared to a stop-and-go driving pattern.
>
> (Barth and Boriboonsomsin 2008, 3–4)

Collective, connected digital systems could regulate vehicles in closely spaced groupings that maintain lower peak speeds and enable higher effective speeds. One estimate is that at 10 percent AV uptake it would reduce fuel intensity by 10 percent (Brown, Repac, and Gonder 2013). Vehicles moving in digitally based harmonization lower fuel consumption by reducing air resistance, or drag, as well as by smoothing movement. Their operation would resemble that of a train even though the individual vehicles are not physically coupled. However, as with trains, such platoons could be managed by a sole individual in the lead vehicle. While it will probably only apply to fleets of trucks, it may benefit neighboring vehicles by increasing road space. Research indicates that lane capacities – measured by vehicles per lane per hour – can be significantly increased through eco-motorization (Herrmann, Brenner, and Stadler 2018, 306).

In the end, even conventionally fossil fuel powered autonomous vehicles would have potential to reduce emissions through individual and collective eco-motorization. The potential impact on congestion likely will not materialize until full automated Level Four is reached. Moreover, deployment may add to congestion for several new reasons. AVs may feature unoccupied return trips and increased travel by non-drivers by former users of public transit (Brenden, Kristoffersson, and Mattsson 2017; Metz 2018). This would be in itself no small matter.

Nonetheless, for vehicles to maximize their environmental sustainability it will require transition to a non-carbon energy source. The present moment offers a propitious opportunity for such a meaningful change. The AV is a potentially innovative motor vehicle that is being introduced in an era of widespread negative reaction to ICVs and their fossil fuel. Combining autonomous vehicle deployment with on-going electric vehicle uptake would be a potentially transformative "two-fer" for reducing emissions: Eco-motorization plus electrification. The automobile may then take on an entirely new character.

2.4 Sustainability opportunity: Electrification

Electrically powered cars have been around for as long as ICVs have. French scientists developed a rechargeable lead-acid battery in the late 19th century, and the first successful electric vehicle debuted in 1880 in the US. By 1900 they accounted for one-third of road vehicles and continued to grow in popularity until the arrival of the gasoline-powered *Ford Motel T*. The cost reductions secured by mass production and newly discovered cheap Texas oil drove electric vehicles (EVs) out of the market. By 1912 they cost about 2.5 times more than the *Model T* (Matulka 2014).

The electric vehicle began to return to prominence in the 1970s in part as a result of the emergence of the environmental movement. However, its revival effectively did not begin until the end of the 20th century. A turning point was the arrival of the *Toyota Prius* in 1997, the world's first mass-produced hybrid electric vehicle. Growing public concern with climate change as a global environmental problem and the subsequent targeting of CO_2 emissions have greatly enhanced the prospects for EVs. Their stock grew from several thousands in just a few countries in 2005 (France, Germany, the UK, and the US) with a virtually nil global market share, to over 2 million vehicles and a 1 percent market share in 2016 (IEA 2017c).

Transportation is the sector of the global economy with the lowest mix of non-GHG emitting renewable energy (IRENA 2015). In 2015 oil comprised 92 percent of motor vehicle energy (IEA 2017a, 47). However, a consulting firm predicts that petroleum demand likely will peak by 2030 due to a rise in electric vehicle sales (*Wood Mackenzie* 2017). Electricity is presently the leading energy for sustainably powering passenger motor vehicles. It can be converted into mechanical energy with high efficiency, and it is emission free at the tailpipe. Thus, electrification is a much more sustainable energy than gasoline, diesel, or natural gas (O'Dea 2018).

A modeling simulation study for a 100-year time horizon compared the environmental benefits of various motor vehicle fuel options to meet the international target for reducing climate change emissions. It concluded that:

> if we are to achieve an 80% reduction in greenhouse gases below 1990 levels, eliminate most oil imports and most urban air pollution, then society must transition to all-electric vehicles powered by some combination of fuel cells and batteries. We cannot achieve our transportation sector goals if most vehicles still rely on internal combustion engines for some of their motive power.
>
> (Thomas 2009, 9279)

There is growing support around the world for vehicle electrification (Milman 2013).

The EV is being promoted by governments in order to reach national GHG emission reduction goals. Public transit agencies are leading the uptake. It is estimated that electric buses will command one-half of the world's fleet by 2015 (Chediak 2018). The Electric Vehicles Initiative is a multinational policy forum created in 2009 at the UN Framework Convention on Climate Change Conference in Copenhagen. Its purpose is to accelerate the deployment of electric vehicles globally (IEA 2017c, 9). As of May, 2017 it had ten member governments, seven of them among the AV9.

Thus, it is apparent that electric vehicles are gaining social momentum: "Most pundits concur that the electrification of mobility will accelerate in the coming decade" (Sumantran, Fine, and Gonsalvez 2017, 115). The impetus is radiating from several compelling sources: Technological development, concern for the environment and climate change, and consumer inclination. A comparative analysis indicates that the nations with the best conditions for promoting EV adoption are those with high GDPs that can provide tax exemptions, purchase subsidies, and ample battery charging infrastructures (Yong and Park 2017). Analysis of the availability of these factors across 24 more developed, developing, and less developed nations found that seven of the AV9 countries are among those most likely to adopt electric vehicles. (The two not included were Italy and the ROK.)

Three of the nine countries leading autonomous vehicle development (China, the US, and Japan) together have over two-thirds of the world's electric vehicle stock (IEA 2017c, 49–51). However, electric vehicles are presently a very small sector of their car markets – less than 1 percent in all three countries. The only nation of the AV9 with more than a miniscule electric vehicle market share is Sweden, at 3.4 percent. However, global electric vehicle stock has been expanding rapidly, increasing by nearly 60 percent between 2015 and 2016, growing its market share by almost 30 percent.

Automobile manufacturers are ramping up their electric-powered vehicle production. Sweden's *Volvo* will produce only electrified models by 2019. Germany's *Volkswagen* plans to launch an EV carshare scheme for locales in Asia, Europe, and the US (Charlton 2018). Change is afoot even at the luxury level – *Ferrari* is planning to bring a battery-powered vehicle to market by late 2019 (Ebhardt 2018). Governments are joining the trend toward the electric vehicle. Norway will prohibit sales of fossil fuel powered cars and vans in 2025 while France, the Netherlands, and the UK have committed to the same policy by 2040 (*National Geographic* 2018). Both production and consumption conditions seem ripe for developing a synergy between AV and EV deployment.

Fuel and emission gains

Numerous LCA studies comparing the operational environmental sustainability of electric vehicles to that of ICVs have shown EVs to be the better option over a wide range of scenarios (i.e., Ma et al. 2012; Onat, Kucukvar, and Tatari 2016; Shi et al. 2016; Wang, Zhang, and Ouyang 2015; Weldon,

Morrissey, and O'Mahony 2016). The electric vehicle stock currently includes three basic modalities:

1   The hybrid electric vehicle (HEV) has an electric drive system and battery but does not have capacity to plug into grids. It relies on liquid fuel and an internal combustion engine to power a generator that provides energy for an electric motor.
2   The plug-in hybrid electric vehicle (PHEV) can connect to grids to recharge and can use energy from its battery or from its backup internal combustion engine.
3   The battery electric vehicle (BEV) is all electric. Energy comes only from a rechargeable battery that plugs into grids.

Even though it relies in part on an internal combustion engine the HEV has greater fuel economy than conventional ICVs. A well-to-wheel assessment of energy sourcing and vehicle operation found that all electric vehicles are more sustainable than internal combustion vehicles (Faria et al. 2013). Moving from the hybrid through the plug-in hybrid to the fully electric vehicle further increases fuel efficiency and lowers emissions at each step.

Thus, the greater the electrification, the lower the vehicle operational energy consumption and emissions (Howey et al. 2011; Lorf et al. 2013; Messagie et al. 2014; Van Mierlo, Messagie, and Rangaraju 2017; Wang 2003). The battery electric vehicle emits no toxic pollutants and hydrocarbons. It is expected to be marketed by 2025 (NRC 2011), with mass production coming after 2030. At this early point the electric vehicle developmental goal is a battery electric vehicle with limited range, such as the city electric vehicle (CEV) that could be used for most household trips. Life cycle assessment of passenger vehicles indicates that BEV substitution over time for internal combustion vehicles will create a progressive reduction in GHG emissions in the use stage (Hawkins et al. 2012). An *EnerData* (2018b) scenario projects by 2040 up to 20 percent of oil production would be avoided through an uptake of electric and hybrid vehicles.

Current deficits

Even the battery electric vehicle at present is not fully sustainable through its full life cycle. A number of WTWAs and LCAs have produced a general consensus as to the sustainability shortcomings of all electric vehicles (Hawkins, Gausen, and Stromman 2012; Hawkins et al. 2012; LCVP 2017; Manjunath and Gross 2017; Qiao et al. 2017; Tagliaferri et al. 2016; Yazdanie et al. 2016). The major problems are the resourcing, production, and disposal of lithium–ion batteries (Zackrisson, Avellan, and Orlenius 2010), and the use of non-renewable electrical energy sources to charge them.

With regard to the battery issue research has determined that sustainability goals require that "electrification of road transportation should be accompanied by an integration of life cycle management in the vehicle manufacturing chain" (Bauer et al. 2015, 871). Ultimately, because of the sustainability limitations of batteries, they may be succeeded by fuel cells that are powered by hydrogen (Thomas 2011; Sharma and Ghoshal 2015; Tagliaferri et al. 2016). However, fuel cells are still in the early development phase and have outstanding issues to be resolved.

Major breakthroughs are needed in hydrogen storage and its environmentally sustainable sourcing (Singh et al. 2015). Most hydrogen is presently produced from fossil fuels (Oge 2015, 212; Sharma and Ghoshal 2015). It then requires rigorous safety oversight in storage and transfer because of its flammability. For this reason fuel cells are largely restricted to highly specialized uses in military and space exploration applications (Greene and Schafer 2003, 271). While fuel cell power for vehicles remains a remote possibility, research continues to improve batteries. The work is seen by an analyst as one of the most important engineering and scientific pursuits going on today in transportation (Levine 2016).

As to the sourcing of energy another consensus finding is that, even though using present EU electricity source mixes, EVs produce significantly lower emissions than ICVs. However, the mixes are only partially sustainably produced (Bauer et al. 2015; Faria et al. 2012; Huo et al. 2015; Onat, Kucukvar, and Tatari 2015; Orsi et al. 2016; Underwood 2014, 67). Electric power is generated by a number of sources, primarily fossil fuels. In 2015 renewables comprised 23 percent of global electric power; nuclear power, 11 percent; and fossil fuels, 66 percent – led by coal with 39 percent (IEA 2017a, 30). There are considerable differences in the electric energy generating profiles of nations, including the AV9. Five of them – Sweden, the UK, Germany, China, and the US – are among the world's 12 leading producers of renewable energy (*Clickenergy* 2017).

However, China (dominated by coal power) has high per kilometer motor vehicle life cycle emissions; its grid-powered EVs produce emissions comparable to conventional ICVs. In Sweden, where renewable energy accounts for over one-half of grid power, electric vehicles produce only about one-third the tailpipe emissions of conventionally powered vehicles (Wilson 2013, 6). The BEV sustainability score will improve as national grid mixes move from fossil fuels to renewable energy sources. One researcher argues that only when interconnected grids are dominated by renewable energy will the electric vehicle be able to claim superiority over the internal combustion vehicle (Moriarity and Wang 2017). When batteries are charged with electricity from renewable sources emissions are considerably reduced (Li, Chen, and Wang 2017).

Renewable energy comprised just 2 percent of global energy consumption in 1973 – by 2015 it rose to double that share (IEA 2017a, 46–7). The major global divide in renewable energy production is between developed and developing nations. In the former it is more advanced. For example, an LCA of vehicle electrification in Malaysia found that "the national electricity supply must be made cleaner before the electrification" of transport can even be contemplated (Onn et al. 2017, 192). There are six renewable energy sources and they can be captured in an acronym, *BiG SHOW*. In 2016 the global share of renewable energy for each was: Bioenergy, 5 percent; geothermal, 1 percent; solar, 15 percent; hydro, 56 percent; ocean, just a trace; and wind, 23 percent. All had significant growth from 2005 to 2016, led by solar and wind. Hydropower, produced by running water, is the dominant renewable energy source, and it has one of the best conversion efficiencies of all energy sources – 90 percent from water to wire (Ellabban, Abu-Rub, and Blaabjerg 2014, 752).

However, it requires the construction of water flow dams that have negative sustainability impacts (Moran et al. 2018). It is important to note in considering electric energy sustainability that the dams which produce hydroelectric power have regressive impacts on their ecosystems. They are case-specific and frequently large in scale and intensity. At present dams are commonly not included in the consideration of the environmental costs of electric energy sourcing (Beck, Claassen, and Hundt 2012).

The major renewable competitor to electric energy for vehicle power today is biofuel. While solid biomass is used to generate electricity it is also used to produce liquid biofuels such as ethanol which power internal combustion engines. They are considered renewable but they have a list of sustainability negatives. Many biofuels "have worse GHG balances than fossil fuels if associated land changes" are considered (WWF 2008, 19). Biofuels emit high levels of air pollution when they are burned and use large amounts of water and land to grow, competing with the food supplies of humans and their domestic animals. Research shows that, contrary to previous assumptions, biofuel in the US is associated with a net increase in CO_2 emissions (DeCicco et al. 2016).

Biofuels do have a practical operating advantage over other renewables in their storage capacity and flexible, on-demand portability (Ellabban, Abu-Rub, and Blaabjerg 2014, 750; Kukreja 2017). This makes them fit for purpose in powering heavyweight transportation of shipping, and in aviation where electrical power is not a practical option (IRENA 2015). Thus, biofuels likely will retain a niche in transport energy (Williams 2013, 3).

Autonomous electric synergies

Surveys as to the AV's public acceptance have found that positive responses associate the vehicles with the use of electric propulsion. A large cross-national survey found among those respondents with the highest level of intent to use an autonomous vehicle "the highest rating was obtained for using a driverless vehicle that is 100% electric" (Nordhoff et al. 2018). The association of automation with electrification is related to environmentalist attitudes. One survey of 40 subjects, following a test drive of an electric vehicle, found that its environmental metrics is a stronger predictor of "attitude and thus purchase intention than price value and range confidence" (Degirmenci and Breitner 2017, 250).

The integrated autonomous and electric vehicle presents a best case future for the evolution of environmentally sustainable motor vehicle operations: The possibility of being fully powered by wind power, thereby producing no CO_2 emissions in energy sourcing and use (Clarke 2017). Moreover, it could significantly reduce the mass of a passenger car, which would serve to further lower emissions throughout its entire life cycle. Lastly, there are functional synergies available in autonomous shared electric vehicles (ASEVs) that could add to the positive environmental profile of the AEV. (See Chapter Four on urban sustainability.) However, despite all these prospective sustainability gains, the potentially transformative path choice of an autonomous electric vehicle deployment has been getting scant attention: "There has been little work done to date on understanding potential transition pathways that include automated vehicles and electrification together, even though it is clear they are both going to happen at the same time" (Offer 2015, 4).

Present circumstances in the automotive industries of the AV9 nations appear favorable to the adoption of autonomous electric vehicles. Integrating the two could mean only one major change in production facilities now instead of two over time. Manufacturers are in the process of developing autonomous electric vehicle models. For example, *General Motors* began testing computer-operated, battery-powered *Chevrolet Bolt* cars in three US cities in 2017 (Vlasic 2017). In the US over one-half of ICV-to-AV refits are now being built over a fully electric powertrain, and a further one-fifth over a hybrid powertrain (McCauley 2017).

The German auto industry may be an especially appropriate venue for an ICV-to-AEV transition, as it is negotiating a path beyond the widely maligned diesel-powered vehicles that constitute one-third of its current production. The Mayor of Stuttgart, the home of *Mercedes Benz* and *Porsche*, underscored the city's new ban on diesel vehicles with these words: "If Germany wants to continue to dominate the car industry, it needs to become a champion of electric cars and autonomous cars" (Bennhold 2018, A6). Other European cities are planning to follow Stuttgart's example, including Athens, Dusseldorf, Madrid, and Munich (Eddy 2018).

The electrification of autonomous vehicles "offers a multitude of synergies" that are "manifest in a higher energy efficiency and a more convenient operation" (Meyer 2016, 187). The most optimistic scenario for autonomous/electric integration is that it can be accomplished by 2030 (Arbib and Seba 2017), probably most effectively across the publicly available vehicle fleets that operate in urban areas. Fleet rather than individual deployment could serve to promote social acceptance by allowing riding in without purchasing an AV. Continuing sustainability benefits will be based on improving battery production and upgrading the renewable share of power grid source mixes.

A boost for autonomous electric vehicle synergy is that the presently deficient battery recharging station infrastructure is much more robust in urban centers where AV testing is largely taking place. The range issue can be addressed in part by the controlling software of the autonomous vehicle, making it more suitable for electrification. For example, the vehicles could be programmed to make trips only within power ranges, as well as to locate the sites of recharging options (Franckx 2016, 87). However, cities still need to promote more extensive deployment of battery recharging stations. A UK survey indicates that in the next decade only 8 percent of charging will be able to use public charging facilities (*Delta-ee* 2018). The great majority takes place at home or at work. Expanding the public infrastructure is important for addressing the "range anxiety" of many potential EV users. Thus, political and social arenas are important to the future of both autonomous and electric vehicles – perhaps at least as much as economic and technological ones (Kotter and Shaw 2013).

Linking the deployments of autonomous vehicles and electric vehicles would be made easier by the fact that they are on a similar upward market trajectory. Mid-range global market forecasts have autonomous vehicles growing from nil in 2010 to about 500,000 by 2025; electric vehicles from 2 million to 55 million. Ten years later, in 2035, it is expected that both will reach a market tipping point, at which there will be 21 million autonomous vehicles and 250 million electric vehicles. In that year there will be 2 billion road vehicles, with AVs comprising 1 percent and EVs 13 percent (IEA 2017c; IHS 2017; Lacey 2017; Voelcker 2014). A helpful support for integration is that the AV9 nations are also leading electric vehicle deployment. In 2016 they had over 80 percent of global EV stock (IEA 2017c, 49).

AEVs could serve as a unifying digital platform to bridge the two competitive wings that exist within electric and autonomous vehicle development – for the US the digital side based in Silicon Valley and the automotive side based in Detroit. The appeal of integration is compelling to both industries. On the digital side electric vehicles would be easier for cyber management than are internal combustion vehicles; on the automotive side, autonomous electric vehicles will be cheaper to resource, manufacture, and assemble (Gardner 2016), based on the fact that they would be much simpler mechanically and so require far fewer moving parts than do ICVs.

Traditionally, automobile manufacturers have used a closed, or independent breakthrough, approach in developing new technologies to replace current ones (Herrmann, Brenner, and Stadler 2018, 330–9). With regard to autonomous vehicles this approach is evolving into a more open, or fusion, approach – in part because AV development also relies on an entirely separate digital industry. Fusion can be achieved by making inter-industry investments, such as *General Motors* has done with *Lyft* (Said 2016) and *Ford* with *Argo AI* (Isaac and Boudette 2017). The fusion strategy serves to promote the production of AEVs as well as AVs.

The AEV, fully electrified from sustainably sourced power, would operate with an energy efficiency level greater than 90 percent (2.7 times the efficiency of the internal combustion engine), require a much simpler and lighter vehicle, and produce no operational emissions and ambient noise (NRC 2013). The marriage of AV eco-motorization and traffic de-congestion with EV energy and vehicle downsizing could become, in the vernacular, a game-changing merger that displaces the 100-year-old fossil fuelled ICV hegemony. The character of the automobile would be thoroughly re-written.

2.5   Sustainability opportunity: Downsizing

Environmental sustainability gains accruing from EVs include considerably lower mass and mechanical complexity, which means less use of natural resources and lower emissions in all stages of their lifespans. Autonomous ICVs could reduce carbon emissions only through operational fuel efficiency gains. What they can achieve, in the words of one analyst, is "to bend the carbon curve down in the intermediate time frame" before motor vehicle stocks become fully electrified (Pyper 2014, 4).

Heavier cars increase wind resistance and inertia, and this makes them less fuel efficient, especially when in the stop-and-go mode of roadway congestion. The potential impact of a vehicle weight reduction is large enough to demonstrate that it "is an effective measure for reducing CO_2 emissions from road transport and can contribute to transport decarbonisation targets" (ITF 2017, 38). Large passenger vehicles such as sport utility vehicles (SUVs) have become "a roadblock in the march toward cleaner cars" because compared with smaller cars they are less fuel efficient, generally by about 30 percent (Tabuchi 2018, D4). Downsizing on a large scale could lead to significant reductions in energy use and its emissions. According to one projection, using fleet-based vehicles for the 87 percent of vehicle trips in the US occupied by just one or two persons would reduce energy consumption by a factor of about 2 (Greenblatt and Saxena 2015).

However, the reality is that national vehicle stocks have been moving in the opposite direction. There is a "global S.U.V. boom," especially in China where the vehicles are predicted to constitute one-half of the cars sold in 2022, and in Western Europe where sales doubled between 2012 and 2017 (Tabuchi 2018, D1). In the UK, because of growth in SUV sales, the Society of Motor Manufacturers and Traders reported that the average new car CO_2 emissions increased in 2017 after 19 years of reductions (LCVP 2018).

The average weight of European Union passenger cars increased by about 40 percent during the development of hyper automobility – in 2015 they weighed 1,400 kgs, compared to 1,000 in 1975. US vehicles are even heavier. Its sport utility vehicles and pick-up trucks are 55 percent heavier than comparable classes of EU vehicles (Miller-Wilson 2013). The escalation of vehicle size has been likened to an "arms race" among drivers on US roads who compete for a safety advantage (White 2004, 333). New car sales there demonstrate a large weight differential among its light duty vehicles, as follows in Table 2.2:

Table 2.2 Weights of selected new passenger cars sold in US in 2012

Car size and model		Weight in lbs (000)	Type
Small:	*Smart* (2-seater)	1.8	Subcompact
	Mini Cooper	2.5	Compact
Mid-size:	*Toyota Camry*	3.2	Sedan
	Audi A-6	3.7	Sedan
Large:	*Dodge Durango*	4.8	SUV
	Cadillac Escalade	6.0	SUV

Source: Miller-Wilson, K. 2013. List of Car Weights. *lovetoknow*. Available at: http://cars.lovetoknow.com/List_of_Car_Weights [Accessed December 6, 2017].

In US regulatory policy SUVs are categorized as light trucks even though they are operated principally as family cars – between 80 and 90 percent are used for personal transport. The country's Environmental Protection Agency (EPA) sets the fuel efficiency standard for light trucks at about 25 percent lower than that for passenger cars (Davis and Truett 2000). This action amplified sustainability problems as it paved the way for the market growth of bigger vehicles with bigger fuel appetites that make bigger contributions to carbon emissions (Oge 2015, 105).

In addition to the SUV another vehicle classified by the EPA as a light truck is the pick-up and it also has been growing in number and weight. Many are used primarily for transporting people. Their heavier four-door models have been increasing relative to their traditional two-door models so they can carry more passengers. They add to emissions over those of the passenger car. For example, in the ROK, new light trucks produce 39 percent more CO_2 emissions than new passenger cars (Kim and Miller 2015).

Sport utility vehicle and pick-up truck growth helps to explain why carbon emissions from highways in US major metropolitan areas increased faster than vehicle miles traveled (VMT) between 2000 and 2005 (Brown, Sarzynski, and Southworth 2008). This increase came despite regulatory and technological advances in reducing emissions. The regulatory fixes, which began with the 1970 Clean Air Act, have lagged behind increases in the number of vehicles, their miles traveled, and their weight. Between 1980 and 2015 motor vehicle CO_2 emissions increased by 18 percent, pulled up by a 25 percent increase in fuel consumption, a VMT increase of 106 percent, and increases in vehicle mass (EPA 2017a).

The contributions of a potential AEV downsizing to environmentally sustainable mobility are substantial. A 10 percent reduction of vehicle mass provides a fuel consumption benefit of 6 to 7 percent (NRC 2011). Electric vehicles require far fewer material resources and far less complex fabrication than do internal combustion cars because they have considerably fewer parts – just 7,000 compared to an ICV's 30,000 (Gapper 2017). While the electric vehicle has three powertrain components, the battery, inverter, and motor, the internal combustion engine powertrain has 2,000 pieces that have to be kept lubricated (Gardner 2016). Smaller and lighter vehicles will provide cumulative environmental sustainability benefits throughout a vehicle's full lifespan (Chester and Horvath 2008; LCVP 2017).

Studies forecast that networked autonomous electric vehicles using smaller vehicles modeled on the city electric vehicle could reduce fuel use by more than double what is forecast for current hybrid electric vehicles (NRC 2011). Pod-sized AEVs (resembling golfing carts in size) are even smaller and lighter vehicles with room for several passengers, and they would reduce vehicle use by greater magnitudes. They likely could be used effectively and safely at first on large university and corporate campuses.

Autonomous electric vehicle technology could be an effective long-term substitute for the ICV's heavyweight safety edge. Vehicle production might then shift from crashworthiness (the "tank" model) to crash avoidance through digital management. It has been projected that downsizing of AEVs can proceed over time in the same successive stages established for an AV deployment. The diffusion of crash avoidance benefits through automation Levels One, Two, and Three could enable incremental vehicle weight reductions – of 20 to 25 percent by 2030 and 32 to 50 percent by 2050 (NRC 2013). Deployment at Level Four automation would then have shifted the safety focus away from crashworthiness, promoting reductions in the number of outsized vehicles, especially SUVs (Anderson et al. 2014, 33).

However, achieving this will require AEV users to have confidence that collisions with conventional vehicles can be avoided and this, in turn, will depend upon their nearly universal adoption. Expert forecasts anticipate that these benefits will not be realized for some considerable time. Until then, the ultralight autonomous electric vehicles operating in an environment alongside much heavier ICVs would likely increase their road crash risk on superhighways (Anderson et al. 2014, 31–3). However, on city streets, autonomous CEVs would not face a similar risk.

2.6 Rebound effects

All the projections of autonomous vehicle environmental sustainability benefits will be negated or qualified by uncertain rebound effects (Groshen et al. 2018, 80). The likeliest rebound effect will be increased vehicle travel. Much of the increase probably will be due to the greater personal convenience provided by AVs – little driving, no parking, etc. Such conveniences will induce more trips, an unknown portion of which would previously not have been taken at all – or would have been taken without driving a vehicle. One estimate is that vehicle miles traveled will increase as autonomous vehicle penetration increases – from a 2 percent increase at 10 percent penetration to a 9 percent increase at 90 percent penetration (Fagant and Kockelman 2013, 8). Another estimate is that at 50 percent market penetration there will be an increase of 5 to 20 percent in VMT; at 95 percent penetration, as much as 35 percent (Bierstedt et al. 2014).

A scenario analysis found a wide range of potential consequences of autonomous vehicle travel increases for greenhouse gas emissions – a reduction of nearly one-half to a near doubling. Perhaps the most interesting finding from this analysis is that "many potential energy-reduction benefits may be realized through partial automation, while the major energy/emission downside risks appear more likely at full automation" (Wadud, MacKenzie, and Leiby 2016, 1). Another expert estimate also indicates a wide range of potential rebounds in fuel use – from nearly 90 percent savings to more than a 250 percent increase. Such a wide range emphasizes the importance of including energy impacts in autonomous vehicle deployment strategies, and adds to the case for their electrification (Brown, Repac, and Gonder 2013). Fuel consumption and GHG tailpipe emissions would be further reduced by combining AV development with that of

EVs and even more so with the use of small ASEVs (Greenblatt and Saxena 2015; Greenblatt and Shaheen 2015), which likely would negate any VMT increases.

There are some possible moderating limits to prospective VMT rebound effects for internal combustion vehicles. Vehicle travel is generally insensitive to energy efficiency improvements because fuel costs are a relatively small part of its total cost – about 20 percent (Greene and Schafer 2003, 23). The bulk of vehicle operating costs in Canada and the US, for example, are for maintenance and repair, tires, insurance, and depreciation. A 10 percent increase in fuel efficiency could reduce fuel cost by 10 percent but total cost would be reduced by only 2 percent, which is likely to result in a small VMT rebound of only 2 percent as well. However, comparative vehicle operating cost profiles support the case for AV-EV integration. The reason is that electric vehicles have considerably lower maintenance, repair, and fuel costs than do ICVs (AAA 2017). This probably would more than compensate for any autonomous electric vehicle VMT mileage increase.

Rebounds can produce rather surprising ripple and ricochet effects that move with even less certainty than the rebound which creates them. For example, while eco-motorization would enhance the fuel efficiency of large truck AVs, it may also result in them taking freighting business away from rail transportation, which is presently 3 to 4 times as fuel efficient (Wang 2015) and consequently more environmentally sustainable. Thus, the rebound of more VMT for trucks ricochets to less tonnage miles for trains.

Unlike ricochets, ripples extend the range of rebound effects without redirecting them. For example, some AV users may utilize their new freedom from driving to engage safely in more productive and entertaining activities while in their vehicles. This could prompt growth in passenger car size to include beds, showers, kitchens, and offices (Anderson et al. 2014, 6), mitigating the downsizing sustainability benefits ensuing from autonomous electric vehicle integration. In a back to the future scenario, the internal combustion SUV could be succeeded by a general purpose AEV office-camper van.

2.7   Conclusion

All the potential environmental sustainability impacts of an AV deployment – their nature and magnitude – are uncertain and likely will take decades to unwind (Litman 2017). The most important path-determining decisions for the technology have not yet been taken. A risk-reward calculus – including qualitative as well as quantitative measures – for each decision would be quite useful. The consensus of research findings relevant to environmental sustainability is that a broad deployment of AVs can be "a turning point in terms of reducing emissions of GHG" (Iglinski and Babiak 2017, 353). This gain can be pocketed while electric vehicle technology continues to enhance the sustainability profiles of its battery and its energy sourcing. This is especially important now, at a data point (2017) when global economic growth concentrated in the developing world has accelerated, abetting an increase in CO_2 emissions after a period of stagnation (*EnerData* 2018a).

Overall, from a purely environmental sustainability perspective the rebound risks of a deployment of autonomous vehicles seem to be smaller than the rewards it is likely to produce. However, an uptake of autonomous electric vehicles would protect sustainability gains.

References

AAA. 2017. *Driving Cost Per Mile*. Heathrow, FL: American Automobile Association. Available at: www.aaa.com/tag/driving-cost-per-mile [Accessed January 8, 2018].

Anderson, J.M., N. Kalra, K. Stanley, P. Sorensen, C. Samaras, and O. Oluwatola. 2014. *Autonomous Vehicle Technology: A Guide for Policymakers*. Santa Monica, CA: RAND Corporation.

Andrieu, C. and G. Saint Pierre. 2012. "Comparing Effects of Eco-Driving Training and Simple Advices on Driving Behaviour." *Procedia: Social and Behavioral Sciences* 54: 211–20.

Arbib, James and Tony Seba. 2017. "Rethinking Transportation 2020–2030." *RethinkX*. Available at: www.rethinkx.com./rethinking-transportation-2020-2030 [Accessed January 5, 2018].

Arlt, Glenn. 2016. *Automotive Navigation Systems*. Gaithersburg, MD: Historic Vehicle Association. Available at: www.historicvehicle.org/automotive-navigation-systems [Accessed October 6, 2018].

Barkenbus, J.N. 2012. "Eco-Driving: An Overlooked Climate Change Initiative." *Energy Policy* 38: 762–9.

Barth, Matthew and Kanok Boriboonsomsin. 2008. *Real-World CO_2 Impacts of Traffic Congestion*. Riverside: Center for Environmental Research and Technology, University of California. Available at: https://pdfs.semanticscholar.org/3664/184/ea936a24d 72604be8183db5674143eb1.pdf [Accessed February 15, 2018].

Bauer, C., J. Hofer, H.-J. Althaus, A. Del Duce, and A. Simons. 2015. "The Environmental Performance of Current and Future Passenger Vehicles: Life Cycle Assessment Based on a Novel Scenario Analysis Framework." *Applied Energy* 157: 871–83. Available at: https://doi.org/10.1016/j.apenerg.2015.01.019 [Accessed January 2, 2018].

Beck, Marcus W., Andrea H. Claassen, and Peter Hundt. 2012. "Environmental and Livelihood Impacts of Dams: Common Lessons across Development Gradients That Challenge Sustainability." *International Journal of River Basin Management* 10: 73–92. Available at: https://doi.org/10.1080/15715124.2012.656133 [Accessed August 20, 2018].

Bennhold, Katrin. 2018. "Germany's Car Capital Reels as Court Allow Ban on Cars." *The New York Times*, February 28, pp. A1, A6.

Bierstedt, J., A. Gooze, C. Gray, J. Peterman, L. Raykin, and J. Walters. 2014. *Effects of Next-Generation Vehicles on Travel Demand and Highway Capacity*. Walnut Creek, CA: Fehr Peers Consulting. Available at: www.fehrandpeters.com/wpcontent/uploads/2015/07/FP_Think_Gen_Vehicle_White_Paper_FINAL.pdf [Accessed December 20, 2017].

BP. 2017. *Statistical Review of World Energy June 2017*. London: British Petroleum P.L.C. Available at: www.bp.com/content/dam/bp/en/corporate/pdf/energy-economics/statistical-review-2017/bp-statistical-review-of-world-energy-2017-full-report.pdf [Accessed December 10, 2017].

Brenden, Anna, Ida Kristoffersson, and Lars-Goran Mattsson. 2017. *Future Scenarios for Self-Driving Cars in Sweden*. Stockholm: KTH Royal Institute of Technology.

Brown, A., J. Gonder, and B. Repac. 2014. "An Analysis of Possible Energy Impacts of Automated Vehicles." Pp. 137–53 in G. Meyer and S. Beiker, eds., *Road Vehicle Automation*. New York: Springer.

Brown, A., B. Repac, and J. Gonder. 2013. *Autonomous Vehicles Have a Wide Range of Possible Energy Impacts*. Washington, DC: National Renewable Energy Laboratory, US Department of Energy. Available at: www.nrel.gov/ [Accessed December 17, 2017].

Brown, A., A. Sarzynski, and F. Southworth. 2008. *Shrinking the Carbon Footprint of Metropolitan America*. Washington, DC: Brookings Institution. Available at: www.brookings.edu/research/shrinking-the-carbon-footprint-of-metropolitan-america/ [Accessed December 1, 2017].

Charlton, Alistair. 2018. "Volkswagen to Launch All-Electric Car Share Scheme in U.S., Europe, Asia." *Salon*, July 7. Available at: www.salon.com/2018/07/07/volkswagen-to-launch [Accessed October 6, 2018].

Chediak, Mark. 2018. "Electric Buses Will Take over Half the World Fleet by 2025." *Bloomberg*, February 1. Available at: www.bloomberg.com/news/articles/2018-02-01/electric-buses [Accessed October 6, 2018].

Chester, M. and A. Horvath. 2008. *Environmental Life-Cycle Assessment of Passenger Transportation*. Berkeley, CA: UC Berkeley Center for Future Urban Transport, Working Paper UCB-ITS-VWP-2008-2. Available at: http://escholarship.org/uc/item/567092q [Accessed March 31, 2015].

Clarke, S. 2017. "How Green Are Electric Cars?" *The Guardian*, December 25. Available at: www.theguardian.com/football/ng-interactive/2017/dec/25/how-green [Accessed December 17, 2017].

Clickenergy. 2017. "Leading Renewable Energy Producers." August 10. Available at: www.clickenergy.com.au [Accessed June 18, 2018].

Davis, S.C. and L.F. Truett. 2000. "An Analysis of the Impact of Sport Utility Vehicles in the United States." Available at: https://citeseerx.ist.psu.edu/viewdoc/download?doi=10.1.1.500.4646&rep=rep1 [Accessed December 5, 2017].

De Aenile, Conrad. 2015. "The Dimming of Diesel Fuel's Future in Cars." *The New York Times*, December 9, Special Section, "Report: Energy for Tomorrow."

DeCicco, J., D. Liu, J. Heo, R. Krishnan, A. Kurthen, and L. Wang. 2016. "Carbon Balance Effects of U.S. Biofuel Production and Use." *Climatic Change* 138: 667–80. doi: 10.1007/s10584-016-1764-4 [Accessed December 29, 2017].

Degirmenci, Kenan and Michael Breitner. 2017. "Consumer Purchase Intentions for Electric Vehicles: Is Green More Important Than Price and Range?" *Transportation Research Part D: Transport and Environment* 51: 250–60. Available at: https://doi.og/10.1016/j.rd2017.01.001 [Accessed February 15, 2018].

Delta-ee. 2018. *Public Chargers to Account for Only 8% of Charging*. Edinburgh: Delta Energy and Environment, May 20. Available at: www.delta-ee.com/press-releases/ [Accessed July 2, 2018].

DOT. 2016. *Diesel-Powered Vehicles as a Share of the Total Fleet*. Washington, DC: US Department of Transportation. Available at: www.rita.gov/bts/sites/files/publications/ [Accessed December 13, 2017].

Eddy, Melissa. 2018. "Stuttgart Ruling Takes Aim at Diesel Industry, Heart of German Car Business." *The New York Times*, February 28, p. A6.

Ebhardt, Tommaso. 2018. "Ferrari Plans Electric Car to Challenge Tesla Roadster." *San Francisco Chronicle*, January 17, p. C6.

EIA. 2017. *Monthly Energy Review*. Washington, DC: US Energy Information Administration. Available at: www.eia.gov/totalenergy/data/monthly/index.php#petroleum/ [Accessed December 16, 2017].

EIA. 2016. *International Energy Outlook 2016*. Washington, DC: US Energy Information Administration. Available at: www.eia.gov/outlooks/ieo/pdf/transportation.pdf [Accessed December 14, 2017].

Ellabban, Omar, Haitham Abu-Rub, and Frede Blaabjerg. 2014. "Renewable Energy Sources: Current Status, Future Prospects and Their Enabling Technology." *Renewable and Sustainable Energy Reviews* 39: 748–64.

EnerData. 2018a. *Global Energy Statistical Yearbook 2018*. Grenoble: EnerData. Available at: https://yearbook.enerdata.net/co2-fuel-combustion/CO2-emissions-data-from-fuel-combustion.html [Accessed August 16, 2018].

EnerData. 2018b. "Up to 50% of the Global Car Fleet Could Be Electric in 2015." February 27. Available at: www.enerdata.net/publications/executive-briefing/half-car-fleet-electric-2050.html [Accessed June 15, 2018].

EPA. 2017a. *Light-Duty Vehicle CO_2 and Fuel Economy Trends*. Washington, DC: US Environmental Protection Agency. Available at: www.epa.gov/fuel-economy-trends/ [Accessed January 17, 2018].

EPA. 2017b. *Fast Facts: U.S. Transportation Sector Greenhouse Gas Emissions 1990–2015*. Washington, DC: Office of Transportation and Air Quality, US Environmental Protection Agency. Available at: www.epa.gov/fastfacts [Accessed December 31, 2017].

EPA. 2017c. *Design for the Environment Life-Cycle Assessments*. Washington, DC: US Environmental Protection Agency. Available at: www.epa.gov/Life-Cycle-Assessments [Accessed February 9, 2018].

Ewing, Jack. 2017. "Across Europe, Diesel's Future Shaky." *The New York Times*, July 17, pp. B1, B6.

Fagant, D.J. and K.M. Kockelman. 2013. *Preparing a Nation for Autonomous Vehicles*. Washington, DC: ENO Center for Transportation. Available at: www.enotrans.org/ [Accessed July 10, 2017].

Faria, R., P. Marques, P. Moura, F. Freire, J. Delgado, and A. de Almeida. 2013. "Impact of Electricity Mix and Use Profile in the Life-Cycle Assessment of Electric Vehicles." *Renewable and Sustainable Energy Reviews* 24: 271–87.

Faria, R., P. Moura, J. Delgado, and A. de Almeida. 2012. "A Sustainability Assessment of Electric Vehicles as a Personal Mobility System." *Energy Conservation and Management* 61: 19–30.

Franckx, Laurent. 2016. *Future Trends in Mobility: The Rise of the Sharing Economy and Automated Transport*. Brussels: MIND-Sets Project. Available at: www.mind-sets.eu [Accessed March 17, 2018].

Freund, Peter and George Martin. 2009. "The Social and Material Culture of Hyperautomobility." *Bulletin of Science, Technology & Society* 29: 476–82.

Gapper, J. 2017. "Germany's Car Industry Suffers Tesla Shock." *Financial Times*, August 3, p. 9.

Gardner, Greg. 2016. "Why Most Self-Driving Cars Will Be Electric." *Detroit Free Press*, September 19, p. 5.

Greenblatt, Jeffery B. and Samveg Saxena. 2015. "Autonomous Taxis Could Greatly Reduce Greenhouse-Gas Emissions of US Light-Duty Vehicles." *Nature Climate Change* 5: 860–63. doi: 10.1038/nclimate2685.

Greenblatt, Jeffrey B. and Susan Shaheen. 2015. "Automated Vehicles, On-Demand Mobility, and Environmental Impacts." *Current Sustainable Renewable Energy Reports* 2: 74–81. doi: 10.1007/s40518-015-0038-5.

Greene, David L. and Andreas Schafer. 2003. *Reducing Greenhouse Gas Emissions from U.S. Transportation*. Arlington, VA: Center for Climate and Energy Solution. Available at: www.c2es.org [Accessed December 30, 2017].

Groshen, Erica, Susan Helper, John MacDuffie, and Charles Carson. 2018. *Preparing U.S. Workers and Employers for an Autonomous Vehicle Future.* Washington, DC: Securing America's Future Energy (SAFE). Available at: https://avworkforce.secureenergy.org/wp-content/uloads/2018/06/Groshen-et-al-Report-June-2018-1.pdf [Accessed September 6, 2018].

Hawkins, Troy R., Ola Moa Gausen, and Anders Hammer Stromman. 2012. "Environmental Impacts of Hybrid and Electric Vehicles: A Review." *The International Journal of Life Cycle Assessment* 17: 997–1014. Available at: https://link.springer.com/article/10.1007/s11367-012-0440-9 [Accessed November 1, 2018].

Hawkins, Troy R., B. Singh, G. Majeau-Bettez, and A. Stromman. 2012. "Comparative Environmental Life Cycle Assessment of Conventional and Electric Vehicles." *Journal of Industrial Ecology* 17: 53–64. doi: 10.1111/j.1530-9290.2012.00532.x.

Herrmann, Andreas, Walter Brenner, and Rupert Stadler. 2018. *Autonomous Driving: How the Driverless Revolution Will Change the World.* Bingley, UK: Emerald.

Howey, A., R. Martinez-Botas, B. Cussons, and L. Lytton. 2011. "Comparative Measurements of the Energy Consumption of 51 Electric, Hybrid and Internal Combustion Engine Vehicles." *Transportation Research Part D: Transport and Environment* 16: 459–64.

Huo, H., H. Cai, Q. Zhang, F. Liu, and K. He. 2015. "Life-Cycle Assessment of Greenhouse Gas and Air Emissions of Electric Vehicles: A Comparison between China and the U.S." *Atmospheric Environment* 108: 107–18.

IEA. 2017a. *Key World Energy Statistics.* Paris: International Energy Agency. Available at: www.iea.org/publications/freepublications/KeyWorld2017.pdf [Accessed December 13, 2017].

IEA. 2017b. *CO$_2$ Emissions from Fuel Combustion.* Paris: International Energy Agency. Available at: www.iea.org/publications/freepublications/publication/CO2Emissionsfrom FuelCombustionHighlights2017.pdf [Accessed December 17, 2017].

IEA. 2017c. *Global EV Outlook.* Paris: International Energy Agency. Available at: www.iea.org/publications/freepublications/GlobalEVOutlook2017.pdf [Accessed January 1, 2018].

IEA. 2016. *World Energy Outlook.* Paris: International Energy Agency. Available at: www.iea.org/publications/freepublications/publication/WorldEnergyOutlook/ [Accessed March 5, 2018].

IEA. 2015. *Key World Energy Statistics.* Paris: International Energy Agency. Available at: www.iea.org/publications/freepublications/publication/KeyWorldEnergyStatistics/ [Accessed August 19, 2018].

IEA. 2009. *Transport, Energy and CO$_2$: Moving toward Sustainability.* Paris: International Energy Agency. Available at: www.iea.org/publications/freepublications/publication/transport2009.pdf [Accessed December 13, 2017].

Iglinski, Hubert and Maciej Babiak. 2017. "Analysis of the Potential of Autonomous Vehicles in Reducing the Emissions of Greenhouse Gases in Road Transport." *Procedia Engineering* 192: 353–8. Available at: www.sciencedirect.com/science/article/pii/S1877705817326073?via%3Dihub [Accessed August 19, 2018].

IHS. 2017. *Autonomous Vehicle Sales Set to Reach 21 Million Globally by 2035.* Santa Clara CA: Information Handling Services. Available at: www.ihs.com/automotive-industry-forecasting.html?ID=115737/ [Accessed December 20, 2016].

IIASA. 2012. "Energy End-Use: Transport." P. 623 in *Global Energy Assessment.* Cambridge: Cambridge University Press. International Institute for Applied Systems Analysis, Laxenburg. Available at: www.iiasa.ac.at/web/home/research/Flagship.Projects/global-Energy-Assessment/ [Accessed December 13, 2017].

INRIX. 2014. *Annual Cost of Gridlock in Europe and the US Will Increase 50 Percent on Average to $293 Billion by 2030.* Kirkland, WA: INRIX Inc., October 14. Available at: http://inrix.com/press-releases/annual-cost-of-gridlock-in-europe-and-the-us-will-increase-50-percent [Accessed August 19, 2018].

IRENA. 2015. *Global Renewable Energy Sources*. Abu Dhabi: International Renewable Energy Agency. Available at: www.irena.org/gateway/dashboard/ [Accessed January 5, 2018].

Isaac, Mike and Neal E. Boudette. 2017. "Ford Invests $4 Billion for a Future of Riders." *The New York Times*, February 17, p. B5.

ITF. 2017. *Lightening Up: How Less Heavy Vehicles Can Help Cut CO_2 Emissions*. Paris: International Transport Forum, Organisation for Economic Co-Operation and Development. Available at: www.itf-oecd/sites/default/files/docs/less-heavy-vehicles-cut-CO2-emissions.pdf [Accessed December 12, 2017].

Jones, C. and D. Kammen. 2011. "Quantifying Carbon Footprint Reduction Opportunities for U.S. Households and Communities." *Environmental Science & Technology* 45: 488–95.

Kim, S. and J. Miller. 2015. "South Korea's New Light-Duty Vehicle Efficiency Standards." In *TransportPolicy.net*. Washington, DC: International Council on Clean Transportation. Available at: www.theicct.org/blogs/staff/south [Accessed January 1, 2018].

Kotter, R. and S. Shaw. 2013. *Work Package 3, Activity: Micro to Macro Investigation*. Viborg: Interreg North Sea Region, EU Regional Development Fund.

Kukreja, Rinkesh. 2017. "What Are Biofuels?" *Conserve Energy Future*. Available at: www.conserve-energy-future.com/advantage-and-disadvantages-of-biofuels.php [Accessed January 5, 2018].

Lacey, Stephen. 2017. "Everyone Is Revising Their Electric Vehicle Forecasts Upward: Except Automakers." In *Green Tech Media*. Edinburgh: Wood Mackenzie. Available at: www.greentechmedia.com/articles/everyone-is [Accessed January 5, 2018].

LCVP. 2018. *SMMT Confirms First Annual Rise in New Car CO_2 Emissions for Nearly 20 Years*. London: Low Carbon Vehicle Partnership, February 27. Available at: www.smmt.co.uk/reports/co2-report/ [Accessed March 1, 2018].

LCVP. 2017. *LowCVP Study Highlights Importance of Measuring Whole Life Carbon Emissions*. London: Low Carbon Vehicle Partnership. Available at: www.lowcvp.org.uk/ [Accessed December 27, 2017].

Levine, Steve. 2016. *The Powerhouse: America, China, and the Great Battery War*. New York: Penguin Random House.

Li, Xiaomin, Pu Chen, and Xingwu Wang. 2017. "Impacts of Renewables and Socio-economic Factors on Electric Vehicle Demands: Panel Data Studies across 14 Countries." *Energy Policy* 109: 473–8. Available at: https://doi.org/10.1016/j.epol.2017.07.021 [Accessed June 24, 2018].

Litman, Todd. 2017. *Autonomous Vehicle Implementation Predictions: Implications for Transport Planning*. Victoria, BC: Victoria Transport Policy Institute, February 27.

Lloyd, A.C. and T.A. Cackette. 2001. "Diesel Engines: Environmental Impact and Control." *Journal of the Air & Waste Management Association* 51: 809–47.

Lorf, C., R. Martinez-Botas, D. Howey, L. Lytton, and B. Cussons. 2013. "Comparative Analysis of the Energy Consumption and CO_2 Emissions of 40 Electric, Plug-in Hybrid Electric, Hybrid Electric and Internal Combustion Engine Vehicles." *Transportation Research Part D: Transport and Environment* 23: 12–19.

Ma, H., F. Balthasar, N. Tait, X. Riera-Palou, and A. Harrison. 2012. "A New Comparison between the Life Cycle Greenhouse Gas Emissions of Battery Electric Vehicles and Internal Combustion Vehicles." *Energy Policy* 44: 160–73.

Maclean, H.L. and L.B. Lave. 2003. "Life Cycle Assessment of Automobile/Fuel Options." *Environment Science and Technology* 37: 5445–52.

Manjunath, A. and G. Gross. 2017. "Towards a Meaningful Metric for the Quantification of GHG Emissions of Electric Vehicles (EVs)." *Energy Policy* 102: 423–9.

Martin, George. 1999. *Hyperautomobility and Its Sociomaterial Impacts*. Guildford: Centre for Environment and Sustainability, University of Surrey, CES Working Paper 02/99.

Matulka, Rebecca. 2014. *The History of the Electric Car.* Washington, DC: US Department of Energy. Available at: https://energy.gov/articles/history-electric-car [Accessed January 4, 2018].

McCauley, Ryan. 2017. "Why Autonomous and Electric Vehicles Are Inextricably Linked." In *FutureStructure.* Washington, DC: Governing. Available at: www.govtech.com/authorss/ryan-mccauley.html [Accessed January 5, 2018].

Messagie, Maarten, F.-S. Boureima, T. Coosemans, C. Macharis, and J. Van Mierlo. 2014. "A Range-Based Vehicle Life Cycle Assessment Incorporating Variability in the Environmental Assessment of Different Vehicle Technologies and Fuels." *Energies* 7: 1467–82. doi: 10.3390/en7031467.

Metz, David. 2018. "Developing Policy for Urban Autonomous Vehicles: Impact on Congestion." *Urban Science* 2: 33. doi: 10.3390/urbansci2020033.

Meyer, Gereon. 2016. "Synergies of Connectivity, Automation and Electrification of Road Vehicles." Pp. 187–91 in G. Meyer and S. Beiker, eds., *Road Vehicle Automation.* New York and London: Springer. Available at: http://link.springer.com/chapter/10.1007/978-3-319-40503-2_14 [Accessed December 20, 2017].

Milakis, D., B. Van Arem, and B. Van Wee. 2017. "Policy and Society Related Implications of Automated Driving: A Review of Literature and Directions for Future Research." *Journal of Intelligent Transportation Systems* 21: 324–48. Available at: https://doi.org/10.1080/15472450.2017.1291351 [Accessed December 27, 2017].

Miller-Wilson, K. 2013. "List of Car Weights." *LoveToKnow.* Available at: http://cars.lovetoknow.com/List_of_Car_Weights [Accessed December 6, 2017].

Milman, Oliver. 2013. "Electric Future? Global Push to Move Away from Gas-Powered Cars." *The Guardian,* September 13. Available at: www.theguardian.com/environment/2018/sep/13/electric-car [Accessed October 6, 2018].

Moran, Emilio, Maria Lopez, Nathan Moore, Norbert Muller, and David Hyndman. 2018. *Sustainable Hydropower in the 21st Century.* Washington, DC: Proceedings of the National Academy of Sciences. Available at: http://doi.org/10.1073/pnas.1809426115 [Accessed November 23, 2018].

Moriarity, Patrick and Stephen Wang. 2017. "Can Electric Vehicles Deliver Energy and Carbon Reductions?" *Energy Procedia* 105: 2983–8.

National Geographic. 2018. "Electric Cars May Rule the World's Roads by 2040." *National Geographic Magazine,* September. Available at: https://news.nationalgeographic.com/2017/09/electric-cars-replace-gasoline-engines-2040.html [Accessed January 3, 2018].

Nordhoff, S., J. de Winter, M. Kyriakidis, B. van Arem, and R. Happee. 2018. "Acceptance of Driverless Vehicles: Results from a Large Cross-National Questionnaire Study." *Journal of Advanced Transportation* Volume 2018, Article ID 5382192. Available at: https://doi.org/10.1155/208/5382192 [Accessed October 25, 2018].

NRC. 2013. "Transitions to Alternative Vehicles and Fuels." In *National Research Council.* Washington, DC: National Academies Press. Available at: http://nap.ed/18264 [Accessed December 13, 2017].

NRC. 2011. "Assessment of Fuel Economy Technologies for Light-Duty Vehicles." In *National Research Council.* Washington, DC: National Academies Press. Available at: http://nap.edu/12924 [Accessed December 13, 2017].

Nwosu, Ikenna. 2017. *When Was Rear-View Camera Technology First Made Available in Vehicles?* Mountain View, CA: Quora Inc., April 20. Available at: www.quora.com/When-was-rearview-camera-technology-first-made-available [Accessed October 5, 2018].

O'Dea, Jimmy. 2018. *Electric vs. Diesel vs. Natural Gas: Which Bus in Best for the Climate.* Cambridge, MA: Union of Concerned Scientists. Available at: https://blog.ucusa.org/jimmy-odea/electric-vs [Accessed October 6, 2018].

Offer, G.J. 2015. "Communication: Automated Vehicles and Electrification of Transport." *Energy & Environmental Science* 8: 26–30. doi: 10.1039/C₄EE02229G.

Oge, Marge T. 2015. *Driving the Future: Combating Climate Change with Cleaner, Smarter Cars.* New York: Arcade.

Onat, N.C., M. Kucukvar, and O. Tatari. 2016. "Uncertainty-Embedded Dynamic Life Cycle Sustainability Assessment Framework: An Ex-Ante Perspective on the Impacts of Alternative Vehicle Options." *Energy* 112: 715–28.

Onat, N.C., M. Kucukvar, and O. Tatari. 2015. "Conventional, Hybrid, Plug-in Hybrid or Electric Vehicles? State-Based Comparative Carbon and Energy Footprint Analysis in the United States." *Applied Energy* 150: 36–49.

Onn, C.C., C. Chai, A. Rashid, M. Karim, and S. Yusoff. 2017. "Vehicle Electrification in a Developing Country: Status and Issue, from a Well-to-Wheel Perspective." *Transportation Research Part D: Transport and Environment* 50: 192–201.

Orsato, R.J. and P. Wells. 2007. "U-Turn: The Rise and Demise of the Automobile Industry." *Journal of Cleaner Production* 15: 994–1006.

Orsi, Francesco, Matteo Muratori, Matteo Rocco, Emanuela Colombo, and Giorgio Rizzoni. 2016. "A Multi-Dimensional Well-to-Wheels Analysis of Passenger Vehicles in Different Regions: Primary Energy Consumption, CO_2 Emissions, and Economic Cost." *Applied Energy* 169: 197–209. Available at: https://doi.org/10.1016/j.apenergy.2016.02.039 [Accessed January 15, 2018].

Parry, Ian, Margaret Walls, and Winston Harrington. 2006. *Automobile Externalities and Policies.* Washington, DC: Resources for the Future, RFF DP 06-26. Available at: www.rff.org/files/sharepoint/WorkImages/Download/RFF-DP-06-26.pdf [Accessed December 30, 2017].

Pyper, Julia. 2014. "Self-Driving Cars Could Cut Greenhouse Gas Pollution." *Scientific American, E&ENews*, September 15. Available at: www.scientificamerican.com/article/self-driving-cars-could-cut-greenhouse-gas-pollution/ [Accessed January 17, 2018].

Qiao, Q., F. Zhao, Z. Liu, S. Jiang, and H. Hao. 2017. "Comparative Study on Life Cycle CO_2 Emissions from the Production of Electric and Conventional Vehicles in China." *Energy Procedia* 105: 3584–95.

Rios-Torres, J. and A. Malikopoulos. 2017. "A Survey on Coordination of Connected and Automated Vehicles at Intersections and Merging at Highway On-Ramps." *IEEE Transactions on Intelligent Transportation Systems* 18: 1066–77. Available at: https://udi.ornl.gov/.survey-coordination-connected-and-automated-vehicles-intersections/ [Accessed December 13, 2017].

Said, Carolyn. 2018. "Uber and Lyft Clog Streets, S.F. Says." *The San Francisco Chronicle*, October 16, pp. A1, A9.

Said, Carolyn. 2016. "Lyft, GM Joining Forces." *San Francisco Chronicle*, January 5, p. D1.

Schaller, Bruce. 2018. *The New Automobility: Lyft, Uber and the Future of American Cities.* Brooklyn, NY: Schaller Consulting. Available at: www.schallerconsult.com/the-new-automobility [Accessed October 7, 2018].

Schrank, D., B. Eisele, and T. Lomax. 2012. *Urban Mobility Report.* College Station: Texas Transportation Institute, Texas A & M University. Available at: http://mobility.tamu.edu/ [Accessed December 16, 2017].

SFCTA. 2018. *TNCs & Congestion.* San Francisco: San Francisco County Transportation Authority. Available at: www.sfcta.org/sites/default/files/content/Planning/TNCs/TNCs_Congestion_Report_181015_Final.pdf [Accessed November 23, 2018].

Sharma, Sunita and Sib Ghoshal. 2015. "Hydrogen the Future Transportation Fuel: From Production to Applications." *Renewable and Sustainable Energy Reviews* 43: 1151–8.

Shi, X., A. Wang, J. Yang, and Z. Sun. 2016. "Electric Vehicle Transformation in Beijing and the Comparative Eco-Environmental Impacts: A Case Study of Electric and Gasoline Powered Taxis." *Journal of Cleaner Production* 137: 449–60.

Singh, Sonal, Shikha Jain, P.S. Venkateswaran, Avanish Tiwari, Mansa Nouni, Jitendra Pankey, and Sanket Goel. 2015. "Hydrogen: A Sustainable Fuel for Future of the Transport Sector." *Renewable and Sustainable Energy Reviews* 51: 623–33. Available at: https://doi.org/101016/j.rser.2015.06.040 [Accessed January 15, 2018].

Sumantran, Venkat, Charles Fine, and David Gonsalvez. 2017. *Faster, Smarter, Greener: The Future of the Car and Urban Mobility.* Cambridge, MA: MIT Press.

Switkes, J. and S. Boyd. 2016. "Connected Truck Automation." Pp. 195–200 in G. Meyer and S. Beiker, eds., *Road Vehicle Automation.* New York and London: Springer. Available at: https://link.springer.com/chapter/10.1007/978-3-319-40503-2_15 [Accessed January 1, 2018].

Tabuchi, Hiroko. 2018. "The World Warms to S.U.V.s, While the Planet Just Warms." *The New York Times*, March 6, pp. D1, D4.

Tagliaferri, C., S. Evangelisti, F. Acconcia, T. Domenech, P. Ekins, D. Barletta, and P. Lettieri. 2016. "Life Cycle Assessment of Future Electric and Hybrid Vehicles: A Cradle-to-Grave Systems Engineering Approach." *Chemical Engineering Research and Design* 112: 298–309. Available at: http://dx.doi.org/10.1016/j.cherd.2016.07.003 [Accessed December 28, 2017].

Thomas, C.E. 2011. "How Green Are Electric Vehicles?" *International Journal of Hydrogen Energy* 37: 6053–62. Available at: https://doi.org/10.1016/j.ijhydene.2011.12.118 [Accessed January 6, 2018].

Thomas, C.E. 2009. "Transportation Options in a Carbon-Constrained World: Hybrids, Plug-in Hybrids, Biofuels, Fuel Cell Electric Vehicles, and Battery Electric Vehicles." *International Journal of Hydrogen Energy* 34: 9279–96. Available at: https://doi.org/10.1016/j.ijhydene.2009.09.058 [Accessed January 5, 2018].

Tsugawa, S., S. Kato, and K. Aoki. 2011. "An Automated Truck Platoon for Energy Saving." IEEE/RSJ International Conference, San Francisco. Available at: http://eeexplore.ieee.org/abstract/document/6094549/ [Accessed December 20, 2017].

TTI. 2015. *Urban Mobility Scorecard.* College Station: Texas Transportation Institute, Texas A & M University. Available at: https://static.tti.tamu.edu/documents/mobility-scorecard-2015/pdf [Accessed February 28, 2018].

Underwood, S. 2014. *Automated, Connected, and Electric Vehicle Systems: Expert Forecast and Roadmap for Sustainable Transportation.* Dearborn, MI: Institute for Advanced Vehicle Systems, University of Michigan. Available at: http://graham.umich.edu/media/files/LC-IA-ACE-Roadmap-Expert-Forecast-Underwood.pdf [Accessed December 15, 2017].

Van Mierlo, J.V., M. Messagie, and S. Rangaraju. 2017. "Comparative Environmental Assessment of Alternative Fuelled Vehicles Using a Life Cycle Assessment." *Transportation Research Procedia* 25: 3435–45.

Vaze, Preshant. 2009. *The Economical Environmentalist.* London: Earthscan.

Vlasic, Bill. 2017. "G.M. to Unveil Driverless Car, Aiming to Get Jump on Rivals." *The New York Times*, November 30, p. B1.

Voelcker, John. 2014. "1.2 Billion Vehicles on World's Roads Now, 2 Billion by 2035." *GreenCarReports.* Available at: www.greencarreports.com/news/1093560_1-2-billion-vehicles-www.greencarreports.com/news/1093560_1-2-billion-vehicles [Accessed January 5, 2018].

Wadud, Zia, Don MacKenzie, and Paul Leiby. 2016. "Help or Hindrance? The Travel, Energy and Carbon Impacts of Highly Automated Vehicles." *Transportation Research Part A: Policy and Practice* 86: 1–18. Available at: http://doi.org/10.1016/j.tra.2015.12.001/ [Accessed March 25, 2018].

Wang, H., X. Zhang, and M. Ouyang. 2015. "Energy Consumption of Electric Vehicles based on Real-World Driving Patterns: A Case Study of Beijing." *Applied Energy* 157: 710–19.

Wang, Michael. 2003. *WTW Analysis in a Complete Energy/Emissions Comparison*. Sacramento: California Air Resources Board, April 14. Available at: https://greet.es.anl.gov/files/ea30hyon [Accessed January 8, 2018].

Wang, U. 2015. "Are Self-Driving Vehicles Good for the Environment?" In *Ensia*. Minneapolis: Institute on the Environment, University of Minnesota, August 17. Available at: https://ensia.com/features/are-self-driving [Accessed December 27, 2017].

Wehrmann, Benjamin. 2018. *'Dieselgate': A Timeline of Germany's Car Emissions Fraud Scandal*. Berlin: Clean Energy Wire, February 28. Available at: www.cleanenergywire.org/factsheets/dieselgate-timeline-germanys-car-emissions-fraud-scandal [Accessed July 1, 2018].

Weldon, P., P. Morrissey, and M. O'Mahony. 2016. "Environmental Impacts of Varying Electric Vehicle User Behaviours and Comparisons to Internal Combustion Engine Vehicle Usage: An Irish Case Study." *Journal of Power Sources* 319: 27–38.

White, Michelle J. 2004. "The 'Arms Race' on American Roads: The Effect of Sport Utility Vehicles and Pickup Trucks on Traffic Safety." *Journal of Law and Economics* 47: 333–55.

Williams, J.H. 2013. *The Technology Path to Deep Greenhouse Gas Emissions Cuts by 2050: The Pivotal Role of Electricity*. Berkeley: Lawrence Berkeley National Laboratory, University of California. Available at: https://escholarship.org/uc/item/2mz2472z [Accessed December 28, 2017].

Wilson, L. 2013. *Shades of Green: Electric Cars' Carbon Emissions Around the Globe*. London: Shrink That Footprint. Available at: www.shrinkthatfootprint.com/shadesofgreen [Accessed December 30, 2017].

Wood Mackenzie. 2017. *World Petrol Demand 'Likely to Peak by 2030 as Electric Car Sales Rise'*. London: Video, *The Rise and Fall of Black Gold*, October 9. *The Guardian*, October 16. Available at: www.theguardian.com/business/2017/oct/16/world-petrol-demand-peak-electric-car-wood-mackenzie-oil/ [Accessed August 15, 2018].

Wu, C., G. Zhao, and B. Ou. 2011. "A Fuel Economy Optimization System with Applications in Vehicles with Human Drivers and Autonomous Vehicles." *Transportation Research Part D: Transport and Environment* 16: 515–24.

WWF. 2008. *One Planet Mobility: A Journey towards a Sustainable Future*. Woking: World Wildlife Fund.

Yazdanie, M., F. Noembrini, S. Heinen, A. Espinel, and K. Boulouchos. 2016. "Well-to-Wheel Costs, Primary Energy Demand, and Greenhouse Gas Emissions for the Production and Operation of Conventional and Alternative Vehicles." *Transportation Research Part D: Transport and Environment* 48: 63–84.

Yong, Taeseok and Chankook Park. 2017. "A Qualitative Comparative Analysis on Factors Affecting the Deployment of Electric Vehicles." *Energy Proceedia* 128: 497–503. doi: 10.1016/j.egypro.2017.09.066.

Zackrisson, Mats, Lars Avellan, and Jessica Orlenius. 2010. "Life Cycle Assessment of Lithium-Ion Batteries for Plug-in Hybrid Electric Vehicles: Critical Issues." *Journal of Cleaner Production* 18: 1517–27. doi: 10.1016/j.jclepro.2010.06.004.

Zhixia, R., M. Chitturi, L. Yu, A. Bill, and D. Noyce. 2015. "Sustainability Effects of Next-Generation Intersection Control for Autonomous Vehicles." *Smart and Sustainable Transport* 30: 342–52. doi: 10.3846/16484142.2015.1080760.

3 Social sustainability

3.1 Introduction: Giving social sustainability its due

Global popularization of the term sustainability as it relates to environments began with United Nations plenary resolution 42/187 in December, 1987: "Sustainable development is development that meets the needs of the present without compromising the ability of future generations to meet their own needs" (UN 1987, 1). The term rapidly became a foundational meme signposting a new direction in environmental science and practice. While the hallmark of the term is its inter-generational focus, it was motivated by concern "about the accelerating deterioration of the human environment and natural resources and the consequences of that deterioration for economic and social development" (UN 1987, 1). Since then social development has become the most amorphous and least considered of the three sides of the sustainability triangle – environment, economy, and society.

The environment, subject of the previous chapter, is the sustainability vector most popularly discussed and scholarly researched – indeed, it is often equated with sustainability. Its realm is relatively straightforward – recovering and maintaining the ecological health of planet Earth in order to sustain human habitation into the future. The economy has been the environment's adjutant in the workings of sustainable development policies and programs – as in determining how monetary costs for repairing degraded ecologies and caring for sound ones will be met. It has come to represent the development half of sustainable development while environment is the sustainable half. The UN resolution put an emphasis on economic growth as the basis for both environmental and social sustainability: "The need for a new approach to economic growth, as an essential prerequisite for eradication of poverty and for enhancing the resource base on which present and future generations depend" (UN 1987, 1). The focus on economic growth has unbalanced the sustainability tripod and has become the subject of a stream of critical analyses in ecological economics that probe its contradictions, limits, and alternatives (Hirsch 2005; Jackson 2009).

While economics are often addressed in this book, for example in considering the external costs of operating a motor vehicle, it does not have its own chapter.

After all, it is given everyday attention in the growing discourse about autonomous vehicles (AVs). For example, business matters related to its technological evolution appear frequently as commentaries in newspapers, e-zines and blogs, and in e-reports of consulting and marketing firms. Many of the sources used in preparing this book illustrate this economic focus in the coverage of AV development – in researches and analyses as well as in commentaries. The social leg of the sustainable development tripod has been hobbled for the most part, leaving it with an unsteady foundation.

Social sustainability has been described aptly as a concept in chaos, a circumstance created in part by official inattention:

> Though the concept of sustainable development originally included a clear social mandate, for two decades this human dimension has been neglected amidst abbreviated references to sustainability that have focused on biophysical environmental issues, or been subsumed within a discourse that conflated 'development' and 'economic growth.'
>
> (Vallance, Perkins, and Dixon 2011, 342)

Analysis and research about autonomous vehicle development thus far are proving to be no exception to this pattern of neglect, a deficiency addressed with this monograph.

As autonomous vehicle development approaches its moment of deployment a focus on society increasingly becomes obligatory. At bottom, economic rewards depend upon public acceptance. This is a challenge that requires substantial attention to understanding social forces. Central to success of the AV transition from development to deployment are the reactions of consumers (public opinion), as well as the positions adopted by interest groups, non-profit organizations, and institutions. Furthermore, public regulatory regimes will have a decisive role in setting the parameters and timing of autonomous vehicle deployment and they are subject to lobbying and campaigning directed at all levels of government by keen parties. The sum output of all these actors will reflect the timbre of reaction to autonomous vehicle mobility. What all interested parties seem to be lacking is comprehensive and evidence-based analyses of its social sustainability attributes.

Autonomous vehicles can be an agent of social change if they are widely deployed. In fact, at the end of the day they are more likely to "herald a greater shift in societal innovation" than they are in technological apparatus or in business practice (Huntington 2015, 3). At present however, despite its manifest importance, society continues to be neglected in the triad of sustainability. This lack of consideration is consistent with the view that programs of sustainable development be led by concern for economic growth and enterprise earnings (Giddings, Hopwood, and O'Brien 2002). This perspective neglects the potential social impacts of AV deployment even though they will have serious economic repercussions. The analysis here is concerned with the deployment's social sustainability prospects, and concentrates on whether they subtract from or add to the social problems in which conventional automobility has a prominent role.

The possible social sustainability impacts of the autonomous vehicle get their full due in this chapter, beginning with a breakdown of the measures used to assess their parameters. This is followed by examination of the public health problems of conventional automobility, including air pollution, and the social sustainability opportunities they present for AV deployment. The next section turns to the conventional vehicle's mobility inequities, including their disproportionate concentrations in some social groups. Existing inequities provide another opportunity for an autonomous vehicle deployment to benefit social sustainability. The final section of the chapter analyzes the rebound effects likely to result from AV use that may moderate these benefits.

3.2   Scoping social sustainability

What are the key areas of life related to autonomous vehicle deployment that likely will bear upon social sustainability (Brain 2014)? The 1987 United Nations resolution had two explicit social goals: Reducing poverty and meeting basic human needs. Since then the organization has expanded and specified an agenda for social sustainability. In 2015 it inaugurated a new program of Social Development for Sustainable Development (SDSD). Following are three of its 16 goals that relate directly to an AV deployment's social sustainability prospects (UN 2017a):

- Good health and well-being – including reduction of air pollution and road traffic deaths
- Reduced inequalities
- Gender equality

Two other objectives in the UN program are addressed in Chapter Four on urban sustainability. They are sustainable cities and communities, which includes urban land use, infrastructure, and transportation. Three other AV-related goals in the SDSD program, affordable and clean energy, climate action, and responsible consumption and production, were addressed in Chapter Two on environmental sustainability. The remaining eight goals lack specific connection to an autonomous vehicle deployment; for example, life on land. Others, such as life below water, have no relevant connection.

The three AV-specific elements of the United Nations Social Development program are addressed by two sections in this chapter, public health and mobility equity. Leading parameters for assessing all social sustainability impacts are equity and equality. They are closely related and often are treated as being interchangeable. However, there are subtle differences (Boschmann and Kwan 2008; MPH 2018). Equality refers to equal treatment with regard to rights and opportunities, while equity is based in fair treatment that may not be equal. For example, fairness provides benefits for selected groups, such as the elderly, the poor, and the disabled. Equitable benefits are allocated under a general principal of "to each according to need." In this analysis of autonomous vehicle deployment, the focus is on equity. It is a prime measure of quality of life in societies (UN 2017a).

3.3 Legacy problem: Public health toll

Cautionary messages are accumulating about an AV "rush to market" and its resultant neglect of public health impacts (Kelley 2017, 1). A former head of the US National Highway Traffic Safety Administration has admonished autonomous vehicle developers for following a "sell now and evaluate later" policy (Claybrook 2017, A22). Public health experts increasingly are being prompted to get more engaged in investigating the potential consequences of the vehicles, including their ethical implications (Fleetwood 2016). (Ethical issues surrounding autonomous vehicle deployment are addressed in Chapter Five.) The present reality is that there has been little analysis of public health implications of AV use – on either personal or population levels (Crayton and Meier 2017).

The accession of an era of hyper automobility based in internal combustion engines powered by fossil fuels has resulted in a batch of social sustainability problems that can be reframed as targets of opportunity for an AV deployment. Two of these were discussed at length in Chapter Two on environmental sustainability – greenhouse gas (GHG) emissions and traffic congestion. Both also have relevance to the public health dimension of social sustainability. Vehicle tailpipe GHG emissions lead to negative social consequences through their contribution to climate change, as in higher probabilities for fire or flooding (IPCC 2007). Also, climate change promotes more frequent and more intense heat waves that result in increased mortality, especially among the poor and elderly (Karl, Melillo, and Peterson 2009). Some vehicle emissions are toxic and thereby directly threaten human health. Thus, they are detrimental to social sustainability and are addressed in this chapter.

Traffic congestion, like GHG emissions, was addressed as an environmental problem in Chapter Two, but is also quite relevant to public health. Road congestion's impacts on health have attracted a growing body of research. A 2010 risk assessment in the US found that the impacts may be significant enough in magnitude, at least in some urban areas, to be included in evaluations of the benefits resulting from policies to mitigate congestion (Levy, Buonocore, and Stackelberg 2010). A 2013 simulation study of risks for on-road and near-road populations found that "the health risks are potentially significant" but further research is needed to "consider travel time, the duration of rush-hour, and congestion-specific estimates" (Zhang and Batterman 2013, 307).

Congestion is frequently considered an economic problem that creates monetarized costs in fuel and time wasted. However, it also contributes to the health problems of ambient air pollution, street noise, and driver stress. These three are examined in detail below. Two additional sustainability issues, unexamined in Chapter Two, are featured in this chapter: Road crash casualties and mobility inequities. Following their analysis all these problems are cast as opportunities for an autonomous vehicle deployment to make positive social sustainability impacts.

Air pollution

The UN's World Health Organization (WHO) has estimated that about 7 million people died worldwide as a result of cumulative air pollution exposure in 2012, roughly one-eighth of all premature deaths that year (UN 2014). Nearly one-half involved exposure to outdoor air pollution. A straight-line projection indicates that global contribution to premature mortality could double by 2050 (Lelieveld et al. 2015). It does not kill directly but does so through its contributions to cardiovascular and pulmonary diseases (UN 2017b). Thus, toxic air pollution in itself is not, categorically, a cause of death that medical examiners list in death certificates (Schumaker 2018).

In the tailpipe emissions soup that internal combustion vehicles (ICVs) produce one ingredient stands out as the most threatening to human health – particulate matter 2.5 ($PM_{2.5}$), consisting of very small soot-like particles that are easily embedded in lungs and bloodstreams (Parry, Walls, and Harrington 2006, 3). Most particles form in the atmosphere as a result of complex reactions of chemicals such as sulfur dioxide and nitrogen oxides, which are pollutants emitted from automobiles (EPA 2018). $PM_{2.5}$ is a designation of microscopic and inhalable particles. In addition to being part of tailpipe emissions, it comes from vehicle tire and brake wear.

Particulates contribute to a range of serious health problems:

> Fine particulate matter is associated with a broad spectrum of acute and chronic illness, such as lung cancer, chronic obstructive pulmonary disease (COPD) and cardiovascular diseases. Worldwide, it is estimated to cause about 25% of lung cancer deaths, 8% of COPD deaths, and about 15% of ischaemic heart disease and stroke.
>
> (UN 2016, 1)

Fine airborne particulate matter is produced by a variety of sources and some of them are domestic, such as burning wood and charcoal. For this reason there are wide differences between nations and within nations with regard to toxic levels in atmospheres and their causes – as there are among the nine that are leading AV development (AV9). For example, deaths are relatively high in China and they stem largely from indoor pollution produced by residential heating and cooking. However, the general fact is that people living close to traffic-heavy roads in any nation are more exposed to breathing in fine particulate matter (Smith et al. 2017).

Within nations elevated health risks from air pollution are often found in the largest urban areas (see Chapter Four). They are locales for multiple sources of toxic emissions, including industrial plants and transportation vehicle facilities, as well as large and often congested roadways (EPA 2017). Roadways appear to be the primary source because of their ubiquity. A global study of air pollution from motor vehicles found that "gasoline and diesel vehicles are among the main sources of toxic air contaminants in most cities and are probably the most important source of public exposure to such contaminants" (Faiz, Weaver, and Walsh 1996, xiv).

In the UK a study in central London illustrated the negative health impacts of toxic air pollution. Using volunteers over age 60 years, researchers compared bio-physical metrics such as blood pressure and lung capacity after their walks along a busy thoroughfare (Oxford Street) and in a leafy retreat (Hyde Park). The results showed that exposure to air pollution on the street countered the positive health effects of walking in the park (Sinharay et al. 2018). Another study in London identified one of the more insidious products of breathing in road traffic air – an enhanced possibility for women to deliver low birth weight (LBW) babies. Maternal residences were assigned average monthly air pollution concentrations using Geographic Information Systems data. LBW was found to be correlated with exposure to polluted air; $PM_{2.5}$ was consistently associated with increased risk (Smith et al. 2017). To some it may sound less serious than it really is – however, LBW is associated with increased lifetime mortality risks for the newly born.

Ambient noise and driver stress

Noise is associated with traffic-congested cities and with good reason – about 80 percent of it is generated by road and street traffic (Lehmann 2010, 276). A high level of ambient noise is considered by the WHO to be an important public health problem (UN 2011). Long-term exposure has been associated with a list of negative health impacts: Auditory system decline, sleep disturbance, impaired cognitive performance, and psychological effects. A developing research stream is focusing on its negative consequences for cardiovascular health, including the development of arterial hypertension (Münzel et al. 2014). With regard to its psychological effects, research using a German population-based longitudinal study found that exposure to residential road noise increases the risk of depressive symptoms in middle-aged and older adults (Orban et al. 2016). Exposure to traffic noise, like exposure to toxic outdoor air, is commonly above regulatory standards. For example, it has been estimated that about 40 percent of the population of European Union nations is consistently exposed to road traffic noise that is defined as high (UN 2017c).

The increased levels and frequencies of traffic congestion induced by hyper automobility have added to the risk of repetitive drive-time stress for commuters and for drivers of commercial vehicles. Perhaps it is motivated by the frustration of frequently having to wait on the way to appointed duties (Wener and Evans 2011). Research literature has indicated positive correlations of traffic congestion with psychological stress (Hennessey and Wiesenthal 1999; Milakis, Van Arem, and Van Wee 2017). In the extreme it can lead to reactionary aggressive driving that may graduate to road rage. Road rage is defined as a road traffic event in which an angry driver becomes aggressive and threatens to harm, or does harm, another driver (Frumkin 2002, 207; Martin 2015, 34).

While driver stress has more often than not been examined as an individual psychological issue, several contributing social factors have been identified, including driving a large number of miles per day in heavy traffic (Ayar 2006; Sansone and Sansone 2010). A study in Toronto found that "road rage perpetration increased significantly with number of weekly kilometres driven and was significantly greater for drivers who are always on busy roads" (Smart et al. 2003, 343). Since the mid-1990s when driver stress, aggression, and road rage first began getting the attention of the news media (Lupton 2002), they increasingly have been considered public health problems. The timing of increased attention was associated with hyper automobility's traffic congestion approaching saturation levels.

Deaths and injuries

The most popularized potential gain of an AV deployment is that it will save lives and prevent injuries resulting from road crashes; this would make a meaningful contribution to social sustainability. The US Department of Transportation has proclaimed that "autonomous vehicle technologies have captured America's imagination" and "the reason is simple: their potential to reduce and even eliminate the devastating loss of life to road deaths globally" (DOT 2017a, 1). Road crash deaths and bodily damages generate substantial emotional and financial costs to societies. The UN's sustainable development program has set a goal for 2020 to reduce worldwide road deaths and injuries by one-half the 2010 figure (UN 2017a). This will be quite difficult to achieve in the face of the increasing motorization featured in developing countries. However, there is potential for autonomous vehicles to slow and eventually reverse the present negative trends in road safety (ITF 2017, 49).

Globally, about 1.3 million people die each year as a result of road traffic crashes (WHO 2018) and deaths are on the increase – largely because of rising automobility and traffic congestion in developing nations. Road deaths also are rising as a cause of death in comparative terms. They were not in the leading ten causes in 2010, rose to being tenth in 2015, and are predicted to become seventh by 2030 (WHO 2018). They are already the leading cause of death among people between 15 and 29 years old. Even the US, a country with well-developed road infrastructures, regulations, driver training, and licensing, is seeing rising levels of deaths – even rising *rates*. Between 2010 and 2016 its road deaths increased by 13.5 percent and its road deaths per 100 million vehicle miles traveled (VMT) increased from 1.1 to 1.2 percent (NHTSA 2016). Road fatalities surged from about 32,000 in 2014 to about 37,000 in 2016, the largest two-year increase since the early 1960s (Lowy 2017).

Road deaths are disproportionately distributed around the world. Higher income countries have far fewer relative to their shares of global population and motor vehicle stock (WHO 2017). Meanwhile, the autonomous vehicle's much touted potential to reduce road deaths will be situated in higher income nations, supporting the validity of the aphorism that "the rich get richer and the poor get poorer." The quality of vehicle stocks, roadway infrastructures, and regulatory protocols comprise the primary supports for road safety – and all reflect the level of national income.

Nearly one-half of the deaths on the world's roads are "vulnerable road users," a designation that features pedestrians and cyclists (WHO 2018). The toll is created by a number of factors but the most general is that vulnerable road users lack the protective shell and mass that a motor vehicle provides for its occupants (SWOV 2012). The comparative risk of harm between a pedestrian or cyclist and a car or van occupant involved in a serious road collision is a 43 to 1 disadvantage for a pedestrian and 32 to 1 for a cyclist. In the US, 16 percent of crash fatalities in 2016 were pedestrians and 2 percent were cyclists (NHTSA 2016), amounting to 6,827 deaths.

Also, some vehicle occupants are more vulnerable than others. Globally, traffic-related deaths among those 65 or older increased by 6.9 percent between 2010 and 2016 (ITF 2018b). Young persons, aged 15 to 24, especially males, have road traffic death rates that are typically twice those for population averages. These two groups would likely profit from an autonomous vehicle deployment. However, the prospects for walkers and cyclists are quite cloudy. One research review estimated their risk factor from a collision with an autonomous vehicle as falling within a range from a 50 percent decrease to a 30 percent increase (Shay, Khattak, and Wali 2018). While AV crash avoidance technology may reduce collision risks for both those inside and outside vehicles, a rebound of increased miles traveled will offset the gains by an uncertain amount.

3.4   Sustainability opportunity: Public health benefit

The negative legacies of hyper automobility and ICVs provide opportunities for autonomous vehicles to make contributions to social sustainability. The signature gain of reduced crashes would apply to all AVs, and driver stress likely would be reduced sharply for occupants of all AVs. However, deployment will substantially reduce the public health problems of vehicle air pollution and ambient noise (even factoring in a rebound vehicle miles increase) only if vehicles are electrified (see Chapter Two).

AV deployment's potential to reduce road crashes is based in its virtual elimination of driver error. Autonomous electric vehicles (AEVs) could lead to additional safety gains for walkers and cyclists, as vehicles might be substantially downsized. This would help to offset the dangers presented by the increasing mass of vehicles, especially sport utility vehicles (SUVs), discussed in Chapter Two. One research study in the US estimated that for every 1 million SUVs that replace smaller cars, "between 34 and 93 additional car occupants, pedestrians, bicyclists, or motorcyclists are killed per year" (White 2004, 333). Autonomous vehicles, even as SUVs, have potential to reduce this social loss by lowering driver error. One scenario study indicates that AV fatality rates could eventually decline to those seen in travel by airplane and rail, or about 1 percent of current road fatality rates (Hayes 2011).

A US national study reported that in over 90 percent of serious car crashes driver error or negligence was a causal or a contributory factor, including inattention, speeding, and alcohol use (NHTSA 1999). These human factors are considered to be preventable by road safety officials (NHTSA 2016). Somewhat ironically, the use of digital devices while driving has become an increasing factor in road crashes: "While cars and phones now offer advanced voice controls and other features intended to keep drivers' eyes on the road, apps like *Facebook*, *Google Maps*, *Snapchat* and others have created new temptations that drivers and passengers find hard to resist" (Boudette 2017, B3). The use of such devices is being increasingly prohibited by regulatory agencies. This ban may not be applied to travel in autonomous vehicles.

Machine-controlling hardware and software are being developed to minimize road crashes, but this is proving to be a difficult and time-consuming process. Detecting and evaluating obstacles in the path of autonomous vehicles is a complex multi-dimensional challenge. Distinguishing vulnerable nearby humans (walkers, cyclists, and children) from other phenomena is the most critical task and it will be more difficult for AV artificial intelligence machines than it is for human drivers (Fagant and Kockelman 2013, 4). However, some commentators argue that we should not wait for the technology to be perfected because even if it is only a bit better than current drivers, it will still save thousands of lives (Anderson et al. 2014).

There are offsetting factors that will reduce the potential of autonomous vehicles to lower the level of road crashes by a large margin. The first is the fact that no digital or machine technology is error free. Thus AV deployment will create an uncertain number of crashes caused by failure of vehicle or system digital apparatus. While machine failure is the cause of just 2 percent of present conventional vehicle crashes, the number of autonomous vehicle crashes will rise with the VMT increase rebound that is expected. With more miles the crash *rate* can be assumed to fall but the *number* of crashes will not fall in the same proportion (Groshen et al. 2018, 79).

The prospect of public health benefits from an autonomous vehicle deployment includes their integration into urban public transit systems (see Chapter Four). The health benefits of public transit begin with user safety. In the US the accident fatality rates for occupants of cars and light trucks are 17 times those for the occupants of trains and 67 times those of transit buses (Savage 2013). Incorporating autonomous vehicle services within transit systems could also alleviate problems that infirm older and disabled persons have traveling because of their regulatory mandate to provide assisted access. A secondary gain from public transit use of AVs could be as a means of reassuring apprehensive and skeptical potential users about their safety.

Public transit AVs could provide for other public health benefits. Modes of mobility have quite different public health profiles. Walking and biking head a health ranking because of the physical exercise both require. Motorized public transit vehicles are grouped together in a second tier, as they offer the opportunity to walk or to bike to their stations. National household survey data in the US show that people who walk from home to public transit stops do so for an average of 21 minutes a day, and that about one-half of transit commuters get an average of 1.7 hours walking per week (Freeland et al. 2013). Additional research has shown that the residents of urban neighborhoods with good access to public transit are more likely to meet or to exceed recommended daily physical activity minimums (Sallis et al. 2009). Bringing up the rear with regard to physical activity are two private motorized vehicles, the car and the motorcycle. A modeling study of six cities around the world found that 30 percent more land use density and diversity made it possible to increase walking and cycling to transit stops by 10 percent, resulting in decreased risk of cardiovascular disease, type-2 diabetes, and respiratory ailments (Stevenson et al. 2016).

3.5   Legacy problem: Mobility equity deficit

The embedding of hyper automobility and auto-centered transport systems has resulted in declines in mobility access for many people (Freund and Martin 1993). A consequence has been the emergence and expansion of another inequitable social exclusion (Freund and Martin 2007). In hyper automobility settings, "the car creates differences in lifestyle practices around time and space, excluding many temporary or permanent non-users from participating in a variety of activities, denying 'citizenship'" (Jain and Guiver 2001, 572).

The number of persons socially excluded is large, comprising as many as one-third of populations in more developed nations (Litman 2002). What's more, the exclusions are disproportionately socially distributed. A lack of mobility access penalizes certain people: "The auto allows the ultimate segregations in our culture – old from young, home from job and store, rich from poor and owner from renter" (Calthorpe 1991, 51). There is a wide swath of groups who are "currently unable or not permitted to use conventional automobiles" (Anderson et al. 2014, 16–17). In auto-centered mobility systems, "people who cannot drive, and who are especially dependent on good pedestrian infrastructure and transit – children, the elderly, people with disabilities – are deeply disenfranchised in a world that is built for automobiles" (Frumkin, Frank, and Jackson 2004, 200). All these groups stand to gain a fairer mobility access from AV deployment – if it addresses their particular needs.

Although mobility-disadvantaged groups are here addressed in a singular, serial fashion it is the case that they are overlapping and cross-cutting in nature. For example, an individual can be ascribed a variety of demographic and social characteristics, such as being simultaneously elderly, disabled, and poor. The variables are categorized here for analysis purposes.

Age

Autonomous vehicles have potential to benefit both the very young and the very old, two demographic sub-groups that have been penalized by hyper automobility. The very young depend on being chauffeured, as do many of the very old, and for this reason both are far more homebound than others. With regard to the young it is likely that safety considerations and social norms will prevent those who are below the present minimum age for getting a driving license – age 16 in many jurisdictions – from managing an AV.

The social inclusion of aged persons is becoming an increasingly salient issue in highly developed nations in part because of the aging of their populations' demographic structures. Persons 60 years old or older as a share of total population in these nations was projected to increase from 24 percent in 2015 to 33 percent in 2050 (UN 2015, 122). High-income Japan is the world leader in the proportion of population that is age 60 or over – 33 percent in 2015, expected to rise to 43 percent in 2050 (UN 2015). The rise can be expected to increase demand for autonomous vehicles. Thus, it is fitting that Japan leads the world in planning for the role of AVs in the lives of older persons (Fitt et al. 2018, 17; McCurry 2018). The potential for improving public health is highlighted by the possible gains for aged persons. In a review of autonomous vehicle status in six nations and the EU, a group which includes all the AV9 countries, analysts concluded that its deployment would be particularly beneficial to older persons as it could help them "overcome physiological barriers to mobility and reduce the risk of collision" (Lim and Taeihagh 2018, 6).

It is a familiar and daunting truth that "many senior citizens (those over age 65) and people with medical conditions often face challenges travelling freely and independently and must rely on family, friends, government, other providers to meet their basic mobility needs" (Harper et al. 2016). Aging often results in declining physiological capacities that are required for driving – reduced capabilities related to vision, manual flexibility, and reaction time (Shaheen and Niemeier 2001). As a result older persons are more likely to suffer road crashes. Many of the "elderly continue to be burdened by disproportionately high rates of collisions (per mile driven) and fatalities (relative to middle-aged drivers)" (Crayton and Meier 2017, 249).

Fatal crash rates increase noticeably starting at age 70 and are highest among drivers age 85 and older (IIHS 2017). The US age ranges with the highest rates of vehicle fatal crash involvements per miles driven are the youngest drivers, 16–19 years old (the teenagers), and the oldest drivers, 80 years and older (the octogenarians). It is important to note that the increased fatality risk among older drivers is partially due to their greater susceptibility to crash-induced bodily harm, particularly chest injuries, and to subsequent medical complications – rather than solely to an increased tendency to get into crashes (Cicchino 2015).

Mobility is a problem for many aged persons not only because of the challenges involved in driving an automobile (especially in dense traffic) but also because of the ordeals of navigating in complex, fast-paced, and crowded public transit systems (Freund and Martin 2001). As a result, older adults are more frequently non-travelers than are younger persons. A study in London found that non-travel increases with age (independent of retirement and disability status) – from 13 percent of 18–49-year-olds, to 19 percent of 60–69-year-olds, and to 40 percent of those over 80 years old (Corran et al. 2018). National household data from the US are comparable. The percent of persons who did not travel on a travel day was just 11 percent for those aged 50–59 but 24 percent for those 60–69, and 38 percent for those 80 and older (NHTS 2011, 55). Access to autonomous vehicles would be a welcome addition to the daily lives of many older persons, as it would eliminate their dependence on being able to secure drivers.

Class and race

Socioeconomic status is a principal determinant of mobility access and in public health analyses it is viewed as being the aspect of quality of life for which interventions result in the greatest health rewards (Frieden 2010). Quality of life is affected by whether or not one is able to take advantage of technological innovations: "Historically, low income and underserved populations are the last to benefit from new technologies" (Richland 2017, 1). Inequitable access to conventional automobiles is a prime example. In the highly motorized US, car travel is in large measure a function of income. Households there with annual incomes less than $25,000 are 8 times as likely as those with higher incomes not to have a motor vehicle (BTS 2016).

Lack of an auto impairs mobility. US national data "clearly shows that more income is related to more travel . . . the highest income households make about two and one-half times as many person trips as the lowest income households" (NHTS 2011, 18). Other highly motorized societies have similar income and car use profiles. In the UK one-half of households in the lowest income quintile have access to a car compared to nearly nine-tenths of those in the highest quintile (DFT 2016, 24). The lack of personal mobility disadvantages poorer persons who reside in places without public transit services and it threatens their health maintenance, including an inability to travel to care facilities (Lutz 2014).

In a nefarious irony, low income persons who are disadvantaged in hyper automobility contexts by not being able to afford cars also are often disproportionately exposed to their toxic emissions. Socially excluded communities are more likely to be proximate to hot spots produced largely by major road interchanges and dense traffic in which ambient air pollution is much higher than in other local areas (Bae 2004; Houston et al. 2004; Grineski, Bolin, and Boone 2007). A local example in San Francisco illustrates this dark paradox. Two neighborhoods were compared on the basis of health metrics (Swan 2017,

A1, A6). One, Bayview, is surrounded by superhighways; the other, West Portal, has none. Bayview has 8 times the asthma emergency room visits as does West Portal. The two differ widely in their socioeconomic profiles (ACS 2011). The median household income in West Portal is 3 times that in Bayview. Less than 1 percent of West Portal's households have no motor vehicle, while 21 percent of Bayview's do not. For AVs to play a role in redressing such disparities, their deployment will need to include shared and affordable vehicles (see Chapter Four).

The class-based lack of access to automobility benefits reflects racial and ethnic disparities in the two San Francisco neighborhoods. The doubly disadvantaged (by having far fewer cars and far more car pollution) neighborhood of Bayview is about 90 percent non-white, while the doubly advantaged (by having far more cars and far less car pollution) neighborhood, West Portal, is about 40 percent non-white. Because of historical racial discrimination and social exclusion in the US people of color are over represented among the poor, subjecting them to such double inequities (Bullard and Johnson 1997; Sheller 2015). Overall in the US, while 22 percent of black households and 12 percent of Hispanic ones do not own automobiles, only 6 percent of white households do not (FHWA 2009). Data show the inequities in practice by the commuting modes of employed Americans. Asian-, Hispanic-, and African-Americans get to work by public transit rather than by automobile at about double the rate that white Americans do (ACS 2015, 11).

The overlap of class and race disparities permeates US society and it contributed to the emergence of its environmental justice movement in the 1980s (Bryant 1995). This campaign was built on opposing inequities in the siting of toxic waste dumps and polluting industries. Since, it has expanded its scope and spawned a transport justice movement. Mobility justice is now a younger sibling in the environmental justice family (Martin 2018). Its reform program is based on the following foundation: "Generally, transportation amenities (benefits) accrue to the wealthier and more educated segment of society, while transportation disamenities (burdens) fall disproportionately on people of color and individuals at the lower end of the socioeconomic spectrum" (Bullard and Johnson 1997, 1).

The linked mobility class and race disparities found in the US are not uncommon in the largely whiter and more prosperous global North nations in which autonomous vehicle development is prominent. This enhances the opportunity for AV deployment to make a major contribution to social sustainability, and it appears that the most direct path to this end would be to provide for vehicles to operate within the framework of public transit systems (see Chapter Four).

Disability

Disability is a status that is officially designated and protected in many countries. In the US, for example, its Federal law defines an individual with a disability as "any person who has a physical or mental impairment that substantially limits one or more major life activities" (DHHS 2018). The Americans with Disabilities Act of 1990 prohibits discrimination against persons with disabilities in all areas of public life, including transportation (ADA 2018). There are four major types of defined disability difficulties: Hearing, vision, cognitive, and ambulatory. Each can be an obstacle to driving a motor vehicle.

In the US about one in five people have a disability and one in ten of these, or about 6 million persons, have difficulties getting the day-to-day transport they need. The consequences of such mobility problems have been researched and found to be significant. Almost one-half of the respondents in an online survey of persons with disabilities reported that they had to cancel appointments because of transport-related conflicts. A majority felt that their lack of transport access hindered their social lives (Bascom and Christensen 2017).

Disabled persons appear to be quite welcoming to the potential AV deployment. However, autonomous vehicles are not presently being developed with consideration for persons who have visual or other impairments. There are a number of developmental hurdles to overcome. For example, managing test vehicles requires a visual ability to read images and data. Perhaps the biggest hurdle many persons with disabilities will face in managing an AV is the capacity to intervene quickly and operate a vehicle when safety demands it.

Of persons with disabilities the visually-impaired are among the most attracted to the possibility of driverless vehicles. For example, a US group that represents the blind is an enthusiastic supporter of driverless cars, which it argues would give their members more independence (AFB 2017). One legally blind person who has ridden in autonomous vehicle prototypes is quoted as saying the following:

> I miss driving . . . and I want it to happen. Everyone in the blind community wants it to happen.
>
> (Stenquist 2014)

However, an AV developer has commented in response that access for the visually impaired could be realized only if the need for a human operator was eliminated. This is not likely to occur until Level Four, Full Self-Driving Automation.

Gender

Gender differentiation has been neglected among mobility equity concerns, in part because "it is often the least understood" of the "variables than can influence travel behaviour" (ITF 2018a, 4). However, the fact is that driving as well as its traffic violations tend to be disproportionately male. Thus, in Sweden men do 70 percent of the driving and comprise 88 percent of those prosecuted for violations (Balkmar 2018; ITF 2011, 7). In all European countries fewer women than men own or use a car (ITF 2011, 7). A study of gender travel behavior in eight cities around the world found that "women tended to travel shorter distances and prefer public transport and taxi services over cars more than men" (Ng and Acker 2018, 1). In the study gender proved to be a more robust determinant of travel mode choice than did age or income.

The research findings suggest that women would be more amenable to use of an AV because it will take driving out of the mobility equation. However, as well as being disproportionately a male activity, driving has become culturally ascribed as masculine. The most prominent of road driving vocations feature vehicles with masculinized machine connotations – big trucks and fast race cars, for example. While testosterone is not required to drive heavy-duty and fast vehicles, it is associated with them. The autonomous vehicle has potential to considerably reduce, perhaps eventually to eliminate, driving. This could make them de-gendered mobility machines.

In more developed nations, travel studies of men and women show a convergent pattern of behavior as a result of the entry of women into paid labor forces in the latter part of the 20th century. However, differences do remain because women have far more complex daily task structures. They often travel more than men because of their continuing disproportionate child care (school and medical trips) and domestic (household shopping trips) responsibilities. Because these responsibilities are now combined with jobs, women would be expected to be more welcoming to the travel flexibility of automobiles. However, they still make more use of walking and public transit than do men for equivalent trips (ITF 2011).

3.6   Sustainability opportunity: Mobility dividend

There is empirical evidence from the US that people who live in communities with good transportation options have greater opportunity to overcome poverty (Kauffman et al. 2015). If an AV deployment eventually eliminates human driving it has potential to bring greater mobility access to excluded social groups. However, low income persons would benefit only if use of autonomous vehicles is affordable, as ownership will not be an option for them. Even though autonomous vehicles will trend downward over time in cost, as with present automobiles they will remain too expensive for poorer persons to buy. Because of higher costs personal ownership will accentuate existing class and race mobility inequities.

However, there are opportunities for AVs to enhance equitable mobility. The least cost and fairest deployment is in inexpensive closed loops in fleets that are part of public transit systems (NCD 2015, 28). The broadest equity contribution of public transit is its affordability compared to other mobility modes. Travel cost is a proxy measure for the degree of equitability across modes, and the automobile is higher by a large margin in per passenger energy cost (in US$) per kilometer. It is followed by, distantly and in order, tram, bus, metro, and motorcycle modes. At the bottom of the sustainability naughty list are cycling and walking, both of which require only human energy (Sumantran, Fine, and Gonsalvez 2017).

Private carshare enterprises provide an increasing number of short journeys via on-demand digital platforms. However, these are services provided for profit and their cost prevents them from contributing to mobility equity. This is a sustainability concern with regard to the present operation of carshare vehicles because their digital platforms' lower use by lower income persons (Kondransky and Lewenstein 2014). These services require possession of internet connections, credit cards, and smartphones, expenses that many poorer urban residents cannot afford.

A prioritizing of financially affordable and physically accessible autonomous vehicles will require major government subsidies and oversight (Kondrasky 2016). This may prove difficult given the rise of austerity regimes in the more developed world since the financial crisis of 2008 (Hayes 2016). Nevertheless, there is a case to be made that government subsidization of autonomous vehicle deployment will benefit private enterprises just as present public transit systems do – for example, in providing affordable transport for their employees.

While autonomous vehicle affordability is a mobility inequity tied to class and race, there are others for the aged, disabled, and women. Aging may present a special hurdle for some, one that is not related to fitness or to affordability but to a lack of opportunity. One way to overcome this obstacle is for AVs to be available in the increasing number of specialized residential communities and retirement homes in the developed world. There is anecdotal evidence that seniors will take advantage of an AV deployment and retirement communities would appear to be fitting sites to begin. One in California has welcomed the autonomous vehicle: "Self-driving cars are the way to keep seniors independent longer," according to an organizer of the service, and one of its users put the autonomous vehicle prospects for older citizens selectively: "To get somewhere close by, it would be helpful . . . but I don't think I'd feel comfortable going out on the freeway in it" (Said 2017a, D7).

An AV deployment offers a possibility for major benefits for people with disabilities, as indicated by research on the role of mobility in supporting independence and full functioning in society (Bradshaw-Martin and Easton 2014). However, in the US, "across the country, autonomous vehicle legislation is being discussed, but little attention is being given to the role this technology can play in serving individuals with disabilities" (Claypool, Bin-Nun, and Gerlach 2017, 4). Unless they are included as stake-holders in regulatory development, some categories of persons with disabilities likely will face licensing and physical access protocols that curtail or prevent their use of an AV (NCD 2015).

The autonomous vehicle raises legal liability and ethical issues regarding the independence of disabled people. A central concern is how the role of driver will be re-defined. It is being argued by some that driving will be made obsolete by the AV. If so, the international Vienna Convention on Road Traffic will require amending so as to shift "drivership" liability to designers who create the software that manages vehicles (Bradshaw-Martin and Easton 2014), or to manufacturers who make them. This change could forestall a liability insurance barrier from preventing the independent use of autonomous vehicles by disabled persons.

Finally, with regard to gender inequity, AV mobility may serve to neutralize the cultural stereotype that driving a motor vehicle is a masculine activity (Martin 2018). (For feminist expositions and critiques of this social bias, see Lezotte 2015; Wajcman 1991.) Autonomous vehicles may be welcomed by many women who have domestic duties that require shopping and chauffeuring trips. In the longer term AVs may become household appendages. However, there will be a cultural lag to any significant change to the present masculinization of driving. At this preliminary stage women are less positive about autonomous vehicles than are men. Surveys have consistently shown that men have a higher interest in, and more positive opinions about, automated cars – and more willingness to use and to buy one (Nordhoff, Van Arem, and Happee 2016).

3.7   Rebound effects

The master autonomous vehicle rebound of more miles driven has a wide range of potential consequences related to social sustainability. For example, an AV deployment that provides an equitable means of everyday motorized mobility will attract new users who previously could not or chose not to own and operate an automobile. The population groups cited in this chapter would comprise many of these *new* users, and they are sizeable in number (Bierstedt et al. 2014, 17). They could provide a considerable add-on to vehicle miles traveled, mitigating gains that might be made in sustainability. Using data from a US national survey, researchers estimated the bounds of the potential VMT increase (in a fully autonomous vehicle environment) due to more travel from current non-drivers, senior citizens and people with travel-restrictive medical conditions (Harper et al. 2016). The projection is for an increase of 14 percent in vehicle miles for members of this population who are age 19 and older.

The wide range of new users will likely serve to create ripples of rebound effects. As an example, a growing stream of research indicates that there will be an over-reliance on AV digital systems, resulting from the fact that many new users may have limitations when dealing with automated machines. Such reliance may interfere with their ability to take control of an autonomous vehicle when necessary (Milakis, Van Arem, and Van Wee 2017, 337). In this case, a positive rebound effect (extending mobility access to non-users) produces a negative ripple effect (increased risk of vehicle crashes).

Providing an escape from the driving task, autonomous vehicles may also promote a rebound of increased consumption of goods. This potential effect has been described as follows in one analysis of AV impacts: "Driverless shared cars will create opportunities to serve their occupants; all of them will be free to be entertained and ready to consume other products" (Hudda et al. 2013). The consumer products will reflect a new domestication of the automobile and could feature additions such as entertainment centers and work stations. This commodity domestication of vehicles could be accompanied by a social aspect as well, in that small group meetings could become regular on-board features.

In addition to the add-on VMT from prior non-users of automobiles, there are at least three other potential rebound effects from an AV deployment that are social sustainability issues. They relate to drinking/driving, jobs, and obesity. Drunk driving is a frequent cause of vehicle crashes. In the US in 2016, 29 percent of the drivers killed in road crashes had blood alcohol concentrations at or above legal limits (IIHS 2017). Progress has been made over the last several decades, spurred in part by public campaigns such as *Mothers Against Drunk Driving*, but "that advancement has been incremental and has stagnated more recently" (Teutsch, Geller, and Negussie 2018, 5). Autonomous vehicle use provides an opportunity to reduce fatalities – perhaps eliminating the need for designated drivers. Some analysts argue that AVs could permanently end drunk driving (Hanna 2015). However, they may increase drunk riding! Here, again, a positive rebound (less drunken driving) could produce a negative ripple (more drinking). Perhaps AVs will be required to have sober keepers – designated managers – who can promptly and correctly intervene in vehicle management if necessary.

With regard to jobs it is likely that an autonomous vehicle deployment will result in ending the need for humans who get paid to drive (Dougherty 2017). The drivers of taxi cabs, delivery vans, and trucks of various sizes are likely to have their jobs threatened (*The Economist* 2018). Some off-road vehicles are already operating autonomously. For example, the Australian mining industry has deployed self-driving trucks for several years (Groshen et al. 2018, 128). They can run for 24 hours a day without a driver and are about 15 percent less expensive to operate (Simonite 2016). Here, the positive outcome of not having to drive produces a ripple threat of eliminating driving for those who do it for a living.

Globally, it is estimated that about 100 million people drive motor vehicles for a living. In the US in 2016 vehicle drivers held some 4.3 million jobs comprising about 3 percent of the labor force (BLS 2017). Moreover, if driving is no longer required other jobs will be at risk of elimination or change, including vehicle dispatchers and parking attendants (Groshen et al. 2018, 7). On the face of it, this would have disproportionate impacts across social and demographic sub-groups. For example, in New York City over 90 percent of *Yellow Cab* drivers are immigrants who use taxi driving as an economic gateway to the US (Englebert 2017). However, not all driving jobs will be threatened. Some autonomous vehicles may still require on-board personnel. For example, driverless public transit buses may have personnel who provide passenger safety oversight and perform tasks such as activating equipment that affords access for disabled and infirm persons.

There are a number of other caveats concerning the job loss threat ensuing from an AV deployment. The first of these is demographic. The International Transport Forum reports that the majority of truck drivers in the more developed world are older and in the latter stages of their careers (ITF 2017). Moreover, fewer are entering the occupation. Furthermore, the job losses would come slowly, over decades, providing some opportunity for drivers to train for different vocations – and for new ones that promise to be created. Driverless vehicles will require in-vehicle operators for some portions of their trips – for example to navigate locally distinctive terminals, docks, and other freight forwarding facilities (Said 2017b). Thus, the effect on jobs constitutes another example of uncertainty about an autonomous vehicle rebound. It is possible that "there is a soft landing, as the current generation of truckers age out and self-driving systems mature and become more widely adopted" (Englebert 2017, 3). There is an additional uncertainty about the possibility that a widespread AV deployment will contribute to the on-going polarization of workforces – between high-level managerial positions and low-level service ones (Autor 2010). An AV deployment is most likely to impact jobs in the middle range, which has been undergoing shrinkage relative to higher and lower labor force strata. This would serve to widen growing socioeconomic disparities in national labor forces.

It is apparent that an autonomous vehicle deployment has negative as well as positive social sustainability prospects. Thus, some of the rebound increase in VMT promised by an AV deployment likely will come from people who have traded walking and cycling for riding. Active personal mobility is associated with increased physical fitness, leading to less chance for obesity and high blood pressure (Gordon-Larsen et al. 2009). Inactive mobility, as in traveling in an automobile, is sedentary and "does not achieve these beneficial outcomes" (DOT 2017b). A travel survey of 11,000 persons in the Atlanta region examined Body Mass Index and other health-related variables and found that "each additional hour spent in a car per day was associated with a 6% increase in the likelihood of obesity" and that "conversely, each additional kilometre walked per day was associated with a 4.8% reducing in the likelihood of obesity" (Frank, Andresen, and Schmid 2004, 87). A number of other public health researchers have found that automobile reliant lifestyles are contributing to the increases in obesity in a number of developed countries (Cohen 2006, 30).

3.8   Conclusion

In summary, the likely social sustainability prospects of an AV deployment's impacts and their rebound effects are a quite broad and variegated lot that features a bounty of uncertainties. This reflects, in part, our present lack of knowledge about the social side of sustainability, including its connections to the complexity and variety of human responses to sociotechnical change in daily life. There are likely to be rebound effects from the social impacts of an AV deployment that are at present unknown. What have been examined here are the identified effects, some of which have been estimated quantitatively. The unknown ones will be generated over the course of an autonomous vehicle deployment and by the contours of its embeddedness in the fabric of societies.

This analysis of AV social sustainability prospects supports the case made in Chapter Two for an integration of autonomous and electric vehicles in a synchronized deployment. Autonomous electric vehicles would substantially reduce tailpipe toxic emissions, offsetting any VMT rebound effect. For example, one global analysis of the varying impacts of four different transport policies and technologies on air quality found that only one, electric/fuel cell vehicles, had a high improvement rating (IEA 2009, 236).

The course of AV deployment will be dynamic in quality, shaped and altered continually by public response, unintended consequences, and government regulation. We are now in the early days, and many of us will get only a glimpse of the AV's fate before our end of days. Their fate will include the degree to which deployment lived up to its potential to make meaningful benefits for social sustainability that counteract the negative legacies of conventional automobiles.

References

ACS. 2015. *Who Drives to Work? Commuting by Automobile in the United States: 2013.* Washington, DC: American Community Survey, US Census Bureau. Available at: www.nhts. ornl.gov/publications.shtml/ [Accessed March 18, 2018].

ACS. 2011. *San Francisco Neighborhoods: Socio-Economic Profiles.* Washington, DC: American Community Survey, Planning Department, US Census Bureau. Available at: www. sf-planning.org/sites/default/files/FileCenter/Documents/8501-SFProfiles/ [Accessed March 18, 2018].

ADA. 2018. *Americans with Disabilities Act.* Available at: www.ada.gov/ [Accessed March 21, 2018].

AFB. 2017. *Riding Driverless on the Highway to Independence.* Arlington, VA: America Foundation for the Blind, July 20. Available at: www.afb.org/blog/afb-blog/riding-driverless-on-the-highway-to-independence/ [Accessed October 12, 2018].

Anderson, J.M., N. Kalra, K.D. Stanley, P. Sorensen, C. Samaras, and O.A. Oluwatola. 2014. *Autonomous Vehicle Technology: A Guide for Policymakers.* Santa Monica, CA: RAND Corporation.

Autor, David. 2010. *The Polarization of Job Opportunities in the US Labor Market: Implications for Employment and Earnings.* Washington, DC: Center for American Progress and the Hamilton Project 6. Available at: https://scholar.google.com/scholar?hi-en&as_sdt=0,5&q=automated+vehicles+impact+labor+force+mid-+rage+jobs#d=gs_qabs&p=&u=%23p%3DhJp7KKS1dm4J [Accessed October 11, 2018].

Ayar, A. 2006. "Road Rage: Recognizing a Psychological Disorder." *Journal of Psychiatry & Law* 34: 123–50.

Bae, Chang-hee. 2004. "Transportation and the Environment." Pp. 356–81 in S. Hanson and G. Giuliano, eds., *The Geography of Urban Transportation*, 3rd ed. New York: Guilford Press.

Balkmar, Dag. 2018. "Violent Mobilities: Men, Masculinities and Road Conflicts in Sweden." *Mobilities*, August 9. Available at: http://doi.org/10.1080/17450101.2018.1500096 [Accessed October 11, 2018].

Bascom, Graydon W. and Keith M. Christensen. 2017. "The Impacts of Limited Transportation Access on Persons with Disabilities' Social Participation." *Journal of Transport & Health Part B* 7: 227–34. https://doi.org/10.1016/j.jth.2017.10.002.

Bierstedt, Jane, Aaron Gooze, Chris Gray, Josh Peterman, Leon Raykin, and Jerry Walters. 2014. *Effects of Next-Generation Vehicles on Travel Demand and Highway Capacity.* Walnut Creek, CA: Fehr and Peers. Available at: www.fehrandpeers.com/wp-content/uploads/2015/07/FP_Think_ Gen_Vehicle_White_Paper_FINAL.pdf [Accessed December 20, 2017].

BLS. 2017. *Labor Force Jobs.* Washington, DC: Bureau of Labor Statistics, US Department of Labor. Available at: www.bls.gov/cps/tables.htm [Accessed March 22, 2018].

Boschmann, Eric and Mei-Po Kwan. 2008. "Toward Socially Sustainable Urban Transportation: Progress and Potentials." *International Journal of Sustainable Transportation* 2: 138–57. doi: 10.1080/15568310701517265.

Boudette, Neal E. 2017. "Traffic Deaths, in Estimate, Pass 40,000 for First Time Since '07." *The New York Times*, February 16, p. B3.

Bradshaw-Martin, Heather and Catherine Easton. 2014. "Autonomous or 'Driverless' Cars and Disability: A Legal and Ethical Analysis." *European Journal of Current Legal Issues* 20, Web JCLI. Available at: http://webjcli.org/rt/printerFriendly/344/471 [Accessed March 21, 2018].

Brain, Joanna. 2014. *The Social Side of Sustainability*. Auckland: New Zealand Planning Institute. Available at: www.planning.org.nz/Folder?Action=View%20File&Folder_id=185&File=Brain.pdf [Accessed February 26, 2018].

Bryant, Bunyan. 1995. *Environmental Justice: Issues, Policies, and Solutions*. Washington, DC: Island Press.

BTS. 2016. *Transportation Statistics Annual Report*. Washington, DC: Bureau of Transportation Statistics, US Department of Transportation.

Bullard, Robert D. and Glenn A. Johnson, eds. 1997. *Just Transportation: Dismantling Race & Class Barriers to Mobility*. Gabriola Island, BC: New Society.

Calthorpe, Peter. 1991. "The Post-Suburban Metropolis." *Whole Earth Review*, Winter, pp. 44–51.

Cicchino, J. 2015. "Why Have Fatality Rates among Older Drivers Declined? The Relative Contributions of Changes in Survivability and Crash Involvement." *Accident Analysis and Prevention* 83: 67–73.

Claybrook, Joan. 2017. "Will Self-Driving Cars Improve Safety?" *The New York Times*, October 25, p. A22, Letters to the Editor.

Claypool, Henry, Amitai Bin-Nun, and Jeffrey Gerlach. 2017. *Self-Driving Cars: The Impact on People with Disabilities*. Boston: Ruderman Family Foundation. Available at: www.rudermanfoundation.org/wp-content/uploads/2017/08/Self-Driving-Cars_FINAL.pdf [Accessed March 21, 2018].

Cohen, Maurie J. 2006. "A Social Problems Framework for the Critical Appraisal of Automobility and Sustainable Systems Innovation." *Mobilities* 1: 23–38. doi: 10.1080/17450100500489106.

Corran, Philip, Rebecca Steinbach, Lucinda Saunders, and Judith Green. 2018. "Age, Disability and Everyday Mobility in London: An Analysis of the Correlates of 'Non-Travel' in Travel Diary Data." *Journal of Transport & Health*, January 6. https://doi.org/10.1016/j.jth.2017.12.008.

Crayton, Travis J. and Benjamin Mason Meier. 2017. "Autonomous Vehicles: Developing a Public Health Research Agenda to Frame the Future of Transportation Policy." *Journal of Transport & Health* 6: 245–52. http://dx.doi.org/10.1016/j.jth.2017.04.004.

DFT. 2016. *Road Use Statistics Great Britain 2016*. London: UK Department for Transport. Available at: www.gov.uk/government/collections/transport-statistics-great-britain/ [Accessed December 5, 2017].

DHHS. 2018. *Disability Services*. Washington, DC: US Department of Health and Human Services. Available at: www.hhs.gov/programs/social-services/programs-for.disabilities/index.html [Accessed March 21, 2018].

DOT. 2017a. *Autonomous Vehicles Driving Us toward a Zero Death Future*. Washington, DC: US Department of Transportation. Available at: www.transportation.gov/connections/autonomous-vehicles-driving-us-toward-zero-death-future [Accessed January 15, 2018].

DOT. 2017b. *Transportation and Health Connection*. Washington, DC: US Department of Transportation. Available at: www.transportation.gov/mission/health/person-miles-traveled-mode/ [Accessed November 28, 2017].

Dougherty, Conor. 2017. "When the CB Radios All Go Quiet." *The New York Times*, November 13, pp. B1, B3.

The Economist. 2018. "Special Report: Autonomous Vehicles." March 3. Available at: https://media.economist.com/news/science-and-technology/21696925 [Accessed April 1, 2018].

Englebert, Cathy. 2017. "Driverless Cars and Trucks Don't Mean Mass Unemployment: They Mean New Kinds of Jobs." *Quartz*, August 1. Available at: www.linkedin.com/pulse/driverless-cars-trucks [Accessed March 22, 2018].

EPA. 2018. *Particulate Matter (PM) Pollution*. Washington, DC: US Environmental Protection Agency. Available at: www.epa.gov/pm-pollution/particulate-matter-pm-basics [Accessed November 27, 2018].

EPA. 2017. *Air Pollution: Current and Future Challenges*. Washington, DC: US Environmental Protection Agency. Available at: www.epa.gov/clean-air-act-overview/air-pollution-current-and-future-challenges [Accessed February 20, 2018].

Fagant, D.J. and K.M. Kockelman. 2013. *Preparing a Nation for Autonomous Vehicles*. Washington, DC: ENO Center for Transportation. Available at: www.enotrans.org/ [Accessed July 10, 2017].

Faiz, Aziz, Christopher Weaver, and Michael Walsh. 1996. *Air Pollution from Motor Vehicles: Standards and Techniques for Controlling Emissions*. Washington, DC: The World Bank.

FHWA. 2009. *National Household Travel Survey*. Washington, DC: Federal Highway Administration, US Department of Transportation. Available at: http://nhts.ornl.gov/2009/pub/stt.pdf [Accessed August 23, 2018].

Fitt, H., A. Curl, R. Dionisio-McHugh, A. Fletcher, B. Frame, and A. Ahuriri-Driscoll. 2018. "Autonomous Vehicles and Future Urban Environments: Exploring Implications for Wellbeing in an Ageing Society." In *Think Piece*, 2nd ed. Christchurch, NZ: National Science Challenge.

Fleetwood, Janet. 2016. "Public Health, Ethics, and Autonomous Vehicles." *American Journal of Public Health* 107: 532–7. doi: 102105/AJPH.2016.303628.

Frank, Lawrence D., Martin A. Andresen, and Thomas L. Schmid. 2004. "Obesity Relationships with Community Design, Physical Activity, and Time Spent in Cars." *American Journal of Preventive Medicine* 27: 87–96.

Freeland, A., S. Banerjee, A. Dannenberg, and A. Wendel. 2013. "Walking Associated with Public Transit: Moving toward Increased Physical Activity in the United States." *American Journal of Public Health* 103: 536–42.

Freund, Peter and George Martin. 2007. "Hyperautomobility, the Social Organization of Space, and Health." *Mobilities* 2: 37–49.

Freund, Peter and George Martin. 2001. "Moving Bodies: Injury, Dis-Ease and the Social Organisation of Space." *Critical Public Health* 11: 203–14.

Freund, Peter and George Martin. 1993. *The Ecology of the Automobile*. Montreal: Black Rose Books.

Frieden, Thomas R. 2010. "A Framework for Public Health Action: The Health Impact Pyramid." *American Journal of Public Health* 100: 590–5. doi: 10.2105/AJPH.2009. 185652.

Frumkin, H. 2002. "Urban Sprawl and Public Health." *Public Health Reports* 117: 201–17.

Frumkin, H., L. Frank, and R. Jackson. 2004. *Urban Sprawl and Public Health*. London: Island Press.

Giddings, Bob, Bill Hopwood, and Geoff O'Brien. 2002. "Environment, Economy and Society: Fitting them Together into Sustainable Development." *Sustainable Development* 10: 187–96. doi: 10.1002/sd199.

Gordon-Larsen, P., J. Boone-Heinonen, S. Sidney, B. Sternfeld, D.R. Jacobs, and C.E. Lewis. 2009. "Active Commuting and Cardiovascular Disease Risk: The CARDIA Study." *Archives of Internal Medicine* 169: 1216–23. doi: 10.1001/archinternmed.2009.1.

Grineski, Sara, Bob Bolin, and Christopher Boone. 2007. "Criteria Air Pollution and Marginalized Neighborhoods: Environmental Equity in Metropolitan Phoenix, Arizona." *Social Science Quarterly* 88: 535–54.

Groshen, Erica, Susan Helper, John MacDuffie, and Charles Carson. 2018. *Preparing U.S. Workers and Employers for an Autonomous Vehicle Future*. Washington, DC: Securing America's Future Energy (SAFE). Available at: https://avworkforce.secureenergy.org/wp-content/uloads/2018/06/Groshen-et-al-Report-June-2018-1.pdf [Accessed September 6, 2018].

Hanna, Katherine L. 2015. "LegalTrac: Old Laws, New Tricks: Drunk Driving and Autonomous Vehicles." *Jurimetrics Journal of Law, Science and Technology* 55: 275. Available at: www.law.asu.edu/jurimetrics/JurimetricsJournal/ [Accessed March 22, 2018].

Harper, Corey D., Chris T. Hendrickson, Sonia Mangones, and Constantine Samaras. 2016. "Estimating Potential Increases in Travel with Autonomous Vehicles for the Non-Driving, Elderly and People with Travel-Restrictive Medical Conditions." *Transportation Research Part C: Emerging Technologies* 71: 1–9.

Hayes, Brian. 2011. "Leave the Driving to It." *American Scientist* 99: 362–6.

Hayes, Graeme. 2016. "Regimes of Austerity." *Social Movement Studies* 16: 21–35. doi: 10.1080/14742837.2016.1252669.

Hennessey, Dwight A. and David L. Wiesenthal. 1999. "Traffic Congestion, Driver Stress, and Driver Aggression." *Aggressive Behavior* 25: 409–23.

Hirsch, Fred. 2005. *Social Limits to Growth*. London: Routledge.

Houston, Douglas, Jun Wu, Paul Ong, and Arthur Winer. 2004. "Structural Disparities of Urban Traffic in Southern California: Implications for Vehicle-Related Air Pollution Exposure in Minority and High-Poverty Neighborhoods." *Journal of Urban Affairs* 26: 565–92.

Hudda, R., C. Kelly, G. Long, J. Luo, A. Pandit, D. Phillips, L. Sheet, and I. Sidhu. 2013. *Self Driving Cars*. Berkeley: College of Engineering, University of California, Fung Technical Report No. 2013.05.29. Available at: www.funginstitute.berkeley.edu/sites/default/files/Self_Driving_Cars.pdf [Accessed July 4, 2017].

Huntington, Scott. 2015. "How Driverless Cars Will Impact the Environment." *Triplepundit*, February 27. Available at: www.triplepundit.com/2015/02/driverless-cars-will-impact-environment/ [Accessed November 17, 2017].

IEA. 2009. *Transport, Energy and CO$_2$: Moving toward Sustainability*. Paris: International Energy Agency. Available at: www.iea.org/publications/freepublications/publication/transport2009.pdf [Accessed December 13, 2017].

IIHS. 2017. *Older Drivers*. Arlington, VA: Highway Loss Data Institute, Insurance Institute for Highway Safety. Available at: www.iihs.org/iihs/topics/t/older-drivers/fatality/facts/older-people [Accessed March 20, 2018].

IPCC. 2007. *Climate Change 2007: Adaptation and Vulnerability*. Intergovernmental Panel on Climate Change, Working Group II. Cambridge: Cambridge University Press. Available at: www.ipcc.ch/publications_and_data/ar4/wg1/en/contents.html/ [Accessed August 23, 2018].

ITF. 2018a. *Understanding Urban Travel Behaviour by Gender for Efficient and Equitable Transport Policies*. Paris: International Transport Forum.

ITF. 2018b. *Road Safety Annual Report 2018.* Paris: International Transport Forum. Available at: www.itf-oecd.org/sites/default/files/docs/irtad-road-safety-annual-report-2018_2.pdf [Accessed July 2, 2018].

ITF. 2017. *Managing the Transition to Driverless Road Freight Transport: Policy Considerations.* Paris: International Transport Forum.

ITF. 2011. *Gender and Transport.* Paris: International Transport Forum.

Jackson, Tim. 2009. *Prosperity without Growth: Economics for a Finite Planet.* London: Routledge.

Jain, Juliet and Jo Guiver. 2001. "Turning the Car Inside Out: Transport, Equity and Environment." *Social Policy and Administration* 35: 69–86.

Karl, T.T., J.M. Melillo, and Thomas C. Peterson, eds. 2009. *Global Climate Change Impacts in the United States.* New York: Cambridge University Press.

Kauffman, Sarah, Mitchell Moss, Justin Tyndall, and Jorge Hernandez. 2015. *Mobility, Economic Opportunity and New York City Neighborhoods.* New York: Wagner School of Public Service, New York University, Research Paper No. 2598566. Available at: https://papers.ssm.com/sol3/papers.cfm?abstract_id=2598566 [Accessed October 11, 2018].

Kelley, B. 2017. "Public Health, Autonomous Automobiles, and the Rush to Market." *Journal of Public Health Policy* 38: 167–84. doi: 10.1057/s41271-016-0660-x.

Kondrasky, Michael. 2016. "Driverless Cars Will Not Solve Inequality in Cities." *Sustainable Transport,* Winter: 25–6.

Kondransky, Michael and Gabriel Lewenstein. 2014. *Connecting Low-Income People to Opportunity with Shared Mobility.* New York: Institute for Transportation & Development Policy. Available at: www.livingcities.org/resources/275-executive-summary-can-shared-mobility-help-low-income-people-access-opportunity [Accessed February 3, 2018].

Lehmann, Steffen. 2010. *The Principles of Green Urbanism: Transforming the City for Sustainability.* London: Earthscan.

Lelieveld, J., J.S. Evans, M. Fnais, D. Giannadaki, and A. Pozzer. 2015. "The Contribution of Outdoor Air Pollution Sources to Premature Mortality on a Global Scale." *Nature* 525: 367–71. doi: 10.1038/nature15371.

Levy, Jonathan I., Jonathan J. Buonocore, and Katherine Von Stackelberg. 2010. "Evaluation of the Public Health Impacts of Traffic Congestion: A Health Risk Assessment." *Environmental Health* 9: 65. doi: 10.1186/1476-069X-9-65.

Lezotte, Christine L. 2015. *Have You Heard the One about the Woman Driver?* Ph.D. Dissertation, Bowling Green State University, Bowling Green, OH.

Lim, Hazel and Araz Taeihagh. 2018. "Autonomous Vehicles for Smart and Sustainable Cities: An In-Depth Exploration of Privacy and Cybersecurity Implications." *Energies* 11: 1062. doi: 10.3390/en11051062.

Litman, Todd. 2002. "Evaluating Transport Equity." *World Transport Policy and Practice* 8: 565.

Lowy, Joan. 2017. "Feds Drop Car-to-Car Wireless Push." *The San Francisco Chronicle,* November 17, p. C2.

Lupton, Deborah. 2002. "Road Rage: Drivers' Understandings and Experiences." *Journal of Sociology* 38: 275–90. Available at: www.researchgate.net/profile/Deborah_Lupton/publication/236111330 [Accessed Marsh 12, 2018].

Lutz, Catherine. 2014. "The U.S. Car Colossus and the Production of Inequality." *American Ethnologist* 41: 232–45. doi: 10.1111/amet.12072.

Martin, George. 2018. "An Ecosocial Frame for Autonomous Vehicles." *Capitalism Nature Socialism,* August 21. Available at: https://doi.org/10.1080/10455752.2018.1510531 [Accessed August 28, 2018].

Martin, George. 2015. "Global Automobility and Social Ecological Sustainability." Pp. 23–37 in A. Walks, P. Hess, and M. Siemiatycki, eds., *The Political Economy and Ecology of Automobility: Driving Cities, Driving Inequality, Driving Politics.* Abingdon: Routledge.

McCurry, Justin. 2018. "Driverless Taxi Debuts in Tokyo in 'World First' Trial Ahead of Olympics." *The Guardian*, August 28. Available at: www.theguardian.com/technology/2018/aug/28/driverless-taxi-debuts-in-tokyo-in-world-first-trial [Accessed September 23, 2018].

Milakis, D., B. Van Arem, and B. Van Wee. 2017. "Policy and Society Related Implications of Automated Driving: A Review of Literature and Directions for Future Research." *Journal of Intelligent Transportation Systems* 21: 324–48. Available at: https://doi.org/10.1080/1547 2450.2017.1291351 [Accessed December 27, 2017].

MPH. 2018. *What's the Difference between Equity and Equality?* Washington, DC: Milken Institute School of Public Health, George Washington University. Available at: http://publichealthonline.gwu.edu/blog/equity-vs-equality/ [Accessed October 11, 2018].

Münzel, T., T. Gori, W. Babisch, and M. Basner. 2014. "Cardiovascular Effects of Environmental Noise Exposure." *European Heart Journal* 35: 829–36. doi: 10.1093/eurheartj/ehu030pmid:24616334.

NCD. 2015. *Self-Driving Cars: Mapping Access to a Technology Revolution.* Washington, DC: National Council on Disability.

Ng, Wei-Shiuen and Ashley Acker. 2018. *Understanding Urban Travel Behaviour by Gender for Efficient and Equitable Transport Policies.* Paris: International Transport Forum, Organisation for Economic Co-Operation and Development.

NHTS. 2011. *Summary of Travel Trends.* 2009 National Household Travel Survey. Washington, DC: Federal Highway Administration, US Department of Transportation. Available at: www.nhts.ornl.gov/2009/pub/stt.pdf [Accessed November 30, 2017].

NHTSA. 2016. *Traffic Safety Facts: Research Note.* Washington, DC: National Highway Traffic Safety Administration, US Department of Transportation. Available at: www.nhtsa.gov/usdot-release-2016-fatal-traffic-crash-data [Accessed March 14, 2018].

NHTSA. 1999. *The Relative Frequency of Unsafe Driving Acts in Serious Traffic Crashes.* Washington, DC: National Highway Traffic Safety Administration, US Department of Transportation.

Nordhoff, S., B. Van Arem, and R. Happee. 2016. "A Conceptual Model to Explain, Predict, and Improve User Acceptance of Driverless Vehicles." Transportation Research Board, 95th Annual Meeting, Washington, DC.

Orban, Ester, Kelsey McDonald, Robynne Sutcliffe, Barbara Hoffman, Kateryna Fuks, Nico Dragano, Anya Viehmann, et al. 2016. "Residential Road Traffic Noise and High Depressive Symptoms after Five Years of Follow-Up: Results from the Heinz Nixdorf Recall Study." *Environmental Health Perspectives* 124: 578–85. doi: 10.1289/ehp.1409400.

Parry, Ian, Margaret Walls, and Winston Harrington. 2006. *Automobile Externalities and Policies.* Washington, DC: Resources for the Future, RFF DP 06-26. Available at: www.rff.org/files/sharepoint/WorkImages/Download/RFF-DP-06-26.pdf [Accessed December 30, 2017].

Richland, Jud. 2017. *Autonomous Vehicles and Public Health.* Ann Arbor, MI: Altarum Institute. Available at: www.altarum.org/sites/default/.publication./Autonomous%20Vehicles/ [Accessed January 21, 2018].

Said, Carolyn. 2017a. "Seniors Hitch Rides in Robot Cars." *San Francisco Chronicle*, December 10, p. D7.

Said, Carolyn. 2017b. "Robot Vehicles Spur Major Shift in Jobs." *San Francisco Chronicle*, December 17, pp. A1, A18.

Sallis, James F., Heather R. Bowles, Adrian Bauman, Barbara E. Ainsworth, Fiona C. Bull, Cora L. Craig, Michael Sjostrom, et al. 2009. "Neighborhood Environments and Physical

Activity among Adults in 11 Countries." *American Journal of Preventive Medicine* 36: 484–90. doi: 10.1016/j.amepre.2009.01.031.

Sansone, Randy A. and Lori A. Sansone. 2010. "Road Rage: What's Driving It?" *Psychiatry* 7: 14–18. Available at: www.ncbi.nim.nih.gov/pmc/articles/PMC2922361/ [Accessed March 12, 2018].

Savage, Ian. 2013. "Comparing the Fatality Risks in United States Transportation across Modes and over Time." *Research in Transportation Economics* 43: 9–22. doi: 10.1016/j.retrec.2012.12.011.

Schumaker, Erin. 2018. "Air Pollution Is Killing Millions Around the Globe Each Year." *HUFFPOST*, January 23. Available at: www.huffingtonpost.com/entry/air-pollution-is-killing-millions-around-the-globe-each-year_us_5a1ed396e4b017a311eb9c5f [Accessed February 1, 2018].

Shaheen, Susan A. and Debbie A. Niemeier. 2001. "Integrating Vehicle Design and Human Factors: Minimizing Elderly Driving Constraints." *Transportation Research Part C: Emerging Technologies* 9: 155–74.

Shay, Elizabeth, Asad Khattak, and Behram Wali. 2018. "Walkability in the Connected and Automated Vehicle Era: A U.S. Perspective on Research Needs." *Transportation Research Record*: 1–11. Washington, DC: National Academy of Sciences. doi: 10.1177/0361198118787630.

Sheller, Mimi. 2015. "Racialized Mobility Transitions in Philadelphia: Connecting Urban Sustainability and Transport Justice." *City & Society* 27: 70–91.

Simonite, Tom. 2016. "Mining 24 Hours a Day with Robots." *MIT Technology Review*, December 28. Available at: www.technologyreview.com/s/603170/mining-24-hours-a-day-with-robots/ [Accessed October 11, 2018].

Sinharay, Rudy, Jicheng Gong, Benjamin Barratt, Pamela Ohman-Strickland, Sabine Ernst, Frank J. Kelly, Junfeng Zhang, et al. 2018. "Respiratory and Cardiovascular Responses to Walking Down a Traffic-Polluted Road Compared with Walking in a Traffic-Free Area in Participants Aged 60 Years and Older with Chronic Lung or Heart Disease and Age-Matched Healthy Controls: A Randomised, Crossover Study." *The Lancet* 391: 339–49.

Smart, Reginald G., Gina Stoduto, Robert E. Mann, and Edward M. Adlaf. 2003. "Road Rage Experience and Behavior: Vehicle, Exposure, and Driver Factors." *Traffic Injury Prevention* 5: 343–48. https://doi.org/10.1080/15389580490509482.

Smith, Rachel B., Daniela Fecht, John Gulliver, Sean D. Beevers, David Dajnak, Marta Blangiardo, Rebecca E. Ghosh, et al. 2017. "Impact of London's Road Traffic Air and Noise Pollution on Birth Weight: Retrospective Population based Cohort Study." *British Medical Journal* 359: 5299. https://doi.org/10.1136/bmj.j5299.

Stenquist, Paul. 2014. "In Self-Driving Cars, a Potential Lifeline for the Disabled." *The New York Times*, November 7. Available at: www.nytimes.com/204/11/09/automobiles/in-self-driving-cars [Accessed November 1, 2018].

Stevenson, Mark, Jason Thompson, Thiago Herick de Sa, Reid Ewing, Dinesh Mohan, Rod McClure, Ian Roberts, et al. 2016. "Land Use, Transport, and Population Health: Estimating the Health Benefits of Compact Cities." *The Lancet* 388: 2925–35.

Sumantran, Venkat, Charles Fine, and David Gonsalvez. 2017. *Faster, Smarter, Greener: The Future of the Car and Urban Mobility*. Cambridge, MA and London: MIT Press.

Swan, Rachel. 2017. "Where Air Pollution Hits the Hardest." *San Francisco Chronicle*, September 5, pp. A1, A6.

SWOV. 2012. "Vulnerable Road Users: The Hague: Institute for Road Safety Research." Available at: www.swov.nl/sites/default/files/publicaties/ [Accessed March 24, 2018].

Teutsch, Steven M., Amy Geller, and Yamrot Negussie. 2018. *Getting to Zero Alcohol-Impaired Driving Fatalities: A Comprehensive Approach to a Persistent Problem*. Washington, DC: The

National Academies Press. Available at: http://nap.edu/24951 [Accessed January 18, 2018].

UN. 2017a. *Social Development for Sustainable Development; Transforming our World: The 2030 Agenda for Sustainable Development.* New York: Department of Economic and Social Affairs, United Nations. Available at: https://unstats.un.org/sdgs/report/2017/goal-11/ [Accessed February 11, 2018].

UN. 2017b. *The Top 10 Causes of Death.* Geneva: World Health Organization, United Nations. Available at: http://who.int/facts-sheets/fs310/en/ [Accessed March 10, 2018].

UN. 2017c. *Noise Data and Statistics.* Copenhagen: World Health Organization, United Nations. Available at: www.euro.who.it/en/health-topics/environment-and-health/noise/data-and-statistics [Accessed March 10, 2018].

UN. 2016. *Global Health Observatory (GHO) Data: Ambient Air Pollution.* Geneva: World Health Organization, United Nations. Available at: www.who.int/gho/phe/outdoor_air_pollution/en/ [Accessed March 10, 2018].

UN. 2015. *World Population Ageing Report.* New York: Department of Economic and Social Affairs, United Nations. Available at: www.un.org/en/development/desa/population/publications/pdf/ageing/WPA2015_Report.pdf [Accessed March 20, 2018].

UN. 2014. *7 Million Premature Deaths Annually Linked to Air Pollution.* Geneva: World Health Organization, United Nations. Available at: www.who.int/2014/air-pollution/en/ [Accessed March 9, 2018].

UN. 2011. *Burden of Disease from Environmental Noise.* Bonn: European Center for Environment and Health, United Nations. Available at: www.euro.who.int/__data/assets/pdf_file/0008/136466/e94888.pdf [Accessed March 10, 2018].

UN. 1987. "Report of the World Commission on Environment and Development." United Nations 96th Plenary Meeting, New York, December 11, A/RES/42/187. Available at: www.un.org/documents/ga/res/42/ares42-187.htm [Accessed February 11, 2018].

Vallance, Suzanne, Harvey C. Perkins, and Jennifer E. Dixon. 2011. "What Is Social Sustainability? A Clarification of Concepts." *Geoforum* 42: 342–8. doi: 10.1016/j.geoforum.2011.01.002.

Wajcman, Judy. 1991. *Feminism Confronts Technology.* University Park: Pennsylvania State University Press.

Wener, Richard E. and Gary W. Evans. 2011. "Comparing Stress of Car and Train Commuters." *Transportation Research Part F: Traffic Psychology and Behaviour* 14: 111–16. https://doi.org/10.1016/j.trf.2010.11.008.

White, Michelle J. 2004. "The 'Arms Race' on American Roads: The Effect of Sport Utility Vehicles and Pickup Trucks on Traffic Safety." *Journal of Law and Economics* 47: 333–55.

WHO. 2018. *Road Traffic Injuries.* Geneva: World Health Organization, United Nations. Available at: www.who.int/factsheets/fs358/en/ [Accessed March 13, 2018].

WHO. 2017. *Global Status Report on Road Safety 2015.* Geneva: World Health Organization, United Nations. Available at: www.who.int/road_safety_status/2015/en/ [Accessed February 12, 2018].

Zhang, Kai and Stuart Batterman. 2013. "Air Pollution and Health Risks Due to Vehicle Traffic." *Science of the Total Environment* 15: 307–16. doi: 10.1016/jscitotenv2013.01.074.

4 Urban sustainability

4.1 Introduction: The city as crossroads

Urbanized areas are the critical locales for autonomous vehicle (AV) deployment and its environmental and social sustainability impacts. Cities historically have emerged where human pathways crossed and over the course of millennia their intersections have multiplied in number and size, volume of use, and types of mobility – and their importance has increased accordingly. Today's cities will be milieus for an autonomous vehicle's interaction with other roadway users, motorized and non-motorized, and will be showcases where it auditions for social acceptance.

While cities are junctions for all modes of mobility they are also interfaces for ecologies and societies. They are habitats for most of humanity and central places for the structural frameworks of civilization – material, cultural, and political. Natural ecologies are heavily impacted by urbanized areas as they are centers for the production and consumption of goods and services, as well as the residues of both. In 2015, while home to about one-half of the world's population, cities were responsible for about three-fourths of its energy-related greenhouse gas (GHG) emissions, and transportation was a principal contributor (Seto et al. 2014). Cities are where a growing majority of humans live, especially in nations where AV activity is taking place. Eight of the nine countries (AV9) in which it is concentrated are highly urbanized – from a low of 69 percent for Italy's population to a high of 93 percent for Japan's (UN 2014). The ninth, China, has a population that is 54 percent urban, about where the global figure stands. However, the country is developing rapidly and will exceed the global urbanization level by a significant margin in 2050. Across the projected time frame for autonomous vehicle deployment – stretching to 2050 – the urban proportion of the world's population is expected to reach about two-thirds from its current level of about one-half.

With increasing urbanization and stasis or decline in available land for expansion, city population densities are rising. Data from metropolitan areas around the world show an overall density increase of 6 percent from 2001 to 2012 (UITP 2016). There are manifold reasons for on-going rural to urban population shifts even in already highly urbanized countries, including generational changes in residential preference. Several social trends have been noted in the Millennial generation that favor city life, including later marriages and longer spans of single living (*Nielsen* 2014).

Cities are the principal venues for motor vehicles as well as for people. Despite the fact that trip distances are longer, often far longer, in rural areas than in urban ones, the share of global urban vehicle miles traveled (VMT) grew from 44 percent in 1965 to 60 percent in 2000 (Mitchell, Barroni-Bird, and Burns 2010, 159). This time span corresponds to the hyper automobility era in cities of the more developed world. While overall vehicle miles have reached saturation levels in a number of countries their urban concentration continues to inch upwards. For example, in the US between 2002 and 2018, the urban share of VMT rose from 58 to 68 percent (FHWA 2018).

Growing urban populations will require ever more motorized transportation that is at the same time more environmentally and socially sustainable. This means transportation that is more affordable and accessible to all and is not dominated by internal combustion vehicles (ICV), goals that may be more achievable with the AV as a new player in the mobility drama. It is arriving at a timely moment that offers opportunities to play a major role because of its relevance to three mega forces in today's world: Urbanization, digitalization, and sustainability.

Several areas of the autonomous vehicles' potential urban impacts were previously examined in Chapter Two, including road congestion, and in Chapter Three, including toxic emissions. This chapter addresses legacy issues bequeathed to cities by hyper automobility and its infrastructures, particularly their contributions to low-density urban sprawl and erosion of public transit. Attention then turns to the sustainability opportunities that may be available for an autonomous vehicle deployment, including its incorporation into public transit systems. The chapter will then examine likely rebound effects of AV deployment as they bear upon land use and transportation in cities.

Parameters for urban sustainability

There are a few spheres of urban life in which an AV deployment promises to have the most intense and lasting impacts. The UN Agenda for Sustainable Development adopted in 2015 includes among its goals several that relate directly to cities and vehicles: Sustainable cities and communities, which includes **land use**; and industry, **innovation**, and **infrastructure**, including **transportation** (UN 2017). With regard to environmental sustainability, lowering the carbon emissions produced in cities focuses on buildings, transportation, and waste (Ghouldson et al. 2015). For the focus here, passenger transportation, there are three specific sustainability goals: Land use change to reduce motorized travel, motorized travel shift to public transit, and vehicle electrification. The first two of these are addressed in this chapter; the third was examined in Chapter Two.

All nine of the UN-derived sustainability vectors addressed in this book bear upon the quality of urban resilience in the face of extreme weather events such as hurricanes and tornadoes, and they are important factors in upgrading urban responses to challenges precipitated by global climate change. Land use and transportation are central concerns in the portfolio of measures for adaptation to and mitigation of climate-based changes (Ford and Blythe 2018). One of the most significant is the rise of sea levels, which poses a slowly developing but inevitable threat to coastal dwelling populations. Cities have been commonly located at seaside for transportation purposes. Historic crossroad junctions frequently are sites where paths and roadways meet waterborne boat and ship channels. Many have evolved into today's major ports. It is estimated that in 2017 over one-half of the world's megacities (having populations of 10 million or more) are at risk from rising sea levels as well as from coastal surges (Baklanov, Molina, and Gauss 2016; Demographia 2018), including Tokyo, Seoul, Shanghai, and New York City in the AV9 group of countries.

A 2018 comprehensive analysis of research findings on urban transportation sustainability supports the recommendations of the UN Agenda. The research consensus is that the most advantageous paths are through public transit in order to increase transport efficiency and through land use change in order to reduce urban sprawl (Wittstock and Teuteberg 2018, 1161). (A third path in this research consensus, adding green technologies to improve the energy efficiency of motorized transportation modes, was examined previously in Chapter Two.) The UN Agenda is a general one and there are more specific goals at local levels. For example, German city planning managers who oversee land use responded to a survey about their concerns regarding an AV deployment with the following recommendations (Fraedrich et al. 2018, 2):

- Changes in the distribution of right of way (ROW) including developing protocols for autonomous vehicle interactions with walkers and bikers
- Changes in the amount and location of parking spaces
- Assessing the opportunities for land use redevelopment

The variety and scope of land use is foundational to all things urban, as the mantra "location, location, location" for valuing property infers. Land use and transportation constitute the principal determinants of the built environments of cities (NAS 2018a), and they have critical bearing on the triad of environmental, social, and urban sustainability. For example, they mediate the effects of cities on public health, a subject addressed in Chapter Three. The most direct connections are traffic congestion, vehicle crashes, and emissions (see Chapters Two and Three).

The prevailing expert consensus among urban transportation specialists for promoting urban sustainability is a straightforward quartet of complementary measures that are consistent with what the German planners recommend (Petersen 2004, 19):

- Reduce the need for automobile trips as well as their length
- Increase walking, biking, and public transit use

- Increase automobile occupancy
- Reduce automobile-related land use

Central to all these measures are public streets and sidewalks; they provide for the lifeblood of cities (Martin 2002). While their right-of-way is public the means of travel are public and private, motorized and motorless. A deployment of autonomous vehicles provides potential to ease the dominance of urban right-of-way by personal automobiles and benefit sustainability. The planning blueprint for deployment should include a rebalancing of ROW rights: "Instead of planning for roadway expansion, reallocate street space to active, sustainable modes and use technology to manage the public realm dynamically" (ITF 2018b, 31).

Efforts to rein in the automobilization of urban land use and transportation have met with some success in a number of cities. Between 1993 and 2017, for example, Berlin, Hamburg, Munich, Vienna, and Zurich employed "a coordinated package of mutually reinforcing transport and land-use policies" to reduce the automobile's share of local trips (Buehler, Pucher, and Altshuler 2017, 257). The five cities averaged a decline from 40 to 32 percent in its share. For all five the most productive policy was controlling and reducing the availability of car parking (Buehler et al. 2017). While these planning efforts led to a decline of one-fifth in the car share it took more than two decades to achieve. This indicates the durability of conventional automobility's embeddedness.

There are common threads in the concerns and recommendations of researchers and urban planners and they form a land use/transportation sustainability path forward: A densification and mixing of land uses to negate urban sprawl's distanciation and specialization of urban landscapes. Enhanced densities and more varieties in land use are routes to more public transit services, and to urban sustainability (Bhat and Guo 2007).

A human ecology of the city

Urban settings that will shape the disposition of AV deployment share some generic characteristics. The parameters of urban sustainability considered here to be most relevant, land use and transportation, are geographic and demographic in nature. They are parsed based on the classic Chicago urban ecology model (Park and Burgess 1970), still used as a basis for analyzing cities (Jiao 2015). Although developed for the pre-World War II industrial city its concept of concentric urban zones remains protean in the study of human settlement. The bones of the Chicago model are three center-to-periphery zones: A core or central business district (CBD), residential areas laying just outside the core, and commuter zones even farther out. Since the model was originally published in 1925 the residential and commuter zones have, respectively, morphed through urban expansion and automobilization into today's metropolitan triad of cities, suburbs, and exurbs.

Suburb is an old term dating from the Latin *suburbium* meaning an outlying part of a city. Exurb, however, is a newer term coined in the 1950s to refer to the additional, extra-urban residences of quite prosperous New Yorkers (Spectorsky 1955). Exurban residence has expanded since to include the middle class as a result of the urban transportation shift from rail-based to road-based, signaled by the arrival of superhighways. The industrial metropolis became the post-industrial metropolitan area. Today the exurb is the most outlying of urban residential areas – a transition fringe zone that verges on the countryside. The city-suburb-exurb nexus matured in the last decades of the 20th century with the ascendancy of hyper automobility. In the course of land and population expansion urban areas experienced a process of decentralized centralization (Hoyt 1941), a sprawling growth in which new outlying business sub-centers nested. While CBDs remained dominant, they became less so. In today's global economies some have evolved into international corporate finance centers. London's City and New York City's Wall Street are leading examples. However, Central Business Districts are no longer the only locales where globally influential enterprises cluster. Thus, Hollywood and Silicon Valley are not located in the CBDs of, respectively, the Los Angeles and San Francisco metropolitan areas.

The key feature of the Chicago model relating to autonomous vehicle deployment is that population density (residents per land unit) decreases as one goes from core to periphery. It applies as well to the density of transportation infrastructures and vehicle miles traveled. Thus, urban road congestion and vehicle emissions are concentrated in the core (and the road arteries serving the core), and they decline as one goes outward. The same general pattern applies as well to the intensity of public transit services. An AV deployment could have a sustainably useful role to play in developing transit service for low-density urban areas. In many metropolitan areas the trips between suburbs, and between exurbs and suburbs, constitute a major share of travel that is dominated by automobiles. Because of sprawl's low densities and residential land use, its transportation is highly dependent on private automobiles for trips to work, to school, etc. The focus in public transit on moving large passenger loads is not functionally efficient for such trips. This is a service gap that may be particularly amenable to additional public transit deployment of right-sized autonomous vehicles.

While they remain oriented primarily to a fixed central place (the CBD), urban built environments are continually evolving, not only because urban populations are increasing but also because of their dynamic use of land. Cities are the sites for innovative relationships between transportation modes and land use, because they are the most intense and concentrated of humanity's built environments. While their primary physical features are buildings and roadways, "natural" constructions such as parks and gardens are also characteristic features. Such urban green spaces could become more plentiful if autonomous vehicle deployment frees up parking and other automobile-dedicated space for redevelopment (see Compact Green Cities below). Alterations to the type and form of both land use and transportation can benefit sustainability even more so than technological developments such as the AV *per se* (Bruun and Givoni 2015). For example, converting land into public green spaces can lead to gains in both environmental and social sustainability – the former through an increase in carbon sequestration and the latter through the provision of outdoor venues which serve public health.

4.2 Legacy problems

The land use and transportation setting for an AV deployment is dominated by three features that bear heavily and negatively upon sustainability: Auto-centeredness, urban sprawl, and erosion of public transit. All three provide opportunities for a deployment to make significant improvements in urban sustainability.

Auto-centered infrastructure

Personal car mobility developed across ranges of scale and intensity in the last third of the 20th century in many cities of the global North, generating an era of hyper automobility. As a result, their transportation systems became dominated by a menu of land-eating support facilities. However, there were some general global differences in the degree to which cities became automobilized. It was more intensive in cities of newer (and larger) nations in the global North. Three cities there (Chicago, Montreal, and Sydney) averaged 488 passenger cars per 1,000 inhabitants in 2012, while three cities in older (and smaller) countries (Berlin, London, and Tokyo) averaged 325. A similar difference exists between cities in less developing and more developing nations. Three cities in developing countries (Hong Kong, Singapore, and Tehran) averaged 185, while three in less developed countries (Lagos, Mumbai, and Nairobi) averaged just 58 (UITP 2015).

Individually owned outsized conventional automobiles are very inefficient users of space. While their purpose is mobility they are typically parked for about 95 percent of their lifetimes (Barter 2013; Herrmann, Brenner, and Stadler 2018, 23; RAC 2012; Shoup 2005). Furthermore, in this meager operating time vehicle occupancy is also low. From 1995 to 2017 average occupancy for all trips in the US declined from 1.59 to 1.54 persons (EERE 2018). Commuter work trips comprise the largest trip category, accounting for about 50 percent, and their occupancy is the lowest of all trips – 27 percent lower than the overall average occupancy (NHTSA 2011). Automobile commuting promotes automobile parking. In a study of land use in 12 US cities McCahill and Garrick (2012) found that each increase of 10 percent in the share of commuters traveling by automobile was associated with an increase of more than 0.25 ha of parking space – in dedicated spots on streets as well as in surface lots and parking structures.

The environmental problem of car-parking space is two-fold: It is a substantial land user, very inefficiently used. It occupies large dollops of the urban landscape that remain vacant for much of the time (Ben-Joseph 2015; Chester et al. 2015; Kim 2018). A study of CBD spatial distributions in 41 cities around the world found that parking uses an average of 31 percent of land (Shoup 2005). With regard to their inefficiency surface parking lots in central Houston for example have daily occupancy rates of only 50 percent (Huntsman, Lasley, and Metaker-Galarza 2018). The surfeit of parking spaces in US cities emerged with the rise of hyper automobility and sprawl; a study of five cities of varying size found lavish amounts of parking space in all but one (Scharnhorst 2018). Four have more space devoted to car parking than to residences. Only one, New York City, has more households than parking spaces, which is likely attributable to its higher population density and more extensive public transit services.

Because the use of parking space is concentrated at particular times of the (working) day demand often exceeds supply, while at other times its lots and structures are virtually empty. This cycle produces more emissions as drivers search for spaces in the high-demand parts of the day and week. The extra travel adds a non-trivial amount of greenhouse gas emissions (Chester, Horvath, and Madanat 2010) and toxic pollutants. A survey conducted in 30 cities in the US, the UK, and Germany found that in the US the average driver spends 17 hours a year driving around in search of a parking spot; in the UK and Germany, the figure is more than 40 hours (*INRIX* 2017). The large difference is due to greater land availability for parking in the more spacious North American cities.

In addition to parking space, cities in the global North commit other large amounts of land use to automobile infrastructure. In US cities the average share of land dedicated to roadways (and their sidewalks) is in the range of 30 to 40 percent. In high density New York City it falls to 17 percent. In London it is 24 percent; in Tokyo, 15 percent (Petersen 2004). One study estimates that roadway footprints could be reduced by as much as 20 percent with a full autonomous vehicle deployment (Wadud, MacKenzie, and Leiby 2016, 25). As well as parking and roadway space, cities devote land to various facilities for the automobile trade and for the operation of motor vehicles, including fuel and repair stations. Overall, in the CBDs of US cities over one-half of land is devoted to motor vehicles (Melosi 2010).

Urban sprawl

A common spatial feature associated with automobilization of land use is low-density settlement sprawl, meaning "to spread irregularly" (Freund and Martin 1993). It is a pattern quite different from the more concentrated and walkable layouts of pre-automobile cities. A comparison of North American with East Asian and Western European cities illustrates the difference. In the historically older cities of Asia and Europe there are higher population densities, less automobility and sprawl, and more public transit. However, the growth of superhighways and automobilization pushed the edges of all metropolitan areas farther and farther from their cores, even those in Europe (EEA 2011). Promoted by the automobile urban sprawl is now dependent on it, as Ivan Illich (1974, 30) noted: "Beyond a certain speed, motorized vehicles create remoteness which they alone can shrink."

The arrival of light rail in the 19th century provided a transportation impetus for developing residential settlement in suburbs. Later, it was the elimination of light rail in the US and its replacement by the automobile that "allowed the suburbs to sprawl more freely and farther" (Hall 1988, 315). This transition from rail to road was highlighted by the dismantling of urban electric railways in Los Angeles in the 1930s, abetted by the political influence of major companies – *General Motors*, *Firestone Tire and Rubber*, and *Standard Oil*. In a historical analysis Yago (1984) detailed the roles played by the corporate car complexes of the US and Germany in compelling the transition from rail/ electric to auto/oil transportation in their cities.

London provides a textbook case of the historical development of sprawl. In 1801, when only non-motorized mobility was available, the inner core of the city was home to 87 percent of its population. One hundred years later, in 1901, following on the establishment of public transit rail service that proportion had declined to 70 percent. The largest growth in sprawl occurred in the next 100 years, pursuant to the popularization of automobiles – in 2001 London's inner core housed 45 percent of the metropolitan city's population (Banister 2012). Automobilization continues to have land use impacts across the whole of London. Thus, between 1998 and 2008 its domestic garden space fell by 12 percent while the area of hard surfacing increased by 26 percent, largely a product of paving over ground to use it for car parking (Smith 2010).

Large-scale urban sprawl got its beginnings in the interwar years of the 20th century and surged after World War II, accelerating to saturation levels from the 1970s to the 1990s. Its peak in the US was reached in 1994 (Barrington-Leigh and Millard-Ball 2015). The sprawl surge was facilitated by hyper automobility, and the two continue to synergize in a positive feedback loop. Population growth and its urbanization have extended the boundaries of settlements globally (UN 2017). Between 2000 and 2015 the rate of urban land expansion outpaced that of urban population increase, led by cities in the global South. Urban sprawl was galvanized by the construction of super-highways with public monies and, in the US, by the erection of pre-fabricated affordable houses by private developers following World War II. The resulting creation of metropolitan areas was detailed in a study of their metro politics (Orfield 1997). The sprawl is described in a contemporary report on its environmental and social impacts as follows: "The development of the interstate highway system facilitated tremendous growth in economic activity occurring over larger distances but also led to a great deal of flight from cities, with deeply negative implications for the environment, income distribution, race relations, etc." (Groshen et al. 2018, 81).

A household survey of residence and travel modes in a representative US metropolitan area (Table 4.1) illustrates the considerable mobility modal differences among the zones of urban residence.

Urban sprawl developed before sustainability became a public issue and its persistently negative profile indicates that it will take time for it to be reformed

Table 4.1 Household travel in Minneapolis-St. Paul metropolitan area by residence

	Residence		
	City	Suburb	Exurb
	("urban")	*("inner ring")*	*("outer ring")*
Number of cars per household	1.26	1.79	2.17
Percentage using **non-auto** travel to work in last seven days:			
Walk	44	24	12
Public transit	45	12	5

Source: Krizek, Kevin J., Jessica Horning, and Ahmed M. El-Geneidy. 2012. "Perceptions of Accessibility to Neighborhood Retail and Other Public Services." Pp. 960–117 in K. Geurs, K. Krizek, and A. Reggiani, eds., *Accessibility and Transport Planning: Challenges for Europe and North America.* London: Edward Elgar.

to reflect present realities. Ewing, Pendall, and Chen (2002, 17) developed an inventory of the sprawl-induced sustainability negatives for US cities:

> As sprawl increases, so do the number of miles driven each day; the number of vehicles owned per household; the annual traffic fatality rate; and concentrations of ground-level ozone, a component of smog. At the same time, the number of commuters walking, biking or taking transit to work decreases to a significant extent.

Sprawl considerably heightens automobile energy consumption and its emissions. A study in Toronto found a large difference between residential densities in their automobile GHG emissions – 3.6 times greater in low-density areas (Norman, MacLean, and Kennedy 2006). A study of metropolitan areas around the world sorted them into a three-fold density/energy grouping: (1) High density coupled with low energy use, i.e., Hong Kong and Taipei; (2) moderate density coupled with moderate energy use, i.e., Madrid and Singapore; and (3) low density coupled with high energy use, i.e., Atlanta and Los Angeles (Bruun and Givoni 2015).

Urban sprawl's negative impacts on social sustainability are evidenced by research that has identified its associations with public health. The automobile-based lifestyle that sprawl promotes increases the risks posed by obesity and its connections to diabetes and cardiovascular ailments (Freund and Martin 2007, 2008). A national study in the US compared the sprawl index of urban areas with the health characteristics of their populations and found that obesity was higher in areas of greater sprawl – regardless of gender, age, education level, or smoking and eating habits (McCann and Ewing 2003). Additionally, as measured by a number of indicators, including residential densities, urban sprawl has been found to feature less household health-supporting walking and biking and more sedentary automobile travel (Frumkin 2002).

The US is the world's leader in the scale of its urban sprawl and also performs poorly in comparison to other developed nations in average life expectancy. While these variables would seem to be unconnected, a national study controlling for sociodemographic characteristics found otherwise – life expectancy was significantly higher in more compact than in more sprawling counties (Hamidi et al. 2018). This association, however, does not speak to causation. The possible causes are hypothesized to include the reduced physical exercise and increased traffic crashes that exist in sprawl living. Cities with higher population densities and more public transit have lower crash fatality rates. However, walkers and cyclists are at greater risk in congested urban cores.

Public transit erosion

Public transit got its start in densely populated 19th century industrial cities and has developed primarily to serve more and more sizeable passenger loads, reaching the level of **mass transit** with the development of rail service. The world's first line was opened in London in 1863 (the underground or tube) with Paris (the metro), Berlin (the *U-bahn*), and New York City (the subway) following suit in 1902–04. Today, six of the busiest systems are in East Asian cities; Tokyo's leads the world with 3.3 billion riders annually (Duddu 2014; Lin 2014).

Public transit has proven to be largely unsuitable for service in urban sprawl because of its low population densities. In the deindustrializing-to-postindustrial transition in the global North over the last decades of the 20th century, economies shifted from manufacturing goods in factories to providing services in offices. Many of their job sites moved from cities to suburbs and exurbs, and to other regions and countries. These changes prompted population dispersion from former industrial cores and their large working class residential districts. Detroit, the renowned Motor City of the US, historical home to *Ford* and *General Motors*, has become the poster city for the phenomenon of post-industrial urban decay (Bluestone and Harrison 1982).

One example of the connection between land use and transportation has been the negative drag on public transit during the post-industrial transition period. Between 1977 and 1994 transit passenger trips per capita declined by 13 percent in the US (APTA 2015). As cities sprawled local transit systems expanded to serve growing peripheral populations and miles of service grew by one-third. However, because urban sprawl features low population density and high automobility, the number of passenger trips per mile declined by 36 percent. The mobility modal differences are reflected in the negative correlation between residential population density and household ownership of vehicles. In densities of 10,000 people per square mile or more (comparable to New York City's Manhattan Borough), 28 percent of households have no vehicle, while the figure is only 4 percent for households in suburban-to-exurban densities of less than 2,000 per mi^2 (NHTSA 2011).

Public transit's decline in the US was reflected in changes of journey-to-work modes. Between 1970 and 2000 the share of commuters who traveled by transit declined from 10 to 5 percent (the number of walkers, from 7 to 3 percent). During the same period the proportion of commuters who traveled alone in their car increased from over two-thirds to over three-fourths (APTA 2015). The urban sprawl locales of automobile-based transportation in North America have come to be referred to as "transit deserts" in which residences, commercial services, and jobs are so widely spread geographically as to be unsuited for present public transit (Hulchanski 2010; Jiao 2017).

Sustainability opportunities for land use and transportation are amplified in the population densities of urban areas. Public transit operates in high density locales, and this is evident in the US. In 2015 the country had 53 metropolitan areas with populations greater than one million, a common floor for public transit systems. However, ridership was concentrated in just six of the densest of these, which accounted for 70 percent of all trips. New York City's metropolitan area alone accounted for 41 percent (Buehler 2018, 11). The older and more compact European-styled cities like New York City (founded in 1624) feature high public transit ridership while younger and more sprawling cities like Dallas (1841) do not.

The strength of a city's public transit network is strongly associated with its transportation sustainability profile. An index of sustainable urban mobility for 100 cities round the world developed by *Arcadis* (2017) rated EU cities as comprising 18 of the top 25. Of the remaining seven only one is in North America (New York City) and six are in East Asia. The leading city on the list is in China (Hong Kong). Presently, the US is at the bottom of the global public transit league table. According to a 2008 survey conducted online in 17 nations it ranked dead last. Only 5 percent of respondents there reported that they used transit every day or on most days, compared to 61 percent who responded that they **never** rode on it. The averaged results for the other 16 countries were strikingly reversed from US levels, with 26 percent reporting that they were regular riders and just 13 percent, non-riders (*Greendex* 2009). In a follow-up survey five years later it remained last (*Greendex* 2014). Among the AV9 nations it also stands out as the public transit laggard. Eight of the nine were included in the survey of 17 (Italy was the exception). China and the ROK led in transit use while the US was far behind. In 2015 the leaders in annual per capita journeys on transit were, in order, Japan, the ROK, and Germany (UITP 2016).

In response to post-industrial sprawl city planning agencies in the global North have been working at a densification of land use. This in-fill process has been prompted in part by sprawl reaching its geographic limits, even in the US – at least in its oldest and largest cities. However, land use alteration is a tenuous and long-term undertaking, slowed by government conflicts with vested political and economic interests. In the meantime, sprawl continues to seep outward. Since the mid-1990s vehicular travel has reached a level of saturation in many metropolitan areas in the global North. In the US between 1995 and 2009 the average annual person trips per household taken by car stabilized (NHTSA 2011) at about four-fifths of trips.

The current parameters of public transit provide background information for assessing how the autonomous vehicle may play a sustainability-promoting role. The land use and transport characteristics of the modalities typically used in urban travel today are as follows in Table 4.2:

Table 4.2 Land use and carrying capacities of urban mobility modalities

Modality	Space per user (m²)	User capacity per hour
Non-motorized:		
Walk	0.7	21,200
Bike	8.0	9,700
Motorized, private:		
Car	40.0	1,500
Motorcycle	17.5	2,400
Motorized, public:		
Bus	4.5	8,300
Tram	1.5	23,000
Metro	2.5	60,000

Sources: Petersen, Rudolf. 2004. "Land Use Planning and Urban Transport." Eschborn: Sustainable Urban Transport Project, German Ministry for Economic Cooperation and Development (*GTZ*); IIASA. 2012. "Energy End-Use: Transport." *Global Energy Assessment.* Cambridge: Cambridge University Press. International Institute for Applied Systems Analysis, Laxenburg, p. 263.

These data clearly illustrate that conventional automobiles are large consumers of urban land, occupying extravagant amounts and doing so in a quite inefficient manner. Their rate of land use per passenger is multiples higher than other surface mobility modes while passenger capacities are much lower by large fractions.

Public transit's scale capacity from moderate (bus) to mass (metro) serves as the pillar of urban multi-modal mobility systems: "Mass transit should serve as the backbone of the transportation network, while autonomous vehicles, biking and walking complement the core parts of the network and provide service where mass transit is not as efficient" (NACTO 2017, 51). Multi-modal transportation infrastructures provide opportunities for reducing the need for personal automobiles – for single trips or for linked ones. It is the linked trip that will likely be the most amenable to autonomous vehicle deployment; for example, in trips from home to station and from station to job, referred to generally as the *last mile* (in commuting). In the US many travelers have become habituated to automobile travel, even for relatively short trips. They are unable or unwilling to walk or to bike to reach public transit stations. They often end up driving in part because transit park-and-ride facilities are available (*CalStart* 2009). Public transit AVs that cover short and moderate distances may be a welcome change for these travelers.

4.3   Sustainability opportunities

Autonomous vehicle deployment has potential to play a meaningful role in advancing urban sustainability by contributing to major alterations in the negative legacies of hyper automobility's land use and transportation dominance. The opportunities fall into three collateral actions: Creating more compact cities, an automobile transformation, and a thickening and digitalization of public transit service.

Compact green cities

Following decades of sprawling urban development in the US another model of urban form emerged in the 1990s – the compact city. Its planning strategies are oriented around densification that shortens distances from home to urban amenities, including public transit, thus reducing individual motorized travel by eliminating the need for it (Boschmann and Kwan 2008, 148). It is inspired by the land use exemplified in older European cities which are "relatively dense and fine-grained" (Montgomery 1998, 93). The compact city is rather like a back-to-the-future application of historical European urban forms to motorized metropolitan areas. Density and local variety of land use are seen as keys to urban sustainability. For these reasons the model is an ideal prospective companion for the deployment of a range of public transit autonomous vehicles.

A US academic center for promoting sustainable and equitable urban transport developed a useful framework for cities that is similar in organization to the UN's program for sustainability goals. The framework features several guiding principles that illustrate the contours of a compact green city: More walking and cycling using extensive networks of connected paths, and promoting mixed land use development within walking distance of public transit (ITDP 2017). One way to promote such development is for public authorities to re-allocate expenditure from automobile infrastructure to public transit, walking and cycling paths (Kenworthy 2007). What about the role of autonomous vehicles in compact green cities? One researcher is reported to have found that if a city's population density is at least 750 persons per mi^2, which would include most US cities, it ensures that a fleet of shared AVs (see below) theoretically could replace 85 percent of conventional personal automobiles (Higgins 2018).

Mixed land use reduces the need for vehicular traffic and increases the potential for walking and cycling, both of which support sustainability. For example, a study of Atlanta residents found that increased levels of mixed land use are associated with reduced odds of obesity. The intervening variable is the increased non-motorized travel that takes place in mixed land use (Frank, Andresen, and Schmid 2004). Another study, a multi-dimensional, multi-level analysis of the 50 most populous US urban areas indicates the environmental sustainability advantages of compactness. The metropolitan areas with greater residential and employment densities have lower automobile dependency and higher use of public transit and non-motorized travel (Nasri and Zhang 2018), which serve to reduce GHG emissions. One calculation of the relationship between housing density and automobile travel in the US is that a reduction from 20 to five dwelling units per acre increases automobile travel by about 40 percent (TDM 2004).

The autonomous vehicle is touted as having potential to open up the automobility-based inefficient land use that is prominent in today's urban areas. Its deployment has potential to do this in several ways: (1) Reducing the number of vehicles and their trips, (2) increasing the occupancy of remaining cars, and (3) reducing space needed for roads, parking, etc. One mathematical model predicts that AVs can decrease the need for parking space by a range of 62 to 81 percent (Nourinejad, Bahrami, and Roorda 2018) based on a projected close packing and stacking of vehicles (with clear pathways for each). Another study estimates that storage of dual-mode vehicles (with or without a driver) would require only one-fourth the space currently used for conventional automobile public garages and lots (Alessandrini et al. 2015, 155). Such alterations provide additional opportunities for densifying in-fill projects. The newly "found" space could make it possible to develop needed affordable housing in many cities in the global North where the costs of living quarters have risen to new highs. This would benefit essential public employees who work in cities but cannot afford to live in them, including teachers, police, fire, and other public sector workers.

Because of pioneering work with the compact city model, sustainability-promoting alterations in urban built environments inspired by the advent of AVs will not have to start from scratch. There is a thriving base of reform-oriented land use and transportation planning projects that focus on transitions to more compact and greener cities, emphasizing a mix of land uses together with healthy public transit systems. Many local governments in the US have adopted these new policies (Barrington-Leigh and Millard-Ball 2015). They have included grid-based street networks and other connectivity-oriented measures to promote in-fill and public transit use. Such actions serve to limit the roadway and ancillary space needed by space-eating conventional automobiles, and at the same time promote travel by foot, bike, and public transit. Because sprawl has slowed to a crawl further new development and retro-fitting of old development are focused inward toward city cores. For example, California is home to a non-profit corporation committed to promoting in-fill, the Council of Infill Builders, a prime target of which is underused parking space in city cores (CIB 2017).

There is an array of models associated with the compact city concept, including new urbanism, smart growth, and more recently, smart (digitalized) city (Caragliu, Del Bo, and Nijkamp 2011). One such is Transit Oriented Development (TOD), an urban design and planning movement that emerged in the US in the late 1980s/early 1990s as a counterforce to the hegemony of low-density, automobile-dominated urban sprawl (Calthorpe 1993; Carlton 2009; Lane 2017). It has some roots in the ideas of Mumford (1956) on urban transportation; Jacobs (1961) on urban land use; Alexander, Ishikawa, and Silverstein (1977) on urban landscapes (1977); and Lynch (1981) on good urban form.

Transit Oriented Development planning promotes sustainability by placing emphasis on urban landscapes that feature high density, mixed land use centered on public transit stations. One example is its estimates of the amount of CO_2 emissions that would be prevented by shifting new urban developments from sprawl to compact form (Ewing, Pendall, and Chen 2002). TOD began with a focus on concentration of residential and retail services around public transit stations. This work advanced to include consideration of the siting of jobs because of the frequency of work-related trips. They constitute about one-fifth of all transportation trips in the US, and they comprise three-fifths of public transit trips (CTOD 2008). Thus, the locations of new work locales are increasingly evaluated in relation to their access by public transit.

Shared vehicles

The sustainability-promoting shared-use transformation of the automobile could lead an autonomous vehicle deployment that includes the following applications (Smolicki and Soltys 2016; NAS 2018b):

- AV: Continuation of the personal automobile's individual mobility, with a connected version that would be digitally linked to other vehicles and to roadway infrastructure
- ASV: Personal use of privately owned rental fleet vehicles that are short range and digitally summoned, such as *ZipCar*
- ARSV: Private carshare fleets with on-demand services, such as *Uber*
- APTV: Public transit fleets with right-sized vehicles for short routes

The basic AV has potential to make environmental sustainability contributions through the eco-motorization of its mobility efficiency (see Chapter Two). The ASV and ARSV could add to this contribution by reducing car ownership and increasing per passenger vehicle operation. Increased loads result in lower per passenger vehicle emissions (Greenblatt and Shaheen 2015; Martin and Shaneen 2011). Simulation studies in Montreal (Morency, Verreault, and Demers 2015) and Auckland (ITF 2017a) indicate that private automobile trips would be halved if substituted for with shared vehicle services. The APTV would promote social sustainability by providing affordable and accessible vehicle use to mobility-disadvantaged persons, while private carshare AVs "could merely perpetuate our individualistic car-centered society by starving public transit of riders" (Anderson et al. 2014, 39).

At this point private enterprises are well ahead of public transit in the potential deployment of shared AVs, exemplified by the collaboration of, for example, *General Motors* and *Lyft* (Isaac 2016). Private sector carshare service is a strong growth business in cities around the world. However, the operation of ride-hailing services operating through digital platforms and personal vehicles has been adding to urban congestion rather than reducing it. A sample survey in seven major US cities found that 49 to 61 percent of their trips would not have been made at all, or would have been made by walking, biking, or public transit (Clewlow and Mishra 2017).

The arrival of private carshare services has also diverted passengers from public transit. One estimate is that in New York City and San Francisco 10 to 30 percent of transit users have switched to carshare services (Sperling 2018, 113). Other research supports this estimate. In New York City ridership in the likes of *Uber* increased by 18 percent between 2014 and 2015, and then by 29 percent between 2015 and 2016 (Schaller 2017). Meanwhile, ridership on transit buses declined in the same spans by 18 and 12 percent. An AV deployment's sustainability prospects will in some measure be determined by whether its digital platforms will be commanded by private enterprises or by public transit systems.

Public transit mobility systems that incorporate affordable and accessible autonomous vehicles will require extensive support of governments at all levels. Private commercial vehicles operate by providing a premium level of service compared to not-for-profit public transit. These premium services include door-to-door non-stop connections and vehicle amenities (NAS 2018c). The costs can be many times as much as public transit service. Governments are guarantors for ensuring that however autonomous vehicles are utilized, the result contributes to sustainability by promoting environmentally efficient and socially equitable mobility (Iacobucci, Hovenkotter, and Anbinder 2017). Many urban planners support an AV deployment via public transit systems, as indicated in a survey in Germany (Fraedrich et al. 2018). Overall, the leading objectives of planners would be to strengthen non-motorized transportation, to improve public transit, and to reduce transportation energy consumption and emissions. While the planners were generally skeptical about the potential of positive impacts from an autonomous vehicle deployment, they did foresee contributions if the vehicles were shared. No respondent saw a positive contribution coming from personal autonomous vehicles.

The automobile role revision from personal to public likely will be staged at first within urban cores, comparable to the locales defined today for congestion charging zones in London and other cities. A geosocial study in the US indicates that autonomous public transit vehicles will be more successful in cores in part because their use will correlate with the presence of work sites for growing occupations, particularly hospital and university complexes (Quodomine 2015). The APTV also could be useful in reducing the high levels of car ownership in outlying suburbs and exurbs. They could service the bulk of household short trips to public transit stations, schools, etc. They could be operated in short loops and being digitally connected their positions could be identified in real time by potential users. Households subsequently might reduce ownership to only one vehicle. For a decade the average number of motor vehicles per household in the US has remained steady at about two (*Statista* 2018). A survey in Canada and the US found that the number of vehicles per household was halved among those who participated in carshare programs (Martin, Shaheen, and Lidicker 2010).

An analysis of US national household data indicates that the average ownership of automobiles could decline significantly as a result of AV deployment – from 2.1 to 1.2 (Schoettle and Sivak 2015). One modeling study predicts that the higher income families who live in suburbs and generate more short trips are more likely to reduce household vehicle ownership (Zhang, Guhathakurta, and Khalil 2018). However, the greatest beneficiaries of a public transit deployment of autonomous vehicles would be the large number of mobility-disadvantaged households that do not possess even one car.

The changes across entire metropolitan areas are likely to be difficult to implement, but not to conceive. One scenario has been developed for the city of Amsterdam (Vleugel and Bal 2017). It is based on 2017 data and projected to end in 2040 with an elimination of individually owned motor vehicles. This full-on transformation would require increases of 30 percent in walking and cycling, and in bus, tram, and metro use. In addition, passengers using ARSVs or APTVs would need to increase from zero to 455,000. Accumulating over the course of several decades these numbers would not be nearly as formidable as they seem. The projected sustainability gains in Amsterdam would include new uses available for 80 percent of the city's vehicle parking space and 50 percent of its roadway space.

One of the consensus points among transportation experts about an AV deployment is "that the first applications are likely to be in fleets rather than individual ownership" (Groshen et al. 2018, 71). According to one expert analysis advantages of autonomous vehicle fleets over individual ownership are likely to be their lower cost, greater ubiquity and flexibility in scheduling, and in routing (Groshen et al. 2018, 83). It is reasonable to expect that if the fleet is part of a public transit system that these advantages could be enhanced. However, current research on the composition and direction of an AV deployment focuses on only two vehicles: The personal version or the private ride-sharing version. There is scant attention given to the possibility of public transit autonomous vehicles. One exception is a research paper that addresses potential "Transit Complementary AVs" (Zhang, Guhathakurta, and Khalil 2018, 65). For sustainability purposes, personal or private shared vehicles ultimately cannot compete with the efficiencies of public transit, as one analysis of carshare mobility in the US has concluded: "Increased investment in mass transit, paired with careful land use planning, holds the best promise for sustainable growth of transportation networks" (Kondransky and Lewenstein 2014, 24).

Public transit systems will need to innovate in order to incorporate the sustainability advantages promised by an autonomous vehicle deployment. Such large public organizations are subject to public transparency and participation as well as to economic constraints, making major change a slow and often interrupted process. One inspiration for innovation is through a public transit fusion of various means of urban mobility (Currie 2018). As an example, subcontracted rail feeder AV services could operate in public–private partnerships (NAS 2018d), perhaps like the shared bike schemes for rail access that are provided by many cities in China and the Netherlands. In this way shared mobility services could be organized to supplement mass transit networks, especially in metropolitan areas with less frequent and lower occupancy services. Rail stations would then need to provide convenient access for varying sizes of vehicles in order to secure safe and timely traveler connections (ITF 2017b, 97).

While public transit contributes to sustainability there is a caveat: Vehicle passenger loads bear upon its efficiency (per passenger). Very low loads of bus trips can be less sustainable in their operation than private vehicles carrying passengers as well as their drivers. The success of APTVs will depend on road-based public transit modes providing integrated routes for a variety of distances and passenger loads, which means also a variety of vehicle sizes. All the categorical uses of the autonomous vehicle will compete for public acceptance on the basis of their cost, convenience, access, and other factors yet to emerge. Data indicate that few motor vehicle users base their choices primarily on environmental or social sustainability factors, although these may be considerations (Pakusch, Stevens, and Bossauer 2018). This puts a sustainability premium on providing public transit AVs acceptable to consumer preferences such as personal comfort.

While a thorough alteration in the car's role can be envisioned thanks to the impending appearance of shared AVs it will be highly problematic to achieve, in large measure because of nearly a century of an embedded personal automobilization in cities of the more developed world. However, the forces of increasing urbanization (with its growing population and congestion densities), and the digitalization of daily life, as well as mounting concerns about sustainability and climate change – all favor fundamental changes in urban mobility. They may be sufficient spurs for societies to awaken "from a reverie to realize that we have been designing cities for cars when we should have been designing cities for people" (Sumantran, Fine, and Gonsalvez 2017, x).

Public transit digitalization

Globally, urban motorized mobility is forecast to have doubled between 2015 and 2050 (ITF 2017b). Personal conventional automobiles will drive the increase and it will be concentrated in the global South. Autonomous vehicles could play a significant sustainability role in this scenario by reducing the level of the expected increases. If they were incorporated into public transit systems they could cover more than 50 percent of the increase. However, for that opportunity to be seized they will need to be financed. Public monies could come from fuel taxes and congestion zone fees that also serve as disincentives for conventional automobility.

In the voluminous discourse about autonomous vehicles little attention is given to the sustainability priority of increased vehicle occupancy, a prime sustainability marker of public transit. Buses appear to be leading candidates for digital eco-motorization. A study of public buses using the Lincoln Tunnel between New York City and New Jersey estimated that the efficiency of connected vehicles would increase the overall passenger capacity by five-fold (Lutin and Kornhauser 2013). The *sohjoa* project in Helsinki provides an example of how transit authorities can launch autonomous bus operational trials (Sisson 2017). Such public sector proactive approaches can serve to stabilize the disruption created by private enterprises. The project is testing automated small buses (with up to 12 passengers) that optimize convenience and rider experience. Right-sized, small and comfortable AV buses could lead to the provision of flexibly routed, door-to-door public transit service (*Canada 2030* 2017).

This is an example of how the AV offers an opportunity to reinvigorate transit by covering service gaps (Green 2018). The gaps are concentrated in suburbs and exurbs and are of differing passenger loads which make them promising sites for using right-sized autonomous vehicles. Currently, according to public transit specialists, there is a substantial difference between fixed route service and flexible on-demand service. It can be narrowed with targeted pilot projects in conjunction with emergent carshare services (*TransitCenter* 2018). Such a scenario for Amsterdam envisions an eventual "daring" replacement of **all** private automobiles with digitally directed public transit shuttles with cars sized for four to five passengers and vans and minibuses for six to 18 (Vleugel and Bal 2017, 510).

Smaller automated vehicles can operate in feeder sub-systems that augment public transit systems' rail and express/rapid bus services and cover the *last mile*. If they were electric vehicles they could recharge on their own when not in use, and could operate on flexible routes based on updated passenger demands. A simulation study has projected the role that shared AVs could play in Lisbon (ITF 2015). The study examined two concept vehicles: *TaxiBots* in which mobility is shared and *AutoBots* which are pick-up/drop-off single passenger vehicles. The simulation showed that in combination the two would replace about 90 percent of the city's automobiles while providing the same volume of mobility service. The sustainability gains would be from vehicle efficiency (more passengers per trip), fewer vehicles, and less traffic congestion, as well as less space needed for vehicles.

Because multi-modal systems are already rich with service connections they provide multiple openings for new short journey travel linkages. Right-sized APTVs offer a fit for these linkages by offering micro scale services. This would add a level to the current meso (bus) and macro (rail) levels of passenger capacity, and it could thicken public transit routes in urban sprawl areas.

While walking or biking to stations is better for personal health and for the environment, it is not always possible for various reasons – bad weather, lack of time, health issues, etc. Mass public transit with its present one-size-fits-all buses, trams, and metros cannot efficiently handle small scale and short distances like the *last mile*. The journey requires smaller vehicles, operating rather like spiders in a web (Weaver 2016). The potential role of the spider-like APTV would be similar to the autonomous pods, minibuses, and shuttles that are being tested in venues in metropolitan areas around the world (Herrmann, Brenner, and Stadler 2018, 157–8). The aforementioned survey of urban planners in Germany (Fraedrich et al. 2018) indicates that any autonomous vehicle deployment needs specific targets and the leading one should be using it to improve public transit's feeder services in areas with low and fluctuating demand.

Some public transit systems already use automated metro trains. As of 2016 there were 55 fully automated lines in 37 cities around the world, operating on 803 km of track (UITP 2016). The kilometers increased by 14 percent over the previous two years and are projected to multiply 2.9-fold by 2025. Seven of the AV9 nations have cities with automated lines – Sweden and the UK are the exceptions, and the UK is planning projects in several cities. In London autonomous operation will allow many more trains to pass through highly congested tracks, as between St. Pancras and Blackfriars stations, increasing space for 60,000 more passengers at peak commuting times (Topham 2018). Among the group of nine, France and the ROK are world leaders in automating conventional metro rail lines. Automation is also coming to tram lines. In 2018 Germany operated the first autonomous tram – in Potsdam (*The Guardian* 2018). It was developed by *Siemens* and its energy is renewably sourced from solar and wind.

Automated metro rail lines provide a number of environmental and social sustainability gains, including enhanced safety and increased energy use efficiency. They also provide beneficial preambles to a roll-out of autonomous roadway vehicles in several ways – first, by providing valuable experience for transit organizations with regard to the complexities of automated mobility. This would facilitate transitions to autonomous trams and buses. Second, they give metro passengers some experience with riding in an automated carrier that may serve to build confidence in their safety.

4.4   Rebound effects

There will be rebound effects from an autonomous vehicle entrance into street traffic (Schlossberg et al. 2018). The space from one side of the street to the other (including curbs and sidewalks) is publicly owned and regulated right of way (ROW). Autonomous vehicle deployment may force a reallocation of its spatial division of use modes. Redistribution could result from a number of factors: Less need for street parking and increased space-efficiency of AV operations. From a sustainability perspective, the ROW focus should shift space away from conventional automobiles and prioritize it for sidewalks, protected bikeways, and public transit lanes. Curb space is increasingly contested due to private carshare services competing for parking and for pick-up/drop-off places (ITF 2018a).

Some rebound effects likely will emerge from AV-produced social interactions of travelers on city streets and sidewalks, already fraught with conflicts among drivers, walkers, and cyclists. Right of way is often negotiated between competitors for the same space. The "way" in ROW refers to three distinctively used "ways" – the street, the curb, and the sidewalk. Present interactions depend on eye contact being made among drivers, walkers, and cyclists. What happens when there are no drivers?

An autonomous vehicle deployment's impact in cities has potential to create a number of uncertainty-rich linked rebounds, ripples, and ricochets leading to negative and positive outcomes that will alter its sustainability profile (Fitt et al. 2018). Following is a hypothetical example:

AV rebound: Fewer vehicles.
↓
Ripple A: Less traffic congestion.
↓
Ripple B: Increase in vehicle speeds.
↓
→ Ricochet: Increase in urban sprawl as commuting distance is lengthened.

Also, as addressed in Chapter Three, freeing vehicle owners of having to drive AVs offers an opening to use their travel time for a range of other activities, including reading or using a phone (Gillespie 2016). This may serve to reduce public transit use because the personal autonomous vehicle will offer an attractive alternative that mimics one of transit's competitive advantages – allowing passengers to engage in activities other than driving while they are traveling (Buehler 2018, 12). Another potential rebound effect of an autonomous vehicle deployment may be a reduction of city revenues. Sizeable automobile-related taxes would face a range of potential threats. Data gathered on the 25 largest US cities project major revenue shortfalls from losses of parking charges and traffic citation fines (*Governing* 2017). Here, the rebound may be positive for social and environmental parameters but negative for the economic sustainability of city governments.

4.5 Conclusion

It is reasonable to conclude that the disruptive potential of an autonomous vehicle deployment could be eased if brought to the public as part of public transit systems. These systems generally have a long-standing brand of service often identified as having convenience and comfort faults that are outweighed by the strengths of safe and affordable mobility. This would provide prospective AV users with opportunities to cheaply experience automated mobility with confidence of safe passage. If the autonomous vehicle does make its debut as a public transit vehicle then its deployment may be more successful if done in locales with decidedly popular transit systems, especially those in which some automation has already occurred. These appear to be in France, Germany, Japan, and the ROK among the AV9 countries. Paris, Berlin, Tokyo, and Seoul are cities with very high public transit use and two (Paris and Seoul) already have automated metro lines.

If an autonomous vehicle deployment is led (only) by the private sector, its leadership in providing digitally based mobility could produce new information and techniques. These could be utilized subsequently more extensively and with affordability and physically assisted access in public transit networks. Private businesses are more nimble in responding to consumer demand because of their small size and lack of public oversight. At the end of the day, according to a comprehensive analysis in the US by its National Academy of Sciences (NAS 2018d, 45), "Expanded public transit service is the best long-term solution to the transparency, service continuity, and civil rights safeguard built into public provision."

A possible outcome of the private–public mobility cleavage is that with AV deployment both private carshare enterprises and public transit agencies will have to increasingly integrate their services with new options. Some argue that all urban mobility may develop into being part of a linked system, an emergent concept known as Mobility as a Service or MaaS (Buehler 2018, 13–14; Barcelo, Montero, and Ros-Roca 2018, 16–19). Travelers could use a single digital application to access and pay for any of various transport modes, providing options to select the most suitable in terms of price, time, comfort, etc. (Li and Voege 2017). New possibilities have emerged from the availability of cash-purchased public transit ride cards in cities around the world, such as the *Oyster* in London and the *MetroCard* in New York City. Chicago's version, the *Ventra*, is being adapted for use with carshare digital options. It will contain a public transit account and a prepaid debit account, with cash being an option for purchasing both (Brown and Taylor 2018).

An important but neglected potential impact of AV deployment is its effect on public right of way in city roads and streets. Presently, right of way is dominated by automobiles. Cyclists and walkers whose travel has the highest possible sustainability profile are accorded the least space and suffer the greatest safety risks. US data in 2016 showed that fatalities are at their highest number since 1990 for pedestrians and highest since 1991 for pedacyclists (NHTSA 2017). The proportion of people killed who were inside a vehicle declined from a high of 80 percent in 1996 to 67 percent in 2016 while the proportion killed outside the vehicle increased from a low of 20 percent in 1996 to a high of 33 percent in 2016. One analyst of the data has put the ROW-based disparity in stark terms: "The vulnerable and the sustainable are disproportionately the victims of the physical powerful and unsustainable" (Hartman and Prytherch 2015, 23). How an autonomous vehicle deployment relates to this issue will be critical to determining its level of public support.

In sum, hyper automobility's growing negative impacts on urban land use and transportation sustainability have led to increased efforts to control and limit it. The individual blessings of travel by personal car are increasingly viewed as a collective blight. A tipping point for such cognitive dissonance might ensue from deployment of autonomous vehicles as electrified public transit vehicles. The dominance of everyday mobility by the personal internal combustion automobile would then face a perfect storm of threatening changes to its traditional character and leading role.

References

Alessandrini, Adriano, Andrea Campagna, Paolo Delle Site, Francesco Filippi, and Luca Persia. 2015. "Automated Vehicles and the Rethinking of Mobility and Cities." *Transportation Research Procedia* 5: 145–60. doi: 10.1016/j.trpro.2015.01.002.

Alexander, Christopher, Sara Ishikawa, and Murray Silverstein. 1977. *A Pattern Language: Towns Buildings Construction.* New York: Oxford University Press.

Anderson, James M., Nidhi Kalra, Karlyn D. Stanley, Paul Sorenson, Constantine Samaras, and Tobi A. Oluwatola. 2014. *Autonomous Vehicle Technology: A Guide for Policymakers.* Santa Monica CA: RAND.

APTA. 2015. *Public Transportation Fact Book: Appendix A: Historical Tables.* Washington, DC: American Public Transportation Association. Available at: www.apta.com/resources/statistics/Documents/FactBook/2015-APTA-Fact-Book-Appendix-A.pdf [Accessed August 30, 2018].

Arcadis. 2017. *Sustainable Cities Mobility Index: Bold Moves.* Amsterdam: Arcadis, NV. Available at: www.arcadis.com/ [Accessed January 15, 2018].

Baklanov, Alenander, Luisa T. Molina, and Michael Gauss. 2016. "Megacities, Air Quality and Climate." *Atmospheric Environment* 126: 235–49. Available at: https://doi.org/10.1016/j.atmosenv.2015.11.059 [Accessed September 6, 2018].

Banister, David. 2012. "Assessing the Reality: Transport and Land Use Planning to Achieve Sustainability." *The Journal of Transport and Land Use* 5: 1–14. doi: 10.5198/jtlu.v5i3.388.

Barcelo, J., L. Montero, and X. Ros-Roca. 2018. *Virtual Mobility Lab: A Systemic Approach to Urban Mobility Challenges.* Karlsruhe and Barcelona: Cooperative Automotive Research Network (CARNET). Available at: http://inlab.fib.upc.eu/en/barcelona-virtual-mobility-lab [Accessed October 3, 2018].

Barrington-Leigh, Christopher and Adam Millard-Ball. 2015. "A Century of Sprawl in the United States." *Scientific Journal of the National Academy of Sciences* 112, July. Available at: www.pnas.org/cgi/doi/10.1073/pnas.1504033112 [Accessed March 15, 2018].

Barter, P. 2013. "Cars Are Parked 95% of the Time: Let's Check!" *Reinventing Parking.* Available at: www.reinventingparking.org/2013/02/cars-are-parked-95%-of-time-lets-check.html [Accessed March 16, 2018].

Ben-Joseph, E. 2015. *Rethinking a Lot: The Design and Culture of Parking.* Cambridge, MA: MIT Press.

Bhat, Chandra R. and Jessica Y. Guo. 2007. "A Comprehensive Analysis of Built Environment Characteristics on Household Residential Choice and Auto Ownership Levels." *Transportation Research Part B: Methodological* 41: 506–26. Available at: https://doi.org/10.1016/j.trb.2005.1.005 [Accessed September 2, 2018].

Bluestone, Barry and Bennett Harrison. 1982. *The Deindustrialization of America.* New York: Basic Books.

Boschmann, Eric and Mei-Po Kwan. 2008. "Toward Socially Sustainable Urban Transportation: Progress and Potentials." *International Journal of Sustainable Transportation* 2: 138–57. Available at: http://dx.doi.org/10.1080/15568310701517265 [Accessed July 30, 2018].

Brown, Anne and Brian Taylor. 2018. "Bridging the Gap between Mobility Haves and Have-Nots." Pp. 131–50 in Daniel Sperling, ed., *Three Revolutions: Steering Automated, Shared, and Electric Vehicles to a Better Future.* Washington, DC: Island Press.

Bruun, Eric and Moshe Givoni. 2015. "Six Research Routes to Steer Transport Policy." *Nature* 523: 29–31.

Buehler, Ralph. 2018. "Can Public Transportation Compete with Automated and Connected Cars?" *Journal of Public Transportation* 21: 7–18. Available at: http://dx.doi.org/10.5038/2375-0901.21.1.2 [Accessed August 30, 2018].

Buehler, Ralph, John Pucher, and Alan Altshuler. 2017. "Vienna's Path to Sustainable Transport." *International Journal of Sustainable Transportation* 11: 257–71. Available at: http://dx.doi.org/10.1080/15568318.2016.1251997 [Accessed September 19, 2018].

Buehler, Ralph, John Pucher, Regine Gerike, and Thomas Gotschi. 2017. "Reducing Car Dependence in the Heart of Europe: Lessons from Germany, Austria, and Switzerland." *Transport Reviews* 37: 4–28. Available at: http://dx.doi.org/10.1080/01441647.2016.1177799 [Accessed September 19, 2018].

CalStart. 2009. *First Mile Compendium.* Pasadena, CA: CalStart. Available at: http://calstart.org/Projects/First-Mile.aspx [Accessed September 29, 2018].

Calthorpe, Peter. 1993. *The Next American Metropolis: Ecology, Community, and the American Dream.* New York: Princeton Architectural Press.

Canada 2030. 2017. *Policy Horizons Canada.* Ottawa: Government of Canada. Available at: www.horizons.gc.ca/en/content/what-ifself-driving-vehicles-were-new-mass-transit-solution-cities [Accessed March 28, 2018].

Caragliu, Andrea, Chiara Del Bo, and Peter Nijkamp. 2011. "Smart Cities in Europe." *Journal of Urban Technology* 18: 65–82. Available at: https://doi.org/10.1080/10630732.2011.601117 [Accessed September 13, 2018].

Carlton, Ian. 2009. *Histories of Transit-Oriented Development: Perspectives on the Development of the TOD Concept.* Berkeley: Institute of Urban and Regional Development, University of California, Working Paper No. 2009.02. Available at: http://hdl.handle.net/10419/59412 [Accessed September 4, 2018].

Chester, Mikhail, A. Fraser, J. Matute, C. Flower, and R. Pendyala. 2015. "Parking Infrastructure: A Constraint on or Opportunity for Urban Redevelopment? A Study of Los Angeles County Parking Supply and Growth." *Journal of the American Planning Association* 81: 268–86. https://doi.org/10.1080/01944363.2015.1092879.

Chester, Mikhail, Arpad Horvath, and Samer Madanat. 2010. "Parking Infrastructure: Energy, Emissions, and Automobile Life-Cycle Environmental Accounting." *Environmental Research Letters* 5: 1–8. doi: 10.1088/1748–9326/5/3/034001.

CIB. 2017. *Wasted Spaces: Options to Reform Parking Policy in Los Angeles.* Sacramento: Council of Infill Builders. Available at: www.councilofinfillbuilders.org/wp-content/uploads/2017/05/Wasted-spaces-May-2017.pdf [Accessed August 28, 2018].

Clewlow, Regina R. and Gouri Shankar Mishra. 2017. *Disruptive Transportation: The Adoption, Utilization, and Impacts of Ride-Hailing in the United States.* Davis: Research Report UCD-ITS-RR-17-07. Institute of Transportation Studies, University of California.

CTOD. 2008. *Transit + Employment: Increasing Transit's Share of the Commute Trip.* Oakland: Reconnecting America, Center for Transit-Oriented Development. Available at: www.reconnectingamerica.org.assets/Uploads/employment202.pdf [Accessed July 3, 2018].

Currie, Graham. 2018. "Lies, Damned Lies, AVs, Shared Mobility, and Urban Transit Futures." *Journal of Public Transportation* 21: 19–30. Available at: http://dx.doi.org/10.5038/2375-0901.21.1.3 [Accessed September 1, 2018].

Demographia. 2018. *World Urban Areas,* 14th annual ed. Belleville, IL. Available at: www.demographia.com/db-worldua.pdf [Accessed September 6, 2018].

Duddu, Praveen. 2014. "The World's Top Busiest Metros." *Railway Technology,* November. Available at: www.railway-technology.com/features/featurethe-worlds-top-10-busiest-metros-4433827/ [Accessed September 20, 2018].

EEA. 2011. "Land Use Conflicts Necessitate Integrated Policy." Copenhagen: European Environment Agency, March 29. Available at: https://www.eea.europa.eu/highlights/land-use-conflicts-necessitate-integrated-policy [Accessed September 3, 2018].

EERE. 2018. *Average Vehicle Occupancy Remains Unchanged From 2009 to 2017*. Washington, DC: Office of Energy Efficiency & Renewable Energy, US Department of Energy. Available at: www.energy.gov/eere/vehiclesarticles/fotw-1040-july-30-2018-average-vehicle-occupancy- [Accessed September 8, 2018].

Ewing, R., R. Pendall, and D. Chen. 2002. *Measuring Sprawl and Its Impact*. Washington, DC: Smart Growth America.

FHWA. 2018. *Travel Volume Trends, June*. Washington, DC: Federal Highway Administration, US Department of Transportation. Available at: www.fhwa.dot.gov/policyinformation/travel_monitoring/18juntvt/ [Accessed August 25, 2018].

Fitt, H., A. Curl, R. Dionisio-McHugh, A. Fletcher, B. Frame, and A. Ahuriri-Driscoll. 2018. *Think Piece: Autonomous Vehicles and Future Urban Environments*, 2nd ed. Christchurch, NZ: National Science Challenge. Available at: www.buildingbetter.nz/resources/publications.html [Accessed August 26, 2018].

Ford, Alistair and Phil Blythe. 2018. "Land-Use Transport Models for Climate Change Mitigation and Adaptation Planning." *The Journal of Transport and Land Use* 11: 83–101. http://doi.org/10.5198/jtlu.2018.1209.

Fraedrich, Eva, Dirk Heinrichs, Francisco Bahamonde-Birke, and Rita Cyganski. 2018. "Autonomous Driving, the Built Environment and Policy Implications." *Transport Research Part A*. Available at: https://doi.org/10.1016/j.tra.2018.02.018 [Accessed September 10, 2018].

Frank, Lawrence D., Martin A. Andresen, and Thomas L. Schmid. 2004. "Obesity Relationships with Community Design, Physical Activity, and Time Spent in Cars." *American Journal of Preventive Medicine* 27: 87–96. doi: 10.1016/j.amepre.2004.04.011.

Freund, Peter and George Martin. 2008. "Fast Cars/Fast Foods: Hyperconsumption and Its Health and Environmental Consequences." *Social Theory & Health* 6: 309–22.

Freund, Peter and George Martin. 2007. "Hyperautomobility, the Social Organization of Space, and Health." *Mobilities* 2: 37–49.

Freund, Peter and George Martin. 1993. *The Ecology of the Automobile*. Montreal: Black Rose Books.

Frumkin, Howard. 2002. "Urban Sprawl and Public Health." *Public Health Reports* 117: 201–212.

Ghouldson, A. et al. 2015. *Accelerating Low-Carbon Development in the World's Cities*. London and Washington, DC: New Climate Economy. Available at: http://newclimateeconomy.report/misc/working-papers [Accessed September 3, 2018].

Gillespie, Matthew. 2016. "Shifting Automotive Landscapes: Privacy and the Right to Travel in the Era of Autonomous Motor Vehicles." *Washington University Journal of Law & Policy* 50. Available at: https://openscholarship.wustl.edu/law_journal_law_policy/vol50/iss1/7 [Accessed September 3, 2018].

Governing. 2017. *Special Report: How Autonomous Vehicles Could Constrain City Budgets*. Washington, DC: Governing the States and Localities. Available at: www.governing.com/gov-data/gov-how-autonomous-vehicles-could-effect-city-budges.html [Accessed September 8, 2018].

Green, Jared. 2018. *ASLA Launches New Guide to Transportation*. Washington, DC: American Society of Landscape Architects. Available at: www.asla.org/sustainabletransportation.aspx [Accessed August 21, 2018].

Greenblatt, Jeffery and Susan Shaheen. 2015. "Automated Vehicles, On-Demand Mobility, and Environmental Impacts." *Current Sustainable/Renewable Energy Reports* 2: 74–81. doi: 10.1007/s40518-015-0038-5.

Greendex. 2014. *Consumer Choice and the Environment: A Worldwide Tracking Survey*. Washington, DC: National Geographic Society. Available at: https://images.nationalgeographic.com/wpf/media-content/file/NGS_2014_Greendex_Highlights_FINAL-cb1411689730.pdf [Accessed September 7, 2018].

Greendex. 2009. *Consumer Choice and the Environment: A Worldwide Tracking Survey*. Washington, DC: National Geographic Society. Available at: https://images.nationalgeographic.com/wpf/media-content/file/NGS_2009_Greendex_Highlights_FINAL-cb1411689730.pdf [Accessed September 7, 2018].

Groshen, Erica, Susan Helper, John Paul McDuffie, and Charles Carson. 2018. *Preparing U.S. Workers and Employers for an Autonomous Vehicle Future*. Washington, DC: Securing America's Future Energy. Available at: https://avworkforce.secureenergy.org/wp-content/uploads/2018/06/Groshen-et-al-Report-June-2018-1.pdf [Accessed September 18, 2018].

The Guardian. 2018. "Germany Launches World's First Autonomous Tram in Potsdam." September 23. Available at: www.theguardian.com/world/2018/sep/23/potsdam-inside-the-worlds-first-autonomous-tram [Accessed September 24, 2018].

Hall, Peter. 1988. *Cities of Tomorrow: An Intellectual History of Urban Planning and Design in the Twentieth Century*. Oxford: Basil Blackwell.

Hamidi, Shima, Reid Ewing, Zaria Tatalovich, James B. Grace, and David Berrigan. 2018. "Associations between Urban Sprawl and Life Expectancy in the United States." *International Journal of Environmental Research and Public Health* 15: 861. doi: 10.3390/ijerph15050861.

Hartman, Laura M. and David L. Prytherch. 2015. "Streets to Live In: Justice, Space, and Sharing the Road." *Environmental Ethics*, March. Available at: www.researchgate.net/publication/280291554 [Accessed August 17, 2018].

Herrmann, Andreas, Walter Brenner, and Rupert Stadler. 2018. *Autonomous Driving: How the Driverless Revolution Will Change the World*. Bingley UK: Emerald.

Higgins, Tim. 2018. "How Driverless Cars Are Going to Change Cities." *Wall Street Journal*, Online, June 27. Available at: https://search.proquest.com/docview/2059340789?ccountid=14496.

Hoyt, Homer. 1941. "Forces of Urban Centralization and Decentralization." *American Journal of Sociology* 46: 843–52. doi.org/10.1086/218799.

Hulchanski, J. David. 2010. *The Three Cities within Toronto: Income Polarization among Toronto's Neighbourhoods, 1970–2005*. Toronto: Cities Centre Press, University of Toronto.

Huntsman, Brett, Phil Lasley, and Madison Metaker-Galarza. 2018. *Finding the Value of Urban Parking: An Analysis of the Impacts of Smart Parking Systems on Congestion and Land Value in Downtown Houston*. College Station: Texas A & M University Transportation Institute. Available at: https://static.tti.tamu.edu/PRC-17-88-F.pdf [Accessed September 4, 2018].

Iacobucci, Joe, Kirk Hovenkotter, and Jacob Anbinder. 2017. "Transit Systems and the Impacts of Shared Mobility." Pp. 65–76 in G. Meyer and S. Shaheen, eds., *Disrupting Mobility: Impacts of Sharing Economy and Innovative Transportation on Cities*. New York: Springer.

IIASA. 2012. "Energy End-Use: Transport." In *International Institute for Applied Systems Analysis*, Laxenburg: Global Energy Assessment. Cambridge: Cambridge University Press.

Illich, Ivan. 1974. *Energy and Equity*. New York and London: Harper & Row.

INRIX. 2017. *The True Cost of Parking: Smart Parking Solutions Can Save Drivers Billions*. London and Los Angeles: INRIX, November 28. Available at: http://inrix.com/blog/2017/11/parking-cost/ [Accessed August 26, 2018].

Isaac, Mike. 2016. "G.M., Expecting Rapid Change, Invests $500 Million in Lyft." *The New York Times*, January 4, pp. B1, B3.

ITDP. 2017. "ITDP's Principles of Development for Transport in Urban Life." In *Sustainable Transport Newsletter 8*, Summer. New York: Institute for Transportation & Development Policy.

ITF. 2018a. *The Shared-Use City: Managing the Curb*. Paris: International Transport Forum. Available at: https://itf-oecd.org/sites/default/file/docs/shared-use-city-managing-curb_5.pdf [Accessed September 11, 2018].

ITF. 2018b. *Safer Roads with Automated Vehicles?* Paris: International Transport Forum. Available at: www.itf-oecd.org/sites/default/files/docs/safer-roads-aitmatedvehicles.pdf [Accessed February 3, 2018].

ITF. 2017a. *Shared Mobility Simulations for Auckland*. Paris: International Transport Forum. Available at: https://itf-oecd.org/sites/default/files/docs/auckland [Accessed September 18, 2018].

ITF. 2017b. *ITF Transport Outlook*. Paris: International Transport Forum. doi: 10.1787/9789282108000-en.

ITF. 2015. *Urban Mobility Systems Upgrade: How Shared Self-Driving Cars Could Change City Traffic*. Paris: International Transport Forum. Available at: www.oecd-ilibrary.org/transport/urban-mobility-system-upgrade_5jlwvzdk29g5-en [Accessed August 27, 2018].

Jacobs, Jane. 1961. *The Death and Life of Great American Cities*. New York: Random House.

Jiao, Junfeng. 2017. "Identifying Transit Deserts in Major Texas Cities Where the Supplies Missed the Demands." *The Journal of Transport and Land Use* 10: 529–40. http://dx.doi.org/10.5198/jtlu.2017.899.

Jiao, Limin. 2015. "Urban Land Density Function: A New Method to Characterize Urban Expansion." *Landscape and Urban Planning* 139: 26–39. Available at: http://dx.doi.org/1.1016/j.landurbplan.2015.02.017 [Accessed September 1, 2018].

Kenworthy, Jeffrey. 2007. "Urban Planning and Transport Paradigm Shifts for Cities of the Post-Petroleum Age." *Journal of Urban Technology* 14: 47–70. doi: 10.108o/10630730701531708.

Kim, John. 2018. "Automated Autonomous Vehicles: Prospects and Impacts on Society." *Journal of Transportation Technologies* 8: 37–50. https://doi.org/10.4236/jtts.2018.83008.

Kondransky, Michael and Gabriel Lewenstein. 2014. *Connecting Low-Income People to Opportunity with Shared Mobility*. New York: Institute for Transportation & Development Policy. Available at: www.livingcities.org/resources/275-executive-summary-can-shared-mobility-help-low-income-people-access-opportunity [Accessed September 6, 2018].

Krizek, Kevin J., Jessica Horning, and Ahmed M. El-Geneidy. 2012. "Perceptions of Accessibility to Neighborhood Retail and Other Public Services." Pp. 96–117 in K. Geurs, K. Krizek, and A. Reggiani, eds., *Accessibility and Transport Planning: Challenges for Europe and North America*. London: Edward Elgar.

Lane, Clayton. 2017. "Inclusive TOD for Sustainable, Equitable Cities." In *Sustainable Transport*, No 28, Winter, pp. 4–5. New York: Institute for Transportation & Development Policy.

Li, Yanying and Tom Voege. 2017. "Mobility as a Service (MaaS): Challenges of Implementation and Policy Required." *Journal of Transportation Technologies* 7: 95–106. doi: 10.4236/jtts.2017.72007.

Lin, Luna. 2014. "A Short History of World Metro Systems." *The Guardian*, September 10. Available at: www.theguardian.com/cities/gallery/2014/sep/10/-sp-history-metro- [Accessed September 9, 2018].

Lutin, Jerome M. and Alain L. Kornhauser. 2013. *Application of Autonomous Driving Technology to Transit: Functional Capabilities for Safety and Capacity*. Transportation Research Board Annual Meeting, Washington, DC. Available at: http://amonline.trb.org/ [Accessed August 25, 2018].

Lynch, Kevin. 1981. *A Theory of Good City Form*. Cambridge, MA: MIT Press.

Martin, Elliot W. and Susan Shaneen. 2011. "Greenhouse Gas Emission Impacts of Carsharing in North America." *IEEE Transactions on Intelligent Transportation Systems* 12: 1074–86. doi: 10.1109/TITS.2011.2158539.

Martin, Elliot W., Susan A. Shaheen, and Jeffrey Lidicker. 2010. "Impact of Carsharing on Household Vehicle Holdings: Results from North American Shared-Use Survey." *Transportation Research Record: Journal of the Transportation Research Board*, No. 2143, pp. 150–8. Washington, DC: Transport Research Board of the National Academies. doi: 10.3141/2143-19.

Martin, George. 2002. "Grounding Social Ecology: Landspace, Settlement, and Right of Way." *Capitalism Nature Socialism* 13: 3–30.

McCahill, Christopher and Norman Garrick. 2012. "Automobile Use and Land Consumption: Empirical Evidence from 12 Cities." *Urban Design International* 17: 221–27. doi: 10.1057/udi.2012.12.

McCann, B. and R. Ewing. 2003. *Measuring the Health Effects of Sprawl: A National Analysis of Physical Activity, Obesity and Chronic Disease*. Washington, DC: Smart Growth America.

Melosi, Martin V. 2010. *The Automobile Shapes the City: The 'Footprint' of the Automobile on the American City*. Dearborn, MI: Automobile in American Life and Society. Available at: www.autolife.umd.umich.edu/the-automobile-shapes-the-city/ [Accessed September 5, 2018].

Mitchell, William J., Christopher E. Barroni-Bird, and Lawrence D. Burns. 2010. *Reinventing the Automobile: Personal Urban Mobility for the 21st Century*. Cambridge, MA: MIT Press.

Montgomery, John. 1998. "Making a City: Urbanity, Vitality and Urban Design." *Journal of Urban Design* 3: 93–116.

Morency, Catherine, Hubert Verreault, and Marie Demers. 2015. "Identification of the Minimum Size of the Shared-Fleet Required to Satisfy Car-Driving Trips in Montreal." *Transportation* 42: 435–47. doi: 10.1007/s11116-015-9605-2.

Mumford, Lewis. 1956. *The Urban Prospect*. New York and London: Harcourt Brace Jovanovich.

NACTO. 2017. *Blueprint for Autonomous Urbanism*. New York: National Association of City Transportation Officials. Available at: https://nacto.org/wp-content/uploads/2017/11/BAU_Moo1_raster-sm.pdf [Accessed August 22, 2018].

NAS. 2018a. *Advancing Obesity Solutions through Investments in the Built Environment: Proceedings of a Workshop*. Washington, DC: National Academy of Sciences, National Academies Press. Available at: http://nap.edu/25074. [Accessed September 23, 2018].

NAS. 2018b. *Between Public and Private Mobility: Examining the Rise of Technology-Enabled Transportation Services*. Washington, DC: National Academy of Sciences, National Academies Press. Available at: http://nap.edu21875 [Accessed September 10, 2018].

NAS. 2018c. *Private Transit: Existing Services and Emerging Directions*. Washington, DC: National Academy of Sciences, National Academies Press. Available at: http://nap.edu/25020 [Accessed April 12, 2018].

NAS. 2018d. *Broadening Understanding of the Interplay between Public Transit, Shared Mobility, and Personal Automobiles*. Washington, DC: National Academy of Sciences, National Academies Press. Available at: http://nap.edu/24996 [Accessed September 15, 2018].

Nasri, Arefeh and Lei Zhang. 2018. "A Multi-Dimensional Multi-Level Approach to Measuring the Spatial Structure of U.S. Metropolitan Areas." *The Journal of Transport and Land Use* 11: 49–65. http://dx.doi.org/10.5198/jtlu.2018.893.

NHTSA. 2017. *Fatal Motor Vehicle Crashes: Overview*. Washington, DC: National Highway Traffic Safety Administration, US Department of Transportation. Available at: www.nhtsa.gov/press-releases/usdot-releases-2016-fatal-traffic-crash-data [Accessed September 22, 2018].

NHTSA. 2011. *Summary of Travel Trends: 2009 National Household Travel Survey*. Washington, DC: National Highway Traffic Safety Administration, US Department of Transportation. Available at: nhts.ornl.gov/209/pub/stt.pdf [Accessed November 30, 2017].

Nielsen. 2014. *Millennials: Breaking the Myths*. New York: The Nielsen Company. Available at: www.slideshare.net/recsportsmarketing/nielsen-millennial-report-2014 [Accessed September 2, 2018].

Norman, J., H. MacLean, and C. Kennedy. 2006. "Comparing High and Low Residential Density: Life-Cycle Analysis of Energy Use and Greenhouse Gas Emissions." *Journal of Urban Planning and Development* 132: 10–21.

Nourinejad, Mehdi, Sina Bahrami, and Matthew Roorda. 2018. "Designing Parking Facilities for Autonomous Vehicles." *Transport Research Part B: Methodological* 109: 110–27. https://doi.org/10.1016/j.trb.2017.12.017.

Orfield, Myron. 1997. *Metropolitics: A Regional Agenda for Community and Stability*. Washington, DC: Brookings Institution. Available at: www.brookings.edu/book/metropolitics/ [Accessed September 19, 2018].

Pakusch, Christina, Gunnar Stevens, and Paul Bossauer. 2018. "Shared Autonomous Vehicles: Potentials for a Sustainable Mobility and Risks of Unintended Effects." *EPiC Series in Computing* 52: 258–269.

Park, Robert E. and Ernest W. Burgess. 1970 [1925]. *The City*. Chicago and London: University of Chicago Press.

Petersen, Rudolf. 2004. *Land Use Planning and Urban Transport*. Eschborn: Sustainable Urban Transport Project, German Ministry for Economic Cooperation and Development (*GTZ*). Available at: https://sutp.org/files/contents/documents/resources/A_Sourcebook/ [Accessed September 3, 2018].

Quodomine, Richard D. 2015. "Further Research into Using Geographic Principles to Analyze Public Transportation in the USA and Maximize the Concept of Induced Transit." Pp. 121–47 in M. Attard and Y. Shiftan, eds., *Sustainable Urban Transport (Transport and Sustainability, Volume 7)*. Bigley, UK: Emerald.

RAC. 2012. *Spaced Out: Perspectives on Parking Policy*. London: Royal Automobile Club. Available at: www.racfoundation.org/reseaarch/mobility/spaced-out-perspectives-on-parking [Accessed February 6, 2013].

Schaller, Bruce. 2017. *Unsustainable? The Growth of App-Based Ride Services and Traffic, Travel and the Future of New York City*. New York: Schaller Consulting. Available at: www.schaller-consult.com/rideservices/unsustainable.pdf [Accessed August 29, 2018].

Scharnhorst, Eric. 2018. *Quantified Parking: Comprehensive Parking Inventories for Five U.S. Cities*. Washington, DC: Research Institute for Housing America, Mortgage Bankers Association. Available at: https://bit.ly/2LfNk4o [Accessed September 10, 2018].

Schlossberg, M., W. Riggs, A. Millard-Ball, and E. Shay. 2018. *Urbanism Next/Research: Rethinking the Street in an Era of Driverless Cars*. Eugene: Sustainable Cities Initiative, University of Oregon.

Schoettle, B. and M. Sivak. 2015. *Potential Impact of Self-Driving Vehicles on Household Vehicle Demand and Usage*. Ann Arbor: Transportation Research Institute, University of Michigan, Report UMTRI-2015-3.

Seto, K.C., S. Dhakal, A. Bigio, H. Blanco, G.C. Delgado, D. Dewar, and L. Huang, et al. 2014. "Human Settlements, Infrastructure, and Spatial Planning." In *Fifth Assessment Report of the Intergovernmental Panel on Climate Change*. Cambridge: Cambridge University Press. Available at: www.ipcc.ch/report/ar5/wg3/ [Accessed September 2, 2018].

Shoup, Donald C. 2005. *The High Cost of Free Parking*. Chicago: Planners Press.

Sisson, Patrick. 2017. "Buses: Small, Electric, and Automated: May Be Transit's Future." *Curbed, Transportation*, November 2. Available at: www.curbed.com/2017/11/2/6593004/bus-autonomous-vehicle-electric-public-transportation [Accessed August 22, 2018].

Smith, C. 2010. *London: Garden City?* London: London Wildlife Trust.

Smolicki, Piotr and Jacek Soltys. 2016. "Driverless Mobility: The Impact on Metropolitan Spatial Structures." *Procedia Engineering* 161: 2184–90. doi: 10.1016/j.proeng.2016.08.813.

Spectorsky, A.C. 1955. *The Exurbanites*. New York: Penguin/Berkeley.

Sperling, Daniel. 2018. *Three Revolutions: Steering Automated, Shared, and Electric Vehicles to a Better Future.* Washington, DC: Island Press.

Statista. 2018. "Number of Vehicles Per Household in the United States from 2006 to 2016." Available at: www.statista.com/statistics/551403/number-of-vehicles-per-household- [Accessed September 11, 2018].

Sumantran, Venkat, Charles Fine and David Gonsalvez. 2017. *Faster, Smarter, Greener: The Future of the Car and Urban Mobility.* Cambridge, MA and London: MIT Press.

TDM. 2004. *Land Use Impacts on Transport: How Land Use Patterns Affect Travel Behavior.* Victoria, BC: Transportation Demand Management, Victoria Transport Policy Institute.

Topham, Gwyn. 2018. "First Self-Driving Train Launches on London Thameslink Route." *The Guardian,* March 26. Available at: www.theguardian.com/business/2018/mar/26/first-self-driving-train/ [Accessed March 29, 2018].

TransitCenter. 2018. *Private Mobility, Public Interest.* New York: TransitCenter. Available at: https://transitcenter.org/publications/private-mobility-public-interest/ [Accessed August 22, 2018].

UITP. 2016. *Statistics Brief: Urban Public Transport in the 21st Century.* Brussels: International Association of Public Transport. Available at: www.uitp.org/sites/default/files/cck-focus-paper-files/UITP_Statistic%Brief_National/ [Accessed September 1, 2018].

UITP. 2015. *Mobility in Cities Database.* Brussels: International Association of Public Transport. Available at: www.uitp.com/MCD [Accessed September 24, 2018].

UN. 2017. *Social Development for Sustainable Development: Transforming Our World: The 2030 Agenda for Sustainable Development.* New York: Department of Economic and Social Affairs, United Nations. Available at: https://unstats.un.org/sdgs/report/2017/goal-11/ [Accessed February 11, 2018].

UN. 2014. *World Population Prospects: Trends in Urbanization.* New York: Department of Economic and Social Affairs, United Nations.

Vleugel, J.M. and F. Bal. 2017. "More Space and Improved Living Conditions in Cities with Autonomous Vehicles." *International Journal of Design & Nature and Ecodynamics* 12: 505–15. doi: 10.2495/DNE-V12-N4-505-515.

Wadud, Zia, Dan MacKenzie, and Paul Leiby. 2016. "Help or Hindrance? The Travel, Energy and Carbon Impacts of Highly Automated Vehicles." *Transportation Research Part A: Policy and Practice,* January: 1–18.

Weaver, Jesse. 2016. "Things That Will Change with Self-Driving Cars." *Medium,* June 8. Available at: https://medium.com/@hairyelephamte/things-that-will-change-17ceeabeff%b [Accessed August 20, 2018].

Wittstock, Rikka and Frank Teuteberg. 2018. "Transforming Urban Public Mobility: A Systematic Literature Review and Directions for Future Research." Proceedings zur Multikonferenz Wirtschaftsinformatik (MKWI), Lüneburg.

Yago, Glenn. 1984. *The Decline of Transit: Urban Transportation in German and US Cities, 1900–1970.* Cambridge: Cambridge University Press.

Zhang, Wenwen, Subhrajit Guhathakurta, and Elias Khalil. 2018. "The Impact of Private Autonomous Vehicle on Vehicle Ownership and Unoccupied VMT Generation." *Transportation Research Part C* 90: 156–65.

5   Scorecards and wildcards

5.1   Introduction

The autonomous vehicle development has attracted great interest but it will be in deployment that it produces great drama. There is no plot for its roll-out and there are sure to be conflicts. What will be the profile of its character as a vehicle – fossil or renewable energy? Which activity will its role feature – traditional personal automobility or new shared mobility? The cast of players in the impending drama will be large – competing business and technology enterprises, conventional car supporters and critics, regulatory bodies, interest groups, etc. The public audience will in the end applaud or boo, making an autonomous vehicle deployment a success or a failure.

On the stage here, the analyses of autonomous vehicle impact in previous chapters provide criteria for a scorecard outlining a best sustainability case for AV deployment – a public transit electric vehicle (EV) that combines an electric-powered character with a shared mobility role. Next, the chapter examines the uncertainties that surround deployment of any variety of autonomous vehicle. These are the wildcards that shadow its social acceptance – car culture, public opinion, cyber failure, loss of privacy, ethical dilemmas, and rebound effects. The chapter ends with an interpretation of the political ecology, or network of players, that likely will shape the path of deployment.

5.2   Scorecards

Students of sustainability and autonomous vehicles could profit from having a scorecard that registers its likely prospects for environments, societies, and cities. It is a resource for weighing potential benefits and harms, providing a guide toward a best case for sustainable deployment. The scorecard (Box 5.1) below outlines nine potential gains distributed among three autonomous vehicles: Internal combustion, electric, and public electric. It does not offer a final scoring but sets a sustainability framework for evaluating deployment. The vehicles are arranged with regard to the rank they presently have in automobility: Internal combustion is dominant, electric is challenging that dominance, and public electric is just emerging.

Box 5.1   Prospective sustainability gains of autonomous vehicles

- Autonomous Internal Combustion Vehicle (AICV):
    - Adding digital motorization =
        - Reduced vehicle crashes
        - Reduced driver stress
        - Increased fuel efficiency

- Autonomous Electric Vehicle (AEV):
    - Adding electrification to digital motorization =
        - Reduced tailpipe greenhouse gas (GHG) and toxic emissions
        - Reduced vehicle size
        - Reduced ambient noise

- Autonomous Public Electric Vehicle (APEV):
    - Adding public accessibility to digital motorization and electrification =
        - Reduced traffic congestion
        - Increased mobility equity
        - Reduced urban sprawl and parking space

There are several points to make about this classification. The sustainability gains overlap to some extent, and their three-tiered staging constitutes an additive progression for achieving sustainability goals. With regard to overlap each gain is placed with the most appropriate vehicle in terms of reach, depth, and value. The following examination of sustainability profiles reveals both the overlap and progression, beginning with the internal combustion vehicle.

The digitally connected *internal combustion* vehicle has potential to make a major social sustainability contribution by reducing crashes and their fatalities and injuries (see Chapter Three). This gain attracts the greatest public attention and support for the autonomous vehicle – with obviously good reason. Another contribution, reduction of driver stress, pales in comparison. A more distant and marginal environmental (see Chapter Two) gain lies in the reduction of materials resourcing stemming from a decline in crashes because vehicles will have longer and more repair-free lives (see Chapter Two). Finally, the fuel efficiency gain of the AICV's digitally connected eco-motorization would contribute to environmental sustainability. All of these gains would be moderated by the rebound effect of an increase in vehicle miles traveled (VMT). Because it is the most anticipated of autonomous vehicle rebound effects, it has its own scorecard. One example scores AV carsharing as decreasing vehicle miles but increasing sprawl – plus increasing autonomous vehicle substitution for public transit (Anderson et al. 2014, 38).

The *electric* autonomous vehicle has potential to enhance the sustainability gains scored by the AICV and to neutralize negative tailpipe emissions from a rebound increase in VMT. An environmental sustainability gain also will accrue from a downsizing of vehicles afforded by electric vehicles – reducing the need for raw materials and the assembly complexity required for ICVs. Social sustainability would get a major public health boost from the electric vehicle's steep reduction in toxic tailpipe emissions. There are yet other gains – AEV quiet operation would reduce ambient noise, making a contribution to urban quality of life (see Chapter Four). The deployment of electric autonomous vehicles apparently has broad support. A global survey found that two-thirds of respondents reported that they expected the vehicle to be electrified (WEF 2015).

However, the present electric vehicle has environmental sustainability shortcomings that beg special consideration. There are two major challenges: Battery production and energy sourcing (see Chapter Two). While both are being improved their drawbacks will take time to overcome. Meanwhile, for sustainability purposes the introduction of electric vehicles should be targeted. Their replacement of older and larger internal combustion automobiles prioritizes the best case reduction in tailpipe GHG emissions, whatever the grid electricity mix (Roland Clift, personal correspondence, October 25 and November 15, 2018). The largest of conventional passenger internal combustion vehicles (ICVs), energy-guzzling sport utility vehicles (SUVs), are expected to double in stock in a few decades and they already consume about one quarter of global primary oil (Sims et al. 2014; Sousanis 2011). A life cycle assessment found that any shift from smaller to larger vehicles increased lifetime emissions whatever powertrain was used (Ellingsen, Singh, and Stromman 2016). The best case to be made, then, for environmental sustainability is to incentivize the replacement of (older) high carbon intensive ICVs with EVs, and to promote a parallel development of renewable energy (see Chapter Two).

The third player in the scorecard, the *public* electric vehicle, would replicate the gains of the AICV and the AEV while adding other benefits. Shared and right-sized affordable public transit trips would be a social sustainability boon as they would inhibit a private autonomous vehicle deployment from swelling present mobility inequities. Fleets of APEVs could lower the use of personal automobiles by extending the coverages of public transit systems. This would also reduce need for parking spaces. Public vehicles would contribute to urban sustainability by reducing inner-city congestion and outlying land use sprawl. This would make secondary contributions to environmental sustainability due to the facts that congestion is an intensifier of tailpipe emissions and sprawl threatens ecological biodiversity. Finally, the public electric vehicle would likely negate the environmental damage from a rebound of added vehicle miles.

In sum, it is reasonable to argue based on this rough scoring that the AICV stage would represent two steps forward on a path to sustainability (reduced crashes, better fuel efficiency) and one backward (a vehicle miles/emissions increase); the AEV stage, two further steps forward (no tailpipe emissions, smaller size) and one backward (EV deficits); and the APEV stage, two more steps forward (reduced sprawl and congestion, greater mobility equity) and none backward. This rough accounting results in the equivalent of very high sustainability prospects for the third, APEV, stage; substantial ones for the second, AEV, stage; and moderate ones for the initial, AICV, stage.

At this writing the front-runner in autonomous vehicle deployment appears to be *General Motors*, which reports that it will have fleets of robot taxis on the road in 2019 (Said 2018a). It will be the *Cruise* car, built at the same plant as the electric *Bolt*, upon which it is based. *General Motors* has petitioned US regulators to approve production of vehicles without steering wheels or braking pedals. This looks to be a promising start from a sustainability perspective, as it would place an initial AV deployment at the second stage in the scorecard.

In the scoring here it appears that sustainability gains will be a bit more numerous on the social side. This result is supported by an analysis of estimated sustainability impacts from an autonomous vehicle deployment in China (Wulkop 2017). The greatest sustainability opportunities there were found among indicators with a social focus. However, the scoring here is not based in a quantitative scaling of sustainability prospects; it is as impressionistic as it is empirical. Moreover, the conceptual categories of environmental and social share a boundary whose measure in reality is continuous, not dichotomous.

5.3   The sustainability case for autonomous public electric vehicles

Using autonomous vehicles in public transit systems offers a best case for their successful deployment as well as for their sustainability. Transit systems provide organizational umbrellas that would serve to democratize an AV deployment and to better ensure safety concerns. A public deployment would also enhance transit coverage and thwart the siphoning off of its riders by private carshare enterprises.

Upgrading public transit

The integration of autonomous vehicle services with public transit systems has empirical support from a modeling scenario based on computational experiments. The modal choices were identified as tram, tram-bus, private car, taxi, autonomous vehicle, AV-tram, and AV-bus. The bases of evaluation were taken from local travelers in Poznan, and they were travel time, cost, comfort, timeliness, availability, reliability, environmental impact, and safety (Owczarzak and Zak 2015). The results showed that autonomous vehicles had the highest status in the rankings of modal choices (exclusive autonomous vehicle use was tied in respondent choice with AV-bus mode) backed by preferences for its shorter travel time, better timeliness and reliability, lower travel cost, and higher comfort. The autonomous vehicle related modes were preferred by good margins over taxis and private cars.

There is a potential AV negative rebound effect on public transit that has garnered little attention compared to the expected VMT rebound. A national online survey in Germany analyzed the preferences of respondents with regard to future travel modal choices. The choices presented were car, automated car, carsharing, automated carsharing, and public transport. The researchers found that carsharing will benefit from automation more than private cars will and that its growth will come at the expense of public transport (Pakusch et al. 2018). (*No* automated public transit option was put to respondents.) This research's conclusion has support from other studies (Krueger, Rashidi, and Rose 2016; Trommer et al. 2016), and it is consistent with results of local studies in the US that found the explosive growth in carsharing use is in large measure coming from public transit riders (see Chapter Four). This potential negative effect can be inhibited or prevented with several changes in public transit: Service improvements, joint agreements, and in-house autonomous vehicle fleets (Coogan et al. 2018).

Public transit systems face substantial problems in the extent and quality of their coverage. The two preferences of travelers most prominent in the online German study were passenger comfort and reliability (Pakusch et al. 2018). It is the older public transit systems that face the largest hurdles in upgrading their infrastructures and services. The older ones in the US are attracting increasing user demands for improvements as patronage grows. An example is the successful political mobilization by a group of users in Boston, *TransitMatters*. It is composed largely of Millennials who use an exhaustive knowledge of service schedules and digital data mining to create empirically based proposals for changes, a number of which have been implemented (Trickey 2018).

The new carshare digital platforms are challenging public transit for the riders taking short connector trips. A major problem is public transit's historic focus on large passenger loads for bus and metro trunk routes. As a result organizations have begun to contract with private carsharing services to cover short journey gaps in their services, especially for *last mile* trips. For example, Dallas Area Rapid Transit collaborates with *Uber* to provide a door-to-door connecting service (Leibowicz 2017). *Lyft* has partnered with public transit in Dayton, Ohio, to provide connections between its stops (Shrikant 2018). An organizational combination of private carshare enterprises with public transit agencies may offer the best first step to sustainable mobility for an autonomous vehicle deployment. For example, an analysis of deployment in China concluded that both private carshare enterprises and public transit systems outperformed a personal ownership-based deployment (Wulkop 2017).

However, such micro transit public–private collaboration has met with mixed results beyond the pilot programs of local transport agencies. One problem is the high per passenger cost of subsidies provided to carshare enterprises (Schmitt 2018). Instead, US cities are increasingly relying on third parties to develop more connectivity between transit modes (Sumantran, Fine, and Gonsalvez

2017a). However, the use of private enterprises in general raises equity issues: Will sub-contractors be required to provide physical and economic accessibility to mobility-disadvantaged persons? These enterprises "are being regulated, but much more lightly than traditional taxi and other for-hire transportation services," according to an analysis by the US National Academy of Sciences (NAS 2018, 17).

One advantage of public transit compared to carshare enterprises is its experience in managing large fleets of motorized vehicles. The consensus position among analysts is that autonomous vehicles will begin deployment in fleets. One reason is cost: Bulk purchase and operation lead to lower per unit expenses. Fleet purchases also enhance the probability for adoption of autonomous electric vehicles because they accumulate higher mileages, swelling the fuel cost (and tailpipe emissions) savings of electricity over gasoline (Leibowicz 2017). Car-sharing services have made public their intention to use fleets of AVs to replace their present use of owner-chauffeured cars (Said 2018b). For example, *Lyft* has a partnership with *General Motors* to develop an autonomous vehicle (Ayapana 2016). There are social sustainability reasons for transit agencies to opt for a similar action. One is that they are mandated to maintain an equitable service for poorer and mobility-challenged persons.

Fleet AVs would add to the automation already underway in some standard public transit bus and rail service (see Chapter Four). The autonomous public stock would include right-sized vehicles, from small to medium, so their utility could match public demand. For example, the US city of Arlington, Texas, is piloting a fixed-route, wheelchair-accessible autonomous shuttle (Rainwater and Dupuis 2018). It has met with positive response and a second phase of on-street testing is planned. In a pioneering effort to create public transit with on-demand inter-connectivity, Singapore is conducting trials with public bus service aimed at commuters living in areas with low ridership (*GovInsider* 2018). Using its transit app available on smart phones, potential passengers can indicate their destinations and an algorithm will calculate the first available bus route from their location. Singapore may provide a model for how autonomous vehicle deployment can correct public transit's lack of fit between large vehicles and small passenger loads. There, "the focus is on public transportation, and the city wants robo-cars to complement rather than replace it" (Herrmann, Brenner, and Stadler 2018, 347).

Right-sized on-demand service

Autonomous vehicles may provide a major improvement in public transit through the extension of services beyond their mass ridership base (Owczarzak and Zak 2015, 474). The autonomous public transit vehicle (APTV) likely will premiere in van fleets operated through a digital platform, possibly in cooperation with carshare enterprises. At some point public transit agencies may opt to operate in-house fleets of micro AVs. Eventually they would operate as public transit on-demand (PTOD) vehicles, perhaps with the following profile:

- Flexible (instead of fixed) stops, routes, and timetables capable of responding to digital passenger requests
- Mixed rather than standardized fleets featuring a range of micro vehicle capacities from two-seat pods through ten-seat vans

In addition to providing more service coverage PTODs could add to public transit's significant role in the sustainability of global passenger transport. From 2015 to 2050, if the current (base) transport energy resourcing mix continues, CO_2 emissions will increase by about one-fourth. However, in a scenario featuring urban integrated land use combined with transport planning that focuses on more and better public transit, the emissions would be reduced by 35 percent (ITF 2017, 136). Large passenger gains would come from enhanced population coverages – as measured by proportions of inhabitants within walking distance (< 1 km) of a transit stop. For example, in European cities average transit coverage would increase from 53 to 85 percent of local populations (ITDP 2016). Coverage is a role that the PTOD could play well in public transit systems. They would provide feeder services to neglected areas located in low-density suburbs and exurbs, offering connections to trunk lines for small to medium groups of passengers (Gruel and Stanford 2015, 28).

PTOD fleets could make a major difference for beggared public transit systems in the US (Nordhoff, Van Arem, and Happee 2016). The decline in its transit over the last century was led by a policy of service cuts, as noted by the following:

> When riders started to switch to the car in the early postwar years, American transit systems almost universally cut service to restore their financial viability. But this drove more people away, producing a vicious cycle until just about everybody who could drive, drove. In the fastest-growing areas, little or no transit was provided at all, because it was deemed to be not economically viable. Therefore, new suburbs had to be entirely auto-oriented.
> (English 2018, 21)

However, US public transit patronage has been on an uptick since the mid-1990s when hyper automobility reached saturation level. Between 1995 and 2014 ridership rose by almost 40 percent, outpacing increases in population and in vehicle miles traveled (APTA 2015). Because transit is becoming more favored by urban populations it provides an opportune channel to introduce autonomous electric vehicle services. In a global survey about autonomous vehicle acceptance, many respondents "could imagine using 100% electric driverless vehicles in connection with public transport" (Nordhoff et al. 2018, 15). These vehicles ultimately may include an on-demand version.

Public transit patrons are experienced in riding with strangers, a background factor that will facilitate their sharing use of automated services. For bus and metro riders, small-to-medium on-demand vehicles could help to allay fears about traveling in autonomous vehicles. It could provide for transitions to AVs on the part of personal automobile users as well. Sharing an autonomous vehicle with a small-ish group or a fellow commuter rather than riding in it alone likely will provide an added sense of security. On the environmental front public fleets would help to resolve several limiting factors in the growth of electric vehicle stocks. Their users would not experience battery-related travel range anxiety, would not have to be concerned with locating and accessing charging stations, and would not have to manage the use of vehicle charge time (Chen, Kockelman, and Hanna 2015).

5.4 Wildcards

All autonomous vehicles, public and private, internal combustion and electric, will face some daunting uncertainties whatever their sustainability prospects. There are a number of wildcard issues which have potential to delay or thwart an autonomous vehicle deployment. In the first instance, AVs will be resisted by people wedded to conventional car driving. On a more general level deployment must deal with public concerns about cyber security and with the ethical judgments needed to program vehicle operational decisions. In the last instance, rebound effects comprise another wildcard, one that features a variety of uncertainties.

Car culture

The culture that has developed around the automobile comprises an embedded nexus of attitudes and lifestyles involving people and their machine mobility, in which emotions and values play a role (Freund and Martin 1993; Marsh and Collett 1986; Sheller 2004). Automobility-dominated societies have produced a cultural meme centered on motoring – including driving to get somewhere, to enjoy oneself, to display social status, and to escape. For many teenagers getting a driver's license became a common symbolic gateway to independence from parents. Car culture developed in the 20th century in varying degree in the nations of the global North. French philosopher Roland Barthes captured the essence of its cultural idealization in 1957:

> I think that cars today are almost the exact equivalent of the great Gothic cathedrals: I mean the supreme creation of an era, conceived with passion by unknown artists, and consumed in image if not in usage by a whole population which appropriates them as a purely magical object.
>
> (Barthes 1957, 1)

The car was elevated in public acclaim with the rise of hyper automobility in the last half of the century when car racing became a widely popular *sport*. In 1982 an editorial in a global magazine called the car the greatest mobile force for freedom in rich democracies, a liberator of women, and a machine that turned the locally bound workman into a free yeoman (*The Economist* 1982).

Driving on an open highway in the countryside is perhaps the most iconic experience of car culture. The classic road trip has been featured in many popular movies. The British Film Institute's (BFI) list of great American road trip movies includes *Bonnie and Clyde* in 1967 and *Thelma & Louise* in 1991 (Quinn 2017a; Wigley 2015). The adventure-ization of road trips has not been limited to North America. For example the BFI lists *Mad Max* in 1979 and *Adventures of Priscilla, Queen of the Desert* in 1994 as distinguished Australian examples (Quinn 2017b). Cars became literary as well as visual cultural icons, featuring individual liberation and experimentation (Dennis and Urry 2009, 37). Kerouac's *On the Road*, published in the US in 1957, is a classic in the genre. Individualism and personal freedom, often expressed as escape from society, are the highlight values of the road trip experience. To some analysts the combination of driver and vehicle represents a major form of machine–human hybridization (Urry 2008).

Those in the automobile industry have been big supporters of the motoring for-the-pleasure-of-it cultural meme. An example is the industrial film and book by Henry Ford II, entitled *Freedom of the American Road* (Ford 1955), which was a quite successful marketing and propaganda tool. It may be the case that in the end the popular success of autonomous vehicles will depend on creating a revised sales message for consumers – the "joy of being driven" (Nordhoff et al. 2018, 7) to replace the bestselling "joy of driving."

More and more, the popularity of the automobile is viewed as having run its course and become defined as a liability in an urbanized world; for example, in the following comment:

> The beloved automobile gradually became a victim of its own success. Urban densification has shifted the emphasis of mobility investment from intercity connections to improved mobility within cities, where cars increasingly find themselves crowded out. Cities compelled to battle congestion and deteriorating air quality have steadily grown more averse to cars.
> (Sumantran, Fine, and Gonsalvez 2017a, 288)

The car culture, featuring a personal internal combustion vehicle, is increasingly viewed as an environmental and social problem. This is magnified by an increase in regulation-evasion scandals produced by some multinational automotive corporations continuing to sell unsustainable diesel engines.

There are two opposing attention-getting public choruses that criticize the automation of automobility. One reveres the conventional car and sings the virtues of driving. This chorus rejects the autonomous vehicle because it threatens to turn driving over to anonymous others, negating all of its valued cultural subtexts. For example, a scholar of automobile design is quoted as saying that "sex, beauty, status, freedom – all the words which advertisers have tried to associate with cars over the past 50 years – have been replaced by mere functionality" (Moss 2015). This anti-AV, pro-car chorus is rooted in the association of driving with personal autonomy; it has been described as a reflection of a hyper-individualism (Paterson 2007, 89). However, opinions are changeable and ultimately it may develop that: "Because even passionate drivers could enjoy being chauffeured in an autonomous vehicle on their daily commute slowed by traffic jams, the passion for driving might be restricted to certain road and traffic conditions" (Becker and Axhausen 2017, 10).

The obverse critical chorus resists autonomous vehicles not because they might replace conventional cars but because they are also cars. In the words of one voice in the chorus: "We don't need self-driving cars – we need to ditch our vehicles entirely" (Solnit 2016). This resistance to AVs repudiates automobile use in favor of walking, cycling, and public transit. Some take that position with regard to electric vehicles as well, as in "our cities need fewer cars, not cleaner cars" (Sumantran, Fine, and Gonsalvez 2017b). Much of the impetus for this chorus is provided by the public health threats posed by urban automobility (see Chapter Four).

Public opinion

Attitudes about a prospective autonomous vehicle deployment are influenced by the culturally embedded legacy of the conventional automobile. Often designated an icon of modernity the personal internal combustion car plays a leading role in the hearts, minds, and practices of many people. For them it represents an admirable totem; for others it is a manifestation of environmental ruination. However, it appears that the bulk of reaction to the arrival of the AV on the public stage is ambiguous, not certain. It is in flux rather than fixed and with good reason – there are many uncertainties that exist about the technology and its use. This makes the parsing of the voluminous public opinion survey data more an auxiliary than a revelatory undertaking. Data on the range and intensity of public attitudes about autonomous vehicles have been examined by academic researchers, think tanks, transportation institutes, blogs, automobile associations, polling organizations, and specialized automotive consultants.

According to one literature review, "There are many different surveys on social acceptance, some that paint a hopeful picture and some a more cautious one" (Valen 2017, 8). The categorization here falls into three clusters: The averse or resistant, the apathetic or reluctant, and the avid or ready. The apathetic display a wait-and-see attitude. The public debate is then between the avid and the averse, with the former cheering the autonomous vehicle as a technological miracle and the latter viewing it as a nanny-state intrusion into individual liberty (Roose 2017), or as a new threat to sustainability.

Generally, mobility decisions by individuals are based in utility considerations (e.g., cost, time) and their attitudes toward sustainable practices "hardly effect mobility behaviour and mode choice in everyday life" (Pakusch et al. 2018, 21). Transportation researchers have identified the travel characteristics that motivate individual decisions as the following: Travel time, cost, comfort, flexibility, availability, and reliability. Choices with regard to the autonomous vehicle likely will be based in the same criteria. Sustainability remains relevant but secondary in *most* consumer decision-making.

In general those who are averse to using autonomous vehicles explain their attitudes with comments such as the following (Fraedrich and Lenz 2016; *Reuters* 2018; Smith and Anderson 2017). (The sentiments have been expressed in slightly different words multiple times in various surveys.)

- I wouldn't feel safe.
- I don't want to be a guinea pig.
- I want to be in control, not have a machine pick what's best for me.

Those who are avid about autonomous vehicles voice reasons such as:

- I appreciate not having to park.
- I'd like to work or relax in the vehicle.
- Drunk drivers – I want my children safe.

A representative sampling of public opinion, pro and con, is the following summary of findings from a survey taken in Berkeley:

> We find that individuals are most attracted to potential safety benefits, the convenience of not having to find parking, and amenities such as multitasking while in route; conversely, individuals were most concerned with liability, the cost of the technology, and losing control of the vehicle.
>
> (Howard and Dai 2013, 1)

There is some evidence that the avid are led by younger adults, particularly the Millennial generation born between 1977 and 1994 (Moor 2016; Etehad and Nikolewski 2016). The car culture has not been as appealing to them as it has to past generations – they display less interest in driving a car and more in living in cities where driving one is not required. While this generational shift has been most often noted in the US, it has been identified in other nations of the global North as well – Australia, Canada, Germany, the Netherlands, New Zealand, and Norway (Delbosc and Ralph 2017). One narrative for the shift portrays Millennials as driving less, moving to (or staying in) cities, and using public transit.

A generational shift is indicated by other data as well. A cross-national study of licensed drivers found that in 1983 about 46 percent of Americans got their licenses in the year following their 16th birthdays but only about one-fourth did so in 2014. A similar pattern was found in seven other nations, five of them in the AV9 group – Germany, Japan, Sweden, the ROK, and the UK. After a statistical analysis of the relationship between licensing and social factors, the researchers noted that a higher proportion of internet users was associated with a lower rate of licensing, a finding "consistent with the hypothesis that access to virtual contact reduces the need for actual contact among young people" today (Sivak and Schoettle 2011, 19). Whether or not this represents a long-lasting trend remains to be seen, but "for now, it appears that many young adults depend on technology-enabled connections as much as, if not more than, those provided by personal vehicles" (NAS 2018, 13).

A meta-analysis of several dozen research studies conducted between 2014 and 2016 that had investigated the public acceptance level of autonomous vehicles found that "men, as well as those currently owning a vehicle with advanced driver assistance, tend to be most positive about using the technology" (Becker and Axhausen 2017, 9).

Fear about autonomous vehicle safety was not as much of a trend as expected in this meta-analysis. Some respondents in the studies did express concern, but others mentioned increased safety as one of the potential benefits of autonomous vehicles. The bulk of the studies showed that individual attitudes wielded more statistical significance with regard to AV adoption than did sociodemographic variables such as age and income.

The first global and large-scale study of the acceptance level of autonomous vehicles was published in 2018. Over 7,000 respondents from 116 countries answered an online questionnaire after being presented with a usage scenario and photographs of an AV (Nordhoff et al. 2018). The dependent variable was acceptance, and stronger correlations were with the following independent variables:

- Being comfortable with technology
- Difficulty of finding parking space
- Frequency of public transportation use
- Living in a city
- Frequency of walking and cycling

Acceptance had only small correlations with age, gender, and income. Males did have a higher acceptance rate but it was not significant within countries.

Public opinion about the autonomous vehicle in general is subject to periodic shifts given that the vehicle is not yet available to the public and its development is producing some crashes. Two well-publicized deaths in the US in 2016 (an AV occupant) and 2018 (a pedestrian) apparently produced such a shift. A national survey in the US conducted before the incidents subsequently was replicated. After the crashes almost one-half of respondents reported that they would never buy a fully autonomous vehicle, while previously this opinion had been held by less than one-third (Baker 2018). Autonomous vehicle developers are aware of the negative public reaction of test crashes. One is quoted as saying, "We recognize the impact this can have on community trust" (Said 2018c, D4). The volatility of opinion likely is based largely on the general public's lack of experience with the AV. Conventional automobiles are not so feared even though their crashes killed over 37,000 Americans in 2016 and again in 2017. The ubiquity of automobility in developed countries has helped to routinize death-by-car. Additionally, the known fact that the great majority of crashes are caused by driver error leads many to believe they are capable of avoiding a crash.

Perhaps skepticism about the AV is a reflection of the *familiarity principle*, a social psychological phenomenon in which "repeated exposure of the individual to a stimulus object enhances his attitude toward it" (Zajonc 1965, 1). Conventional cars are quite familiar to people, and most have become habituated to their (normal) use. It will take decades after autonomous vehicles are initially deployed for them to accumulate a similar level of familiarity. There is some evidence that it will breed AV-like rather than dislike. For example, one survey found that present cruise control users are more confident about autonomous vehicles, likely because they are familiar with automated automobile technology and have had positive experience with it (Sanaullah et al. 2017).

Digital security and privacy

Cyber security and privacy are concerns of the public that may put a ceiling on the social acceptance prospects for autonomous vehicles. The threats of losing control of the vehicle and of having one's privacy invaded are widespread and present high hurdles to overcome (Fagant and Kockelman 2015; Griffin 2018, 99). In a global survey evaluating public acceptance of autonomous vehicles, respondents gave their highest rating to being able to take control by using a button inside the vehicle to stop it. This indicates that AV users will have a strong preference for reserving ultimate control over their vehicle at whatever level of automation (Nordhoff et al. 2018, 15).

The relation of sustainability to cyber security and privacy is being explored on several fronts. One analyst makes an argument for including cyber security in the remit of Corporate Social Responsibility for sustainability programs as a way of safeguarding the public. Applying techniques developed in the environmental movement such as integrated reporting is suggested as a way to share anti-hacking information and security protocols (Shackelford, Fort, and Charoen 2016). AV cyber sabotage has potential negative impacts for environmental sustainability. For example, a scenario study has found that the energy consumption of an autonomous vehicle platoon could increase by 20 to 300 percent as a result of an attack launched from one vehicle that would circulate among surrounding AVs and impact their braking and acceleration (Gerdes, Winstead, and Heaslip 2013).

Security threats to shut down or to manipulate digital systems emanate from a number of sources: Computer hackers, hostile nations, disgruntled employees, and terrorist organizations. If successfully developed and widely popularized AVs will operate within large digital systems. Unlike desktop and laptop computers AV computers will direct vehicle movements, creating a new category of risk.

Autonomous vehicle digital security must address several sorts of threats, including the possibilities of espionage and sabotage (Fagant and Kockelman

2013). Espionage threatens the privacy of personal information that is shared in digital systems; data can be accessed and used surreptitiously. Sabotage threatens digital operations with complete shutdown, constituting a life-threatening situation if a vehicle is in motion. A third threat is the most familiar one – the unintended collapse or well-known crash of a computer or a system.

Espionage, sabotage, and crash will threaten autonomous vehicle digital systems as they do those used in air traffic control and energy grids. As a critical national infrastructure, AV digital systems will be defended by rigorous security measures. However, even the most secure systems do not have a "silver bullet" to prevent invasions and collapses. At its best, autonomous vehicle digital security, like that of other vital systems, will make unwanted incursions very difficult and will limit their reach (Fagant and Kockelman 2013, 13). AV computer error will replace the driver error of the conventional automobile but likely with less frequency and loss of life.

As with their computers and smart phones, individuals using autonomous vehicles will be required to share personal data digitally. It can then be captured and possibly manipulated by identity thieves, commercial enterprises, and regulatory overseers. Data security systems and passwords can act as barriers, but they can be breached, legally (as in court approved governmental surveillance) as well as illegally. While vehicle travel data can be harvested for business purposes, such as advertising and market research, it is more annoying than threatening. Private data could also be used to improve the performance, safety, and oversight of AV-connected systems. In the end, personal data cannot be stonewalled but surveillance should be continually monitored and regulated in order to balance individual privacy and public utility.

Gathering (some) personal data for the benefit of all autonomous vehicle users will be needed to enhance system sustainability. For example, AV operations can continuously feed systems with updated visual recognition data of ever-changing roadway environments (Karnouskos and Kerschbaum 2018). An autonomous vehicle can then upgrade its performance by utilizing the data on the road, which would be a key contribution to projected crash reductions (Griffin 2018, 88–9). The public debate about this conflict of interests is on-going (Musolesi 2014). An AV deployment will ratchet up the increasing digitalization of life that tends to override the privacy of personal data. The internet and smart phones, social media, and digital search engines all have relegated privacy to a secondary concern. Users have largely tolerated this because of the low cost and convenience of these digital products (Oppetit 2017).

Each nation where the autonomous vehicle is deployed will develop its own regulatory protocols for protecting security and privacy. In 2016 the US National Highway Traffic Safety Administration produced a document, "Cybersecurity Best Practices for Modern Vehicles," which made it clear that the government will have oversight of digital systems for both security and privacy purposes (Page and Krayem 2017). The resolution of privacy issues, like AV deployment, will take decades to mature. The major questions will have to be resolved by law:

> Infrastructure design and safeguarding measures can be put into place to protect data both within the vehicle and at stakeholder sources, but the key element for privacy control will be creating laws that make any breach of data or misuse of data illegal.
>
> (Surakitbanharn et al. 2018, 24)

Perhaps the most perplexing and portentous safety issue for autonomous vehicles will be the quality and speed of a passenger's reaction to any system malfunction. The human reaction will be critical to determining the outcome of an unexpected and threatening event. Two specific components of reaction time will be the situational awareness and skill level of the human occupant (Endsley and Garland 2000). With the exception of trained professionals such as airplane pilots research has demonstrated that "humans are notoriously poor at automation monitoring and their ability to step in and take over functionality shortly after an automation failure is very low"; and "this is particularly an issue if the automation fails quickly, where the human would be required to take over full control of the systems within 30 seconds or less" (Surakitbanharn et al. 2018, 24). Analysts of personal safety issues surrounding AVs suggest that a temporary disengagement of all vehicles must be assured in order to protect the safety of their on-the-move users: "A completely autonomous vehicle should include a fail-safe mode where the vehicle returns to a safe state, e.g., parking road side" (Karnouskos and Kerschbaum 2018, 5).

At the end of the day a mature autonomous vehicle deployment will need to wrestle with the threats confronted by all digitally based systems. The fact is that the more we depend on digital technologies for everyday life the more our societies and environments become vulnerable to potential catastrophes, intended or not (Samuelson 2017). Cyber failure and privacy invasion may be caused less by external exotic threats than by more mundane ones such as "less cautious behaviour of vehicle occupants and road users, system errors, and the lack of regulation of crash algorithms that determine life or death situations during inevitable accidents" (Taeihagh and Lim 2018). Routine human errors and normal accidents that occur in complex systems (Perrow 1984) likely will be more prevalent problems for AVs, as they are in the operation of conventional automobiles. Ultimately, data security and privacy are major stumbling blocks for an autonomous vehicle deployment. According to one survey of development insiders, the security needs of AV communication requirements are a potential roadblock to a mass uptake, alongside a successful resolution of data ownership rights (Anderson et al. 2014, 93–4).

Ethics and safety

There is an ethical dilemma that has been re-popularized in autonomous vehicle discourse – moral philosophy's hypothetical Trolley Problem, involving a binary choice between killing one or more than one person (Engber 2018; Foot 1967). Its application to AVs has been criticized as an unnecessary diversion: "Focus should be on the practical technological solutions and their social consequences, rather than on idealized unsolvable problems such as much discussed trolley problem" (Holstein, Dodig-Crnkovic, and Pelliccione 2018). Despite the low probability of such an event happening autonomous vehicle digital applications may be mandated to take them into account. In surveys about such a choice, respondents tended to make utilitarian responses that minimized loss of life – the "greatest good" outcome. Vehicle passenger sacrifice was not approved when only one pedestrian would be saved but approval rates increased as the number of lives saved was increased (Surakitbanharn et al. 2018).

A straightforward way to handle this moral issue is for regulators to implement a minimal loss of life rule for autonomous vehicle digital programming (Edmonds 2018). Reaching a social agreement that is legally codified for decision-making protocols in autonomous vehicles does seem to favor a utilitarian ethic. However, individuals appear to have strong cognitive dissonance regarding the parameters of utilitarian approaches. Surveys indicate that people desire AVs to sacrifice their passengers if necessary but they themselves want vehicles that opt to save them if they are passengers. Surveys have found that "respondents would also not approve regulations mandating self-sacrifice, and such regulations would make them less willing to buy an autonomous vehicle" (Bonnefon, Shariff, and Rahwan 2016, 1573).

Other moral assessment research has produced similar findings. A virtual reality experimental study in Germany required 189 subjects to make a series of binary decisions (Bergmann et al. 2018). One result was that children were saved at higher rates than either adults or elderly persons. The data suggested that subjects did not acknowledge sidewalks as safe zones for pedestrians in a dilemma situation. However, Germany's recently constituted ethical rules for autonomous vehicles makes a clear distinction between those who create traffic risks (vehicle occupants driving onto sidewalks) and those who do not (pedestrians on sidewalks). The code prohibits sacrificing pedestrians for occupants in this example (*BMVI* 2017). With regard to the equity aspect of sustainability, ethical issues are relevant to the principle of fairness in the treatment of persons.

Utilitarianism seems to carry the day around the world although there are cultural differences. Using an online experimental platform, the *Moral Machine*, researchers gathered millions of decisions in ten languages in over 200 countries (Awad et al. 2018). The authors did the work with the goal of adding to the discourse about the interplay of moral values, artificial intelligence, and autonomous vehicles. They documented three clusters of countries with regard to differences in individual value preferences, geographically sorted into Western, Eastern, and Southern groups. The division was based on utilitarian choices and rankings about saving lives. One finding was that the Western group, which included the US and much of Europe, showed a marked preference for saving children. The Eastern cluster, including China, Japan, and the ROK, was more likely to save older people. Another finding was that most populations in the Eastern group strongly preferred saving pedestrians as opposed to vehicle passengers and countries in the Western group were less likely to choose saving pedestrians.

Of course, the research question was staged. It would be rare for a vehicle to actually confront such binary choices and individuals may react differently than predicted when confronted by a real, in the heat of the moment, choice. Drivers of conventional automobiles rarely face moral decisions that have to be made in the moment – for example whether or not to swerve off the road at speed (with unknown consequences) in order to avoid crashing into another vehicle, a cyclist, a walker, or an animal. A problem with this comparison is that autonomous vehicles may not have attentive operators, thus requiring a programmed default decision: Protect vehicle passenger safety or the safety of (unknown) others.

From a legal perspective resolving the ethical content of autonomous vehicle digital programming is advised to stress inclusion and access in order to avoid adding to illegal discrimination against those who are disadvantaged because of age or disability. The international treaty, Vienna Convention on Road Traffic Law (*USLegal* 2018), includes the notice that drivers shall allow extra care with regard to the most vulnerable road users. For an AV deployment the convention will need to update the definition of driver to read persons or things which drive (Bradshaw-Martin and Easton 2014). A driver's license may be replaced by an operator's license, a document that verifies capacity to handle a range of situations while in an autonomous vehicle. Will groups of people who presently do not qualify for a driving license be accepted as operators – for example, infirm elderly, persons with certain disabilities, and adolescents? Resolution of such issues will have to be achieved before autonomous vehicles can be deployed (Shwebel 2018). Regulatory approval of AV operators will take considerable time to promulgate. It is important to include the whole range of decisions relevant to potential ethical issues in the present design and development stage, and to provide for their public notification, or they likely will not gain public trust.

Ethical and safety issues are connected at a new level in autonomous vehicle machines. We have grown accustomed to accept, with some qualification, machine control of operational decisions in our travels. Airplanes are frequently flown by autopilot digital systems, and they have proven to be quite safe and trustworthy. Operationally based crashes are the result of pilot error (over one-half of crashes), aircraft mechanical failure, or weather conditions (Oster, Strong, and Zorn 1992). Although airplanes are fast moving vehicles, their machine intelligence protocols minimize a risk of failure. The autopilot does not steer an airplane on the ground. Taxiing, take-off, and landing are manual. Additionally, a pilot or co-pilot remains attentive at all times to assure proper computing operation, intervening immediately if necessary (FAA 2017).

However, like legacy automobiles autonomous vehicles will present more safety risk than do airplanes. Moving in road traffic will require considerably more complex software code than does operation of even the most advanced airplane (Litman 2017). Many conventional motor vehicles presently are fitted with automatic cruise control for use on long trips taken on major highways, but autonomous vehicles present major divergences from both airplane auto-pilots and automobile cruise control technologies. Unlike pilots and co-pilots, AV managers will not be well-trained and experienced professionals, and unlike cruise control vehicles AVs will not be restricted to limited-access highways. Moving at speed in congested traffic presents a rapidly changing diversity of interactions and surroundings, demanding more decisions to be made quickly than does flying an airplane, and there will be no trusted pilot in a personal AV.

Like conventional motor vehicles AVs will pose a safety threat to outsiders as well as occupants. What software or regulation could enable autonomous vehi-cle users (assuming they are alert) to signal recognition to a cyclist or a walker at an intersection when eye contact may no longer be an option? Vehicle sensors will need to decipher intent by reading body language and understanding social norms. A start-up in Boston, *Perceptive Automata*, is applying techniques from neuroscience and psychology to program a human-like intuition – but can any artificial intelligence be taught to accurately anticipate human actions? Using game theory decision-making, one analysis found that because autonomous vehicles will be programmed to be risk averse, walkers should be able to behave with impunity. However, AV deployment would then be limited by a disad-vantage that slows them down (Millard-Ball 2016). They likely will be deemed "slow and clunky," an unappealing feature to potential users (Coppola 2018).

Human–machine interaction and communication have been experimentally developed for decades. However, the autonomous vehicle represents a unique challenge:

> Automated driving involves an evolution . . . in a high stakes context with new implications for trust generation. Building a trusting human–machine relationship in automated driving inevitably means dealing with social robotics and affective computing where anthropomorphism in technol-ogy has been explored for many years. But the specificity of the automatic driving moment must be attended to: this is the only robot with an interior private mobile space.
>
> (Reilhac, Millett, and Hottelart 2016, 73)

It is becoming apparent from research findings that incorporating ethical decision-making into autonomous vehicle operations will require a notoriously difficult capability – reducing moral values into algorithms for a computer to follow across a wide range of possibilities (Lin 2015, 69).

The current development and testing of autonomous vehicles and their digi-tal coding is an entirely private (business) concern, even though many of the tests are taking place on public roads. Regulators generally have taken a low intervention approach, in part to allow a speedier development of the technology. Perhaps national competition over potential economic rewards contributes as well. This means that there is no society-wide input into the intricacies of AV development. As one analyst has pointed out, there is no experimental approach being adopted to assess various social outcomes for autonomous vehicles, including their degree of social acceptance (Marres 2018). The analyst suggests that street testing be revised in order to elicit and then assess the consequences of being a new AV passenger. The data on the safety of robot-driving provide no definitive answer to date as to whether or not autonomous vehicle systems will be safer than human drivers. "Most comparisons between human drivers and automated vehicles have been at best uneven – and at worst unfair" (Hancock 2018). Perhaps regulators need to take a more active and stringent approach to the experimental vehicles that private enterprises are placing on public roads.

Rebound effects

The rebound is a construct that has evolved from energy economics and is based in a standard economic mantra: As cost declines, demand rises. In typical research usage the rebound effect focuses on the increase in use of a technology as a result of an improved technical efficiency (Matiaske, Menges, and Speiss 2012). Thus, for example, the autonomous vehicle's higher motoring safety margins and lower fuel use may induce passengers to travel at higher speeds (assuming they can control speed), resulting in an estimated fuel consumption increase of 7 to 30 percent (CSS 2017). The focus on AV miles traveled illustrates the general concern with energy use, harking back to the rebound effect's first application – to coal-powered steam engines (see Chapter One). VMT is generally recognized as being the most likely and most pervasive of rebound effects (Bordoff 2016). Fuel's importance has been magnified by the large contribution of tailpipe GHG emissions to climate change. However, the consensus research position is that it is likely "the potential energy savings estimated from AVs are much larger than the estimated worst-case growth in energy use" (Greenblatt and Shaheen 2015). Moreover, the savings probably would be guaranteed with deployment of autonomous electric vehicles and autonomous public EVs.

The focus on energy economics is insufficient for examining secondary effects that are common and sometimes positive in assessments of overall sustainable consumption (Hertwich 2005). The complexity of autonomous vehicle potential rebound effects illustrates this. In addition to the vehicle miles rebound the analysis here has identified a shopping cart full of other spheres of potential effects, relating to alcohol consumption, physical exercise, transport sector employment, urban sprawl, right of way, street interactions, onboard activities, and urban tax revenue.

Thus, in addition to energy gains and losses, AV sustainability prospects will be impacted by a number of rebound effects, along with their ripples and ricochets, all of which will prove difficult to assess. For example, autonomous vehicle accessibility by new users, including the disabled and infirm elderly, will add VMT (negative effect) but benefit equity (positive effect); and the high cost of vehicles will add less vehicle miles (positive) but penalize poorer persons (negative). Some rebounds will appear rather quickly in an AV deployment while others will take a longer time to be realized. Some potential benefits such as less congestion and increased fuel efficiency could be realized at lower levels of automation but others, such as crash reduction, will require higher levels at which mixed traffic is considerably reduced (Litman 2016).

An example of uncertain rebound effects concerns the found time that may be had by autonomous vehicle users. Will the vehicle become a new and expanded driverless version of the mobile home? One commentator suggests the following prospect:

> The automobile of the future might not even have traditional car seats – instead it might have couches or beds. Perhaps it will even have small kitchens or entertainment centers; cars could easily become mobile living rooms with all the amenities.
>
> (Biba 2016)

There is a general expectation that AV users will be attracted by the possibility of doing something productive, entertaining, or relaxing to replace often tedious and taxing driving (Herrmann, Brenner, and Stadler 2018, 211–19). Autonomous vehicles could serve as mobile offices, even mobile bedrooms – perhaps for "commuter sex" (Larson 2016). However, a survey of research findings indicates that this effect will materialize only in the long run and probably only for long-distance trips (Becker and Axhausen 2017, 10). Another survey found that AV users will replicate activities that are frequent in conventional vehicles such as window gazing (Heinrichs 2015).

At present the projections and scenarios about potential autonomous vehicle rebound effects, particularly their ripples and ricochets, are based in informed speculation and surmise. At this early stage specification of their origins, directions, and magnitudes are daunting, if not impossible. However, thoughtful consideration of AV rebound effects does provide motivation to learn more about what may evolve as a result of vehicle uptake.

5.5   Conclusion: Political ecology of an autonomous vehicle deployment

This chapter (and book) concludes with an examination of the likely political ecology parameters that will shape and shadow an autonomous vehicle deployment. The particular perspective used here focuses on a network of potential actors who will play leading roles in decision-making about how to address its environmental and social sustainability prospects.

The sustainability of human civilization depends on promoting integration of its environmental and social realms, as well as its individual and collective needs, amounting to a negotiation of individual ("me"), social ("us"), and environmental ("it") dimensions of life. Mobility is a key factor in this integration as it plays a big role in daily human life. Governments collect transport-related fees and make regulations that go towards improving quality of life for people and for sustaining their earthly home. Decision-making with regard to taxes and regulations is at the heart of the political process. This means that autonomous vehicle deployment will add a political cast to its sustainability ramifications (Martin 2018). It is already apparent, for example, that business interests will have outsized political influence. Private enterprise goals are leading AV development, not social and environmental ones. Carshare enterprises illustrate this in their successful disruptions, featuring *act now/regulate later* tactics (McGrath 2018). These enterprises are being regulated with a light touch (NAS 2018, 17).

A pessimistic outcome of this business-first scenario is that autonomous vehicle ownership will be only for elites who can buy them and for riders who can afford trip fares, credit cards, and smart phones (Papa and Ferreira 2018). Moreover, private carshare fleets likely will not be subject to physical access protocols for infirm and disabled persons. Thus, an autonomous vehicle deployment may reinforce the dominant role in mobility held by the personal automobile. This dominance is individual-focused, highlighted by convenience and comfort, while sustainability is collective-focused, led by fairness concerns for mobility-disadvantaged persons, and for conserving the environment in which all individuals live.

One indication of business-as-usual practice is illustrated in the opinions of autonomous vehicle developers. Members of a panel who were interviewed about AV progress rank-ordered the seven barriers they faced as follows (Underwood 2014, 78):

1 Technology development
2 Legal liability assignment
3 Government regulations
4 Cost of vehicles
5 Roadway and digital infrastructure preparation
6 Consumer acceptance
7 Social acceptance

Thus, to autonomous vehicle developers public acceptance is last on their list of concerns. One can imagine that task will be left to marketing and sales employees.

However, other scenarios are conceivable as alternatives to business as usual. They can be assessed by researchers, spurred by interest groups, developed by regulators, and tabled by public transit systems and their governing bodies. The political ecology of the autonomous vehicle could represent a new perspective on the singular powers of business and tech giants (Bissell 2018). Carshare disruptive innovation creates business risks from social transformations. Such possibilities are not manageable by elites because social change has an entropic quality, multiplying and diversifying at will. One result of this dynamic scenario may be a rippling emergence of resistance and reform aimed at autocratic business decisions. Moreover, the power of big business/tech in autonomous vehicle deployment will face numerous legacy challenges from the many interest groups and non-governmental organizations (NGOs) that campaign for socially excluded people and for environmental sustainability.

A key to promoting a sustainable deployment for autonomous vehicles will be to change the embedded automobile's character from internal combustion to electric motor and its role as a personal car to one as a public vehicle. In addition to research and analysis this will require the development of a wide and effective range of effective government transport policies and regulations. The fact of the matter is that "despite its revolutionary flavour, the AV does not change much when it comes to deciding on the main principles for transport policy" (Thomopoulos and Givoni 2015, 14). Government oversight is required in order for the public interest in sustainability to influence an autonomous vehicle deployment. An analysis of deployment in Chinese cities concluded that "regulators need to develop their own vision of autonomous vehicles in the urban mobility system in order to avoid car makers and high-tech start-ups imposing their dream" (Wulkop 2017, 54). It is reasonable to assume that the dreams of business leaders are dominated by visions of monetary gain. It will take an effective public regulatory regime for deployment to conform to the broad contours of transport and sustainability policies, including elimination of vehicle tailpipe emissions and provision of fully equitable mobility services. If the deployment is left to business and technology interests it risks reinforcing ICV legacy problems (Papa and Ferreira 2018), putting motorized road transport at a further remove from sustainable practices.

This monograph has addressed the issue of autonomous vehicle deployment impacts as they relate to environmental, social, and urban sustainability. The general conclusion is that a diffuse social learning is just beginning and needs to continue to expand at the present cusp of AV development rather than wait for its deployment. This learning needs to go beyond consumer opinions about the vehicle itself to include all aspects of human transportation, especially its public transit systems. It should include learning more about potential impacts of autonomous vehicles on urban spatial uses and infrastructures, on the needs of mobility-disadvantaged groups, and on the health and well-being of non-AV users as well as users.

The political ecological analysis ends with a trio of sustainability spheres in which an autonomous public electric vehicle deployment would have excellent prospects. They are banner issues that are based in science, pursued by transportation and urban planners, and common in public discourse:

- Decarbonization – to address climate change
- Public health – to save human lives
- Mobility equity – to promote social justice

Public transit has been the historical alternative to unsustainable automobility's dominance and remains so today. Its modes are critical to decarbonization efforts, especially their electrified services, and it has superior public health and safety records compared to personal automobility. Finally, public transit is the essential component in providing equitable motorized mobility. The present passenger transportation scene presents an autonomous vehicle deployment with historical opportunities to end the automobile's pernicious legacies with a new environmental character and a new social role. The moment will be difficult to seize but a transformative mobility for humanity and the maintenance of its home are its prizes.

References

Anderson, James M., Nidhi Kalra, Karlyn D. Stanley, Paul Sorenson, Constantine Samaras, and Tobi A. Oluwatola. 2014. *Autonomous Vehicle Technology: A Guide for Policymakers.* Santa Monica CA: RAND.

APTA. 2015. *Status of Public Transportation Ridership.* Washington, DC: American Public Transportation Association. Available at: www.apta.com/mediacenter/ptbenefits/Documents/Ridership%20Points%20Final.pdf [Accessed October 29, 2018].

Awad, Edmond, Sohan Dsouza, Richard Kim, Jonathan Schulz, Joseph Henrich, Azim Shariff, Francois Bonnefon, et al. 2018. "The Moral Machine Experiment." *Nature* 563: 59–64. Available at: www.nature.com/articles/s41586-018-0637-6/ [Accessed November 15, 2018].

Ayapana, Erick. 2016. "*Lyft* Co-Founder: In 5 Years Most Rides Will Be in Autonomous Cars." *Motortrend.* Available at: www.motortrend.com.new/lyft-founder-in-5-years-most-rides-will-be-in-autonomous-cars/ [Accessed January 4, 2018].

Baker, David R. 2018. "After Uber Accident, Fewer People Want Self-Driving Cars." *The San Francisco Chronicle*, August 16, Biz & Tech/Business. Available at: www.sfchronicle.com/business/article/After-Uber-accident-fewer-people-want-13159087.php?utm [Accessed August 17, 2018].

Barthes, Roland. 1957. *Mythologies.* Paris: Editions du Seuil. Available at: www.citronet.org.uk/passenger-cars/michelin/ds/32.html [Accessed November 7, 2018].

Becker, Felix and Kay Axhausen. 2017. "Literature Review on Surveys Investigating the Acceptance of Automated Vehicles." *Transportation* 44. Available at: http://doi.org/10.1007/s11116-017-9808-9 [Accessed October 20, 2018].

Bergmann, Lasse T., Larissa Schlicht, Carmen Meixner, Peter Konig, Gordon Pipa, Suzanne Boshammer, and Achim Stephan. 2018. "Autonomous Vehicles Require Socio-Political Acceptance: An Empirical and Philosophical Perspective on the Problem of Moral Decision Making." *Frontiers in Behavioral Neuroscience* 12: 1–12. doi: 10.3389/fnbeh.2018.00031.

Biba, Erin. 2016. "What the World Will Look Like Without Drivers." *Newsweek*, Online, January 22. Available at: www.newsweek.com/26/02/22/driverless-cars-and-future-getting-around-415405.html [Accessed November 7, 2018].

Bissell, David. 2018. "Automation Interrupted: How Autonomous Vehicle Accidents Transform the Material Politics of Automation." *Political Geography* 65: 57–66. Available at: https://doi.org/10.1016/j.polgeo.2018.05.003 [Accessed July 14, 2018].

BMVI. 2017. *Automated and Connected Driving.* Berlin: Bundesministerium fur Verkehr und digitale Infrastruktur (Federal Ministry of Transport and Digital Infrastructure). Available at: www.bmvi.ed/report-ethicscommission [Accessed November 17, 2018].

Bonnefon, Jean-Francois, Azim Shariff, and Iyad Rahwan. 2016. "The Social Dilemma of Autonomous Vehicles." *Science* 352: 1573–6. doi: 10.1126/science.aaf2654.

Bordoff, Jason. 2016. "How Driverless Cars Could End Up Harming the Environment." *The Wall Street Journal*, April 27. Available at: http://blogs.wsj.com/experts/2016/04/27/how-driverless-cars-might-actually-harm-the-evironment/ [Accessed February 14, 2018].

Bradshaw-Martin, Heather and Catherine Easton. 2014. "Autonomous or 'Driverless' Cars and Disability: A Legal Ethical Analysis." *European Journal of Current Legal Issues* 20. Available at: https://webjcil.org/rt/printerFrindly/344/471 [Accessed November 14, 2018].

Chen, Donna, Kara Kockelman, and Josiah Hanna. 2015. "Operations of a Shared, Autonomous, Electric Vehicle Fleet: Implications of Vehicle & Charging Infrastructure Decisions." *Transportation Research Part A: Policy and Practice* 94: 243–54. Available at: https://doi.org/10.1016/j.tra.2016.08.020 [Accessed November 5, 2018].

Coogan, Matthew et al. 2018. *Understanding Changes in Demographics, Preferences, and Markets for Public Transportation.* Washington, DC: Transit Cooperative Research Program, Report 201, National Academy of Sciences. Available at: www.nap.edu/red/25160/chapter/1?utm_sou rce=Sustainability+Mailing+LIst&utm_ [Accessed November 5, 2018].

Coppola, Gabrielle. 2018. "Can Neuroscience Teach Robot Cars to Be Less Annoying?" *Hyperdrive*, October 9. Available at: www.bloomberg.com/news/articles/2018-10-09/can-neuroscience- [Accessed November 5, 2018].

CSS. 2017. "Autonomous Vehicle Factsheet." Ann Arbor: Center for Sustainable Systems, University of Michigan. Available at: http://css.umich.edu/factsheets/autonomous-vehicles-factsheet [Accessed July 5, 2018].

Delbosc, Alexa and Kelcie Ralph. 2017. "A Tale of Two Millennials." *The Journal of Transport and Land Use* 10: 903–10. Available at: http://dx.doi.org/10.5198/jtlu.207.1006 [Accessed November 6, 2018].

Dennis, Kingsley and John Urry. 2009. *After the Car.* Cambridge: Polity Press.

The Economist. 1982. "The Unfinished Revolution." January 25, pp. 12–13.

Edmonds, David. 2018. "Cars without Drivers Still Need a Moral Compass: But What Kind?" *The Guardian*, November 14. Available at: www.theguardian.com/commentis-free/2018/nov/14/cars-drivers- [Accessed November 16, 2018].

Ellingsen, Linda, Bhawna Singh, and Anders Stromman. 2016. "The Size and Range Effect: Lifecycle Greenhouse Gas Emissions of Electric Vehicles." *Environmental Research Letters* 11. doi: 10.1088/1748-9326/11/5/04010.

Endsley, Mica and Daniel Garland. 2000. *Situation Awareness Analysis and Measurement.* Mahwah, NJ: Lawrence Erlbaum Associates.

Engber, Daniel. 2018. "Does the Trolley Problem Have a Problem?" *Slate*, June 18. Available at: https://slate.co/technology/2018/06/psychologys-trolley-problem-might-have-a-problem.html [Accessed November 1, 2018].

English, Jonathan. 2018. "Why Did America Give Up on Mass Transit? (Don't Blame Cars)." *Citylab*, August 31. Available at: www.citylab.com/transportation/2018/08/how-america-killed-transit/568825 [Accessed October 29, 2018].

Etehad, Melissa and Rob Nikolewski. 2016. "Millennials Not Racing for Cars." *Los Angeles Times*, December 23, p. C1.

FAA. 2017. "Automated Flight Control." Chapter 4 in *Advanced Avionics Handbook.* Washington, DC: Federal Aeronautics Administration, US Department of Transportation.

Fagant, Daniel and Kara Kockelman. 2015. "Preparing a Nation for Autonomous Vehicles: Opportunities, Barriers and Policy Recommendations." *Transportation Research Part A: Policy and Practice* 77: 167–81. Available at: https://doi.org/10.1016/j.tra.2015.04.003 [Accessed November 11, 2018].

Fagant, Daniel and Kara Kockelman. 2013. *Preparing a Nation for Autonomous Vehicles: Potential Benefits.* Washington, DC: ENO Center for Transportation.

Foot, Philippa. 1967. "The Problem of Abortion and the Doctrine of the Double Effect." *Oxford Review,* No. 5. Available at: https://philpapers.org/archives/FOOTPO-2.pdf [Accessed November 16, 2018].

Ford II, Henry. 1955. *Freedom of the American Road: The Case for More Highways.* Documentary film DVD. Available at: https://youtu.be/N9FRxORjzDY [Accessed November 12, 2018].

Fraedrich, Eva and Barbara Lenz. 2016. "Taking a Drive, Hitching a Ride: Autonomous Driving and Car Usage." Pp. 665–85 in M. Maurer, J. Geddes, B. Lenz, and H. Winner, eds., *Autonomous Driving: Technical, Legal and Social Aspects.* Berlin: Springer.

Freund, Peter and George Martin. 1993. *The Ecology of the Automobile.* Montreal: Black Rose Books.

Gerdes, Ryan, Chris Winstead, and Kevin Heaslip. 2013. "CPS: An Efficiency-Motivated Attack against Autonomous Vehicular Transportation." Proceedings of the 29th Annual Computer Security Applications Conference, New Orleans, pp. 99–108.

GovInsider. 2018. "Singapore Trials On-Demand Buses and Hands-Free Ticketing." Available at: https://govinsider.asia/smart-gov/singapore-trials-on-demand-buses-and-hands-free-ticketing/ [Accessed October 1, 2018].

Greenblatt, Jeffrey B. and Susan Shaheen. 2015. "Automated Vehicle, On-Demand Mobility, and Environmental Impacts." *Current Sustainable Renewable Energy Reports* 2: 74–91. doi: 10.1007/s40518-015-0038-5.

Griffin, Melissa L. 2018. "Steering (or Not) through the Social and Legal Implications of Autonomous Vehicles." *The Journal of Business, Entrepreneurship & the Law* 11: 80–114. Available at: https://digitalcommons.pepperdine.edu/jbel/vol11/iss1/4 [Accessed November 14, 2018].

Gruel, Wolfgang and Joseph Stanford. 2015. "Assessing the Long-Term Effects of Autonomous Vehicles: A Speculative Approach." *Transport Research Procedia* 13: 18–29. doi: 10.1016/j.trpro.2016.05.003.

Hancock, Peter. 2018. "Are Autonomous Cars Really Safer than Human Drivers?" *Scientific American,* February 3. Available at: www.scientificamerican.com/article/are-autonomous-cars-really-safer- [Accessed November 16, 2018].

Heinrichs, Dirk. 2015. "Automated Driving: How It Could Enter our Cities and How This Might Affect Our Mobility Decisions." *The Planning Review DISP,* April. Available at: www.researchgate.net/publication/280711966 [Accessed July 25, 2018].

Herrmann, Andreas, Walter Brenner, and Rupert Stadler. 2018. *Autonomous Driving: How the Driverless Revolution Will Change the World.* Bingley, UK: Emerald.

Hertwich, Edgar G. 2005. "Consumption and the Rebound Effect: An Industrial Ecology Perspective." *Journal of Industrial Ecology* 9: 85–98.

Holstein, Tobias, Gordana Dodig-Crnkovic, and Patrizio Pelliccione. 2018. "Ethical and Social Aspects of Self-Driving Cars." *arXiv'18,* January, Gothenburg. Available at: https://arxiv.org/pdf/1802.04103.pdf [Accessed November 16, 2018].

Howard, Daniel and Danielle Dai. 2013. "Public Perceptions of Self-driving Cars: The Case of Berkeley, California." 93rd Annual Meeting, Transportation Research Board, Washington, DC. Available at: www.ocf.berkeley.edu/ djhoward/reports/Report%20-%20 Public%20Perspectives- [Accessed March 20, 2018].

ITDP. 2016. *People Near Transit: Improving Accessibility and Rapid Transit Coverage in Large Cities.* New York: Institute for Transportation & Development Policy. Available at: www.itdp.org/publication/people-near-transit/ [Accessed November 3, 2018].

ITF. 2017. *Transport Outlook 2017.* Paris: International Transport Forum/OECD. Available at: www.itf-oecd.org/transport-outlook-2017 [Accessed August 1, 2018].

Karnouskos, Stamatis and Florian Kerschbaum. 2018. "Privacy and Integrity Considerations in Hyperconnected Autonomous Vehicles." *Proceedings of the IEEE* (Institute of Electrical and Electronics Engineers). doi: 10.1109/JPROC.2017.2725339.

Kerouac, Jack. 1957. *On the Road: The Original Scroll.* New York: Viking/Penguin.

Krueger, Rico, Taha Rashidi, and John Rose. 2016. "Preferences for Shared Autonomous Vehicles." *Transportation Research Part C: Emerging Technologies* 69: 343–55. Available at: https://doi.org/10.1016/j.trc.2016.06.015 [Accessed October 21, 2018].

Larson, Selena. 2016. "Experts Say Sex in Self-Driving Cars Is Inevitable." *The Daily Dot,* May 4. Available at: www.dailydot.com/debug/driverless-car-sex-autonomous/ [Accessed November 5, 2018].

Leibowicz, Benjamin. 2017. "There Are Uncertain Effects with the Rise of Shared Autonomous Vehicles." Austin: UT News, University of Texas. Available at: www.utexas.edu/2017/12/14/shared-autonomous-vehicles-have-uncertain-effects/ [Accessed October 1, 2018].

Lin, Patrick. 2015. "Why Ethics Matters for Autonomous Cars." Pp. 69–85 in M. Maurer, J. Gerdes, B. Lenz, and H. Winner, eds., *Autonomes Fahren.* Berlin: Springer. Available at: https://doi.org/10.1007/978-3-662-45854-9_4 [Accessed November 16, 2018].

Litman, T. 2017. "The Many Problems with Autonomous Vehicles." *Planetizen.* Available at: www.planetizen.com/blogs/95445-many-problems-autonomous-vehicles [Accessed December 4, 2017].

Litman, T. 2016. *Autonomous Vehicle Implementation Predictions.* Victoria, BC: Victoria Transport Policy Institute, September 1. Available at: http://vtpi.org/AVIP.pdf [Accessed March 16, 2017].

Marres, Noortje. 2018. "What If Nothing Happens? Street Trials of Intelligent Cars as Experiments in Participation." In press. In S. Maassen, S. Dickel, and C. Schneier, eds., *TechnoScience in Society.* Niimegen: Springer/Kluwer. Available at: http://wrap.warwick.ac.uk/95442/ [Accessed November 16, 2018].

Marsh, Peter and Peter Collett. 1986. *Driving Passion.* London: Jonathan Cape.

Martin, George. 2018. "An Ecosocial Frame for Autonomous Vehicles." *Capitalism Nature Socialism,* August 21. Available at: https://doi.org/10.1080/10455752.2018.1510531 [Accessed August 28, 2018].

Matiaske, Wenzel, Roland Menges, and Martin Speiss. 2012. "Modifying the Rebound: It Depends! Explaining Mobility Behaviour on the Basis of the German Socio-Economic Panel." *Energy Policy* 41: 29–35. Available at: https://doi.org/10.1016/j.enpol.2010.11.044 [Accessed November 13, 2018].

McGrath, Michael. 2018. *Autonomous Vehicles: Opportunities, Strategies, and Disruptions.* Independently Published. ISBN-13: 978–1980313554. Available at: www.amazon.com/Autonomous-Vehicles Opportunities . . . /dp/1980313857 [Accessed August 13, 2018].

Millard-Ball, Adam. 2016. "Pedestrians, Autonomous Vehicles, and Cities." *Journal of Planning Education and Research,* October 26. Available at: https://journals.sagepub.com/doi/pdf/10.1177/0739456X16675674# [Accessed April 10, 2017].

Moor, Robert. 2016. "What Happens to American Myth When You Take the Driver Out of It?" *New York,* October 17–30, pp. 36–44.

Moss, Stephen. 2015. "End of Car Age: How Cities Are Outgrowing the Automobile." *The Guardian,* Online, April 28. Available at: www.theguardian.com/cities/2015/apr/28/end-of-the-car-age- [Accessed November 6, 2018].

Musolesi, Mirco. 2014. "Big Mobile Data Mining: Good or Evil?" *IEEE Internet Computing* 18: 78–81.

NAS. 2018. *Between Public and Private Mobility: Examining the Rise of Technology-Enabled Transportation Services.* Washington, DC: National Academy of Sciences. doi: 10.17226/21875.

Nordhoff, S., J. De Winter, M. Kyriakidis, B. Van Arem, and R. Happee. 2018. "Acceptance of Driverless Vehicles: Results from a Large Cross-National Questionnaire Study." *Journal of Advanced Transportation* Volume 2018, Article ID 5382192. Available at: https://doi.org/10.1155/208/5382192 [Accessed October 25, 2018].

Nordhoff, Sina, Bart Van Arem, and Riender Happee. 2016. "A Conceptual Model to Explain, Predict, and Improve User Acceptance of Driverless Vehicles." 95th Annual Meeting of Transportation Research Board, Washington, DC.

Oppetit, Ernest. 2017. "Autonomous Vehicles and the End of Privacy." *Hackernoon*, February 4. Available at: https://hackernoon.com/autonomous-vehicles-and-the-end-of-privacy_9c3712f349f [Accessed July 13, 2018].

Oster, C., J. Strong, and C. Zorn. 1992. *Why Airplanes Crash*. Oxford: Oxford University Press.

Owczarzak, Lukasz and Jacek Zak. 2015. "Design of Passenger Public Transportation Solutions Based on Autonomous Vehicles and Their Multiple Criteria Comparison with Traditional Forms of Passenger Transportation." *Transport Research Procedia* 10: 472–82. doi: 10.1016/j.trpro.2015.09.001.

Page, Frderick D. and Norma M. Krayem. 2017. "Are You Ready for Self-Driving Vehicles?" *Intellectual Property & Technology Law Journal* 29: 14+. Available at: http://link.galegroup.com/apps/doc/A489255945/LT?u=ucberkeley&sid=LT&xid=1c910a6d [Accessed March 6, 2018].

Pakusch, Christina, Gunnar Stevens, Alexander Boden, and Paul Bossauer. 2018. "Unintended Effects of Autonomous Driving: A Study on Mobility Preferences in the Future." *Sustainability* 10, 2404. doi: 10.3390/su10072404. Available at: www.researchgate.net/publication/326312355_unintended_/ [Accessed October 22, 2018].

Papa, Enrica and Antonio Ferreira. 2018. "Sustainable Accessibility and the Implementation of Automated Vehicles: Identifying Critical Decisions." *Urban Science* 2. doi: 10.3390/urbansci2010005. Available at: www.mdpi.com/journal/urbansci/ [Accessed October 22, 2018].

Paterson, Matthew. 2007. *Automobile Politics: Ecology and Cultural Political Economy*. Cambridge: Cambridge University Press.

Perrow, Charles. 1984. *Normal Accidents: Living with High-Risk Technologies*. New York: Basic Books.

Quinn, K. 2017a. "10 Great American Road Trip Films." Available at: www.bfi.org.uk/news-opinions-news-bfi/features/10-great-american-/ [Accessed December 5, 2017].

Quinn, K. 2017b. "10 Great Australian Road Movies." Available at: www.smh.com.au/enterntainment/movies/the-10-best-australian-/ [Accessed December 5, 2018].

Rainwater, Brooks and Nicole Dupuis. 2018. "Cities Have Taken the Lead in Regulating Driverless Vehicles." *Citylab*, October 23. Available at: www.citylab.com/perspective/2018/10/cities-led-regulating-driverless-vehicles/573325/?utm_source=newsletter&silvereid=%25%25RECIPIENT_/ [Accessed October 24, 2018].

Reilhac, Patrice, Nick Millett, and Katharina Hottelart. 2016. "Shifting Paradigms and Conceptual Frameworks for Automated Driving." Pp. 73–89 in G. Meyer and S. Beiker, eds., *Road Vehicle Automation 3*. Heidelberg: Springer, Cham. Available at: https://doi.org/10.1007/978-3-319-40503-2_7 [Accessed March 28, 2018].

Reuters. 2018. "Self-driving cars still trouble many Americans." Reuters/Ipsos Poll, January. Available at: http://fingfx.thomsonreuters.com/gfx/rngs/AUTO-SELFDRIVING-SURVEY/010060NM16V/AUTO-[Accessed November 3, 2018].

Roose, Kevin. 2017. "Cars of Future? Lawmakers (Gasp!) Agree." *New York Times*, July 22, pp. B1, B6.

Said, Carolyn. 2018a. "As Cruise Builds Up, Giant GM Downsizes." *San Francisco Chronicle*, November 27, pp. D1, D4.

Said, Carolyn. 2018b. "Lyft Pushes Shared Rides, Transit Links." *San Francisco Chronicle*, June 7. Available at: www.sfchronicle.com/business/article/Lyft,Hussain,Amjad,Chaud-pushes-shared-rides-transit-link-12973543.php [Accessed June 8, 2018].

Said, Carolyn. 2018c. "Robot Car in a Crash: With Human at the Wheel." *San Francisco Chronicle*, November 6, pp. D1, D4.

Samuelson, Robert J. 2017. "Driverless Cars May Be Appealing: But They Could Be Used against Us." *The Washington Post*, Opinions, September 24. Available at: www. washingtonpost.com/opinions/driverless-cars- [Accessed September 12, 2018].

Sanaullah, I., A. Hussain, A. Chaudry, K. Case, and M. French. 2017. "Autonomous Vehicles in Developing Countries: A Case Study on User's View Point in Pakistan." Pp. 51–69 in N. Stanton et al., eds., *Advances in Human Aspects of Transportation*. Berlin: Springer. doi:10.1007/978-3-319-41682-3.

Schmitt, Angie. 2018. "The Story of 'Micro Transit' Is Consistent, Dismal Failure." *USA Today*, June 26. Available at: https://usa.streetsblog.org/2018/06/26/the-story-of-micro-transit [Accessed November 16, 2018].

Shackelford, Scott, Timothy Fort, and Danuvasin Charoen. 2016. "Sustainable Cyber-security: Applying Lessons from the Green Movement to Managing Cyber Attacks." *University of Illinois Law Review* 2016: 1995–2932. Available at: www.researchgate.net/publication/310504691_Sustainable_cybersecurity [Accessed November 10, 2018].

Sheller, Mimi. 2004. "Automotive Emotions." *Theory, Culture & Society* 21: 221–42. Available at: https://doi.org/10.1177/0263276404046068 [Accessed July, 2017].

Shrikant, Aditi. 2018. "The Bus Gets a Lot of Hate: American Cities Are Trying to Change That." *Vox*, November 5. Available at: www.vox.com/the-goods/2018/11/5/18057352/bus-stigma- [Accessed November 13, 2018].

Shwebel, David C. 2018. "Child/Adolescent Development and Autonomous Vehicle Opera-tion: 'Operator's Licenses' Instead of Driver's Licenses." *Journal of Injury and Violence Research* 10: 61. doi: 10.5249/jivr.v10i2.1054.

Sims, Ralph et al. 2014. "Transport." Pp. 590–670 in O. Edenhofer et al., eds., *Climate Change 2014: Mitigation of Climate Change*. Cambridge and New York: Cambridge University Press. Available at: www.ipcc_wg3_ar5_chapter8/ [Accessed August 15, 2018].

Sivak, Michael and Brandon Schoettle. 2011. *Recent Changes in the Age Composition of Drivers in 15 Countries*. Ann Arbor: Transportation Research Institute, University of Michigan. Available at: https://deepblue.lib.umich.edu/bitstream/handle/2017.42/86680/102764. pdf [Accessed November 7, 2018].

Smith, Aaron and Monica Anderson. 2017. *Americans' Attitudes toward Driverless Vehicles*. Washington, DC: Pew Research Center. Available at: www.pewinternet.org/2017/10/04/americans-attitudes-toward-driverless-vehicles/ [Accessed November 1 2018].

Solnit, Rebecca. 2016. "We Don't Need Self-Driving Cars: We Need to Ditch Our Vehicles Entirely." *The Guardian*, April 6. Available at: www.theguardian.com/commentisfree/2016/apr/06/self-driving-car-/ [Accessed July 30, 2017].

Sousanis, J. 2011. *World Vehicle Population Tops 1 Billion Units*. Detroit: Wards Auto, August 15. Available at: www.wardsauto.com/news-analysis/world-vehicle-population-tops-1-billion [Accessed October 27, 2018].

Sumantran, Venkat, Charles Fine, and David Gonsalvez. 2017a. *Faster, Smarter, Greener: The Future of the Car and Urban Mobility*. Cambridge, MA and London: MIT Press.

Sumantran, Venkat, Charles Fine, and David Gonsalvez. 2017b. "Our Cities Need Fewer Cars, Not Cleaner Cars." *The Guardian*, Online, October 16. Available at: www.theguardian.com/environment/2017/oct/16/0ur-cities-[Accessed July 22, 2018].

Surakitbanharn, Caitlin A. et al. 2018. *Preliminary Ethical, Legal and Social Implications of Connected and Autonomous Transportation Vehicles (CATV).* West Lafayette, IN: Policy Research Institute, Purdue University Online. Available at: www.purdue.edu/discoverypark/ppri/catv/Literature Review_CATV.pdf [Accessed November 12, 2018].

Taeihagh, Araz and Hazel Si Min Lim. 2018. "Governing Autonomous Vehicles: Emerging Responses for Safety, Liability, Privacy, Cybersecurity, and Industry Risks." *Transport Reviews.* Available at: https://doi.org/10.1080/01441647.2018.1494640 [Accessed September 27, 2018].

Thomopoulos, Nikolas and Moshe Givoni. 2015. "The Autonomous Car: A Blessing or a Curse for the Future of Low Carbon Mobility? An Exploration of Likely vs. Desirable Outcomes." *European Journal of Futures Research* 3: 1–14. doi: 10.1007/s40309-015-0071-z.

Trickey, Erick. 2018. "'They're Bold and Fresh': The Millennials Disrupting Boston's Transit System." *Politico Magazine,* October 25. Available at: www.politico.com/magzine/story/2018/10/25/what-works-boston-transit-221839 [Accessed October 26, 2018].

Trommer, Stefan et al. 2016. *Autonomous Driving: The Impact of Vehicle Automation on Mobility Behaviour.* Munich: Institute for Mobility Research. Available at: www.ifmo.de/files/publications_content/2016/ifmo_2016_Autonomous_Driving_2035_en.pdf [Accessed October 24, 2018].

Underwood, Steven. 2014. *Automated, Connected, and Electric Vehicle Systems.* Dearborn: Institute for Advanced Vehicle Systems, University of Michigan. Available at: http://graham.umich.edu/media/files/LC-IA-Final-Underwood.pdf [Accessed August 6, 2017].

Urry, John. 2008. *Mobilities.* Cambridge: Polity Press.

USLegal. 2018. *Vienna Convention on Road Traffic Law.* Available at: https://definitions.uslegal-com/Vienna-convention-on-road-traffic/ [Accessed November 16, 2018].

Valen, A. 2017. *The a Taxi Revolution: Autonomous Vehicle Implementation and Rise-Sharing Optimization in the United States and China.* Princeton, NJ: B.S. Thesis, Department of Operations Research and Financial Engineering, Princeton University. Available at: http://orfe.princeton.edu/~alaink/ThesesSeniorTheses%2717/Antigone-VAlen-Te%20ATaxi%20Revolution.pdf [Accessed November 28, 2017].

WEF. 2015. *Self-Driving Vehicles in an Urban Context.* Geneva: World Economic Forum. Available at: www3.weforum.org/docs/wef_press%2release.pdf [Accessed November 4, 2018].

Wigley, S. 2015. *10 Great American Road Trip Films.* London: British Film Institute. Available at: www.bfi.org.uk/news-opinion/news-/ [Accessed December 4, 2018].

Wulkop, Annika. 2017. *Sustainability Opportunities and Risks of Future Mobility Systems Based on Autonomous Vehicles in Chinese Cities.* Masters Thesis, Strategy and International Management, Universitat St. Gallen, Zurich.

Zajonc, Robert B. 1965. *The Attitudinal Effects of Mere Exposure.* Ann Arbor: Research Center for Group Dynamics, Institute for Social Research, Technical Report No. 34, University of Michigan. Available at: www.psc.isr.umich.edu/dis/infosrve/osrpub/pdf/Theattudinaleffects_2306_.PDF [Accessed November 1, 2018].

Index